Trade Paper Back ISBN: 978-0-9998354-7-0
E-Book/Kindle ISBN: 978-0-9998354-9-4

Copy Editing by: Kirstin Madigan with Bleepnwabbit Ventures
Cover and Interior Design by: Melanie Sanchez
Cover Art by: iStock.com/francescoch

Printed in the United States

*Trigger Warning: Some of the chapters in this book may discuss or share stories of assault and physical violence, use profanity and or discuss nudity or adult content.

**Note about chapter formatting: Each chapter is written by a different author who chose how they wanted their layout to appear, in terms of italics, spoken words, conversations, etc. We have tried to create consistency when possible. Individual voices/writers present differently, and the editors desired to respect their choices as it reflects their tone and style.

Lessons Learned The Hard Way

Personal escapades through the trials,
glitches, and hitches life offers up.

Table of Contents

Forward
By Vanda Mikoloski

I believe there's a poem by the poet Rumi about someone dumping a truckload of shit on your front lawn.

Welcome everything!' he wrote—or something like that. *"Manure will help you grow trees, and then you can share your fruit."* I paraphrase, of course, but you get the idea. Rumi meant that the most challenging crap in life, the crap that makes your insides broil, can become your best lessons—your best fruit to share.

In this book, we invite you into our hard-fought-for harvest—not neatly packaged aphorisms that come *after* the hellish dark night of the soul, but the walk *through* that night into a kind of exhausted daybreak. I found the writers courageously forthcoming, funny, and generous, having endured unimaginable adversity—the stuff great souls are made of.

I could talk about the big-ticket items: alcoholism, bulimia, cancer, or depression. (As I list them alphabetically, I fear I may have one for every letter in the alphabet.) Sometimes, however, the hardest stuff is not festooned with pink ribbons and social awareness campaigns.

One of my hardest lessons has been simply allowing people to be. Giving them space—quite possibly the best gift a human can give a human.

Recently, I had a falling out with my dear childhood friend, Freddy, a super-smart guy with thick glasses he hiked up by squeezing all his facial muscles together and still does. He and I shared troubled childhoods back in the '60s and '70s, as our culture went from buttoned-down to psychedelic. We adored each other for decades and then suddenly in this decade of polarity, Freddy got political. My mild-mannered friend turned our normally fun conversations into diatribes promoting his positions.

When he started posting his "research" on social media, I got triggered. We used to call it *surfing the web*. Now, it's *research*.

"Freddy, you're being so arrogant," I said, which didn't help.

I talked to a friend I trusted about it.

"Pointing out your friend's ostensible limitations won't help when it's coming from judgment," he said.

"I thought I was helping!" I said.

"Want to know how to tell if you're judging? Either you are 100% at peace with him or you're judging him." Ouch.

At first, mutual friends from our hometown engaged him in spirited discussions. As his moral outrage escalated, his posts crossed the fine line between propriety into self-righteous bloviating. He lost clients and had to find new work with like-minded people.

"I've realized most people don't really want to know the truth. I highly commend those who do," he said as if he were the great arbiter of truth.

"Mark my words! Everything I've said has come true!" he railed.

"Sounds authoritative," I said sarcastically.

"Oh, it is. I've never gotten a fact wrong!"

Our conflict escalated and before long, my friend and I stopped talking. Our old friends on Facebook began to disengage, too, and I am not proud to say I had a little glee about that. I was still making him wrong.

In Freddy's mind, he was being passionate and brave—all about truth and justice. But it only looked that way to the people who already agreed with him.

I didn't want to lose Freddy, so I began to look in the last place humans are prone to look.

Lesson #1: Turn it around.

The crazy-hard thing to practice when irritation arises is *nothing*—to put some space between trigger and forefinger. A little bit of impartial self-observation buys the grace to ask the question: *Where do I do this? Have I ever been strident?* The answer is yes, Alex.

More honestly, I have alienated my best friend and most of my family by being devoted to my point of view, unable to turn around and see what I had to do with the conflict.

The spiritual teacher Byron Katie has a worksheet to begin what she calls "The Work." It's called the "Judge your Neighbor Worksheet" which I just love because it isn't the new-age nicey-nice school of covering a pile of feces with sweet frosting.

Step four of the worksheet is "The Turnaround," which rests on the idea that a stressful thought, however true it may sound to you, could be equally true if you formulated the exact opposite thought.

I wanted Freddy to stop being so self-righteous, but where was I being self-righteous about him? I stood in that question.

My answer came when a friend pointed out that I was doing the same thing I was accusing Freddy of. I was stridently making him wrong. And who knows? He may be right. Hell, the Scientologists may be right, I don't know. I began to soften toward Freddy.

Lesson #2: Put a Little Maybe in it.

We have no clue—about reality or about what is right for another person.

One of my favorite thinkers, Robert Anton Wilson, is this laid-back Massachusetts academic guy I love. When intelligent people have a

Massachusetts accent, it's funny. He's a regular guy who rails against experts with broad A's and missing R's.

Wilson said, "*All perception is a gamble.*" In other words, we don't know shit. Photons and sound waves hit our eyeballs and ears interpreted by the filter of our dirty brains and we call that an accurate gauge for reality.

I say "dirty brain" because many of our beliefs are shaped by nothing more than falling off a swing in childhood (life is dangerous!) or being bullied (people are mean!) These are ideas that, for survival reasons, become hard-wired into our operating systems unbeknownst to us. These contexts we hold are decisive. We grow to live our lives constrained by mental stuff we don't even remember deciding. Our point of view creates more evidence for our point of view.

Aren't we all a little guilty of relating to our point of view as if it were the truth?

I once had a joke in my stand-up act about perception: *Ever notice how right we are? Ever notice we never argue that we're wrong? Shouldn't it be 50/50?* Then I did an act-out of a couple fighting, screaming: '*This relationship is failing because I don't listen!*'

In the very big scheme of things, we don't know what a soul's trajectory involves. Maybe there's a reason to go all in on an idea that leaves you ostracized—I mean in a soul's evolution sort-of-way. We just can't know. I wanted my friend to put a little 'maybe' in it. I wanted him not to be such a frigging know-it-all, but where could I do that?

The only way I have learned to inspire someone to action is by modeling. If I stop judging him, he might notice his old pal beaming love rays at him.

Lesson #3: Stand in their shoes.

I became willing to move away from my well-defended position about Freddy's "craziness" just long enough to wonder: What was motivating his "bloviating?" Freddy was beaten up at school. A lot. Now he had the perfect conditions to redress that by standing up to the bullies from the other party. Maybe it was that. I don't know, but simply wondering about his world gave me compassion for him.

I had called him crazy, but didn't they call Galileo crazy? I don't know what's crazy and what isn't. We all ended up here on a planet and took a few guesses as to how and why life happened and how we're supposed to behave. Some people worshipped the sun. Others worshipped some dude. All guesses, some of which grew into full-blown belief systems, but no matter how big they got, everyone knows down deep that beliefs are conjectures. That's what faith is—believing it before you see it.

However crazy a belief is, I would defend your right to have yours. The greatest thing about America is that it was designed to include all faiths. Maybe I'm still mad about Catholic school. But why wouldn't I support Freddy's new "religion?" I began to see myself as a hypocrite and love Freddy for his ferocity.

Finally, I called him. I got curious, asking him about his resources. The more curious I got, the more he softened and made sense. I saw where I was strident and unmovable. I considered his point of view. Yes, even QAnon. I am now concerned the deep state is sacrificing children for their blood. I'm kidding, but could I be open to some truth being censored by mainstream media? You betcha. Couldn't I assume anything that is called a 'conspiracy theory' might contain some truth? Yes.

I had a breakthrough that day that opened me up to real conversations, not the polarized venom we see so much of on social media.

The ego relates to agreement like it's love. It isn't. I didn't need to agree with Freddy to love him. My love for Freddy and his wild mind returned. I even relate to him as a resource—a thinker who is exploring a whole bunch of stuff I rarely think of. I am so happy he is in my life.

So, here's our harvest. Jump into it as you would a pile of leaves. Let it surround you as each writer accesses their humanity, their humility, their fear, and their grit. May you also access yours.

Vanda Mikoloski was a voice-over artist, professional stand-up comic, yoga teacher for the Dixie Chicks, Ayahuasquera, and personal growth enthusiast before becoming a full-time writer. She lives in Philadelphia and publishes on vanda.substack.com

Introduction
By Betsy Chasse

The morning after my accident, when I realized I could not plant my feet on the floor and take on the day with my normal tenacity, grit, and grind, a thought popped into my head. What lesson am I now learning the hard way?

I turned fifty-three just a few weeks prior to this event, which happened in late March, and have spent some time reflecting on my life and the decisions I have made that led me to this very moment. Splayed out on my bed, my ankle a dangling particle, I consider that I am a victim of my own stubbornness.

I go back to the evening of the accident. I had just ended a phone call with someone who was supposed to be my business partner and more importantly, a friend, who had done something so unethical and abusive to me that I finally stood up for myself. This may sound surprising since I am a strong, independent woman; to most, I seem like the type of woman who always stands up for herself.

What I was awakening to was that I am a strong woman who often accepts what is and makes it work instead of standing up and saying no at the onset. In my moment of standing up and saying no, I quite literally fell to the ground and broke my ankle. Clearly, I needed practice at this new art of setting boundaries and respecting myself—lessons I had yet to learn so late in life.

The irony is that after that call, I had a choice: either consume a bottle of wine or take a short walk to the hot tub and submerge my hurt in a boiling bowl of bubbles. I am a Pieces; we like water. I chose the latter, which came as a surprise because usually wine was my go-to, but I had decided almost a year earlier to slow the roll on the drinking. I had been working out three times per week and was trying to focus on my body and my health.

The accident was a catalyst for what on the surface appeared to be a series of unfortunate events but would later be revealed as a reminder that the forces of nature (or the Universe, source, God, whatever your name for it) mean business and if one refuses its call, it will take you there anyway.

After the accident, I had major surgery, could not work or walk for four months, gained ten pounds, lost all my money, was evicted from my apartment, and lost most of my friends. If it was able to be lost, I lost it and added it to my ass.

And so, I did what I always do in a crisis; I went into survival mode—a skill I have honed over my entire existence. Crisis is my sweet spot; it's where I shine. Like a magician, I have always been able to pull a rabbit out of my hat in what seems like the darkest of hours.

But this time it felt different. I was tired of producing roses from my shirtsleeves to cover the stench of shit I found myself surrounded by. I fought hard for a few weeks until the day I went to court and lost my case, after which I sat in my car alone and cried. I had nothing left, no more hidden aces. I honestly didn't care anymore. I didn't.

I screamed "FUCK YOU, BoB!" (BoB is my nickname for the invisible source we all know exists but shall be unnamed).

"Fuck you, BoB." I am an awesome mom, who has provided for my kids on my own in a world that does everything in its power to force suffering on women who don't play by the rules.

"Fuck You, BoB." I am an award-winning filmmaker who has created works that have legit shifted the paradigm.

"Fuck You, Bob." I am a writer, a creative, an artist who has been able to survive and sometimes even thrive in a world that has no appreciation for the arts and prefers our artists starving and begging.

14

"Fuck you, BoB." I am a force of nature! A change maker. I create BIG THINGS!

Snot ran from my nose, my throat burned, and my vision was blurred by searing hot tears of rage. Passersby moved as far away as possible as they walked past my car, probably wondering if I was armed and dangerous.

At this point, I had nothing left in me and so I just sat there in my car outside the Ventura County Courthouse, utterly broken.

And I heard a voice within me. "I know you are; I've been waiting for you to remember..."

"Remember what?" I asked.

"...remember that you are a force of nature, that you have the capacity and the abilities to create change—to create beautiful, impactful, profound things that change the world."

And it all came flooding back. In 2004, I was young, bold, and filled with the belief that I could do anything. I was a co-creator of a film that made a major impact, and for a while, I rode that wave until the self-doubt crept in. When I began to wonder if it was a fluke, this sense of imposter syndrome hit hard. I got divorced in 2012 and the world I had built came crashing down. The fear of failure took hold, and with it came the belief that I wasn't enough to be the person who made great things. I didn't have the pedigree; I was just a girl faking it who would never actually make it. I didn't deserve to have it all.

And so, for the next ten years, right up until March 23, 2023 (the one-year anniversary of my mother's death) I ran a race to the finish line in survival mode, hustling my way through, producing ponies out of piles of manure, existing the only way I thought I knew how based on what I believed I deserved.

I spent a little over 10 years accepting "what is" and making it work, forgetting who I was and what I was capable of. I pretended to be strong while allowing people, places, things, times, and events to force me into survival mode instead of taking charge, speaking up, and using my innate gifts to create from the fire in my soul.

The voice of BoB echoes through me, "You forgot that trust and faith are verbs and that we are a team. You've been going it alone for too long. I'm sorry it had to be so violent, but It's time for you to wake up again; the world needs you. YOU need you."

And I let go and let BoB. And ya know what? I ended up finding my dream apartment with gorgeous natural light and a huge patio. And my old apartment complex is mired in a series of lawsuits about nasty mold spewing up from the sinks.

I found my true friends and a love of just being on my own and doing my thing.

I started projects I actually enjoy—endeavors I love that inspire me to WANT to create instead of feeling I need to out of desperation.

On the darkest night, I stopped running, I had no choice; BoB literally took me down to the ground to remind me to slow down, trust the process, and listen more deeply to the messages showing up for me. I will be OK. It won't always be easy, but I will be OK.

As you read the chapters in this book, written by brave humans willing to share their darkest moments that brought them to light, remember that. You will be OK, too.

––––––––––––––––––

Betsy Chasse is an award-winning filmmaker best known for *What The Bleep Do We Know?!*, and a bestselling author of multiple books including *Killing Buddha* and *Tipping Sacred Cows*. Learn more at www.betsychasse.net

CHAPTER 1

Flat
By Vienne Cordet

There have been moments in my life when I blamed all my self-love issues on my well-meaning parents, crazy, loud-mouthed, evil bullies, or insensitive misogynistic men/boys. My mind can pinpoint memories from my past that seem like logical pathways to insecurity and self-hate. Through the years, therapists, self-help books, and gurus pushed me to dive deep into how things felt. To change behaviors and create differently. I used my new tools and became adept at monitoring my thoughts. But it dawned on me fairly recently that my reaction towards my insecurities, coupled with the strength I hold towards my ideas, mattered. My identity and what I think others think of me have been paramount in my navigation through the abyss of my insecurity. Throw in a brain that is usually highly focused but not always highly organized, and life has sometimes gotten messy.

I am 57. This summer, I had my beautiful size 34 DD breasts removed. I loved having large breasts and thought they would be with me forever. However, my immune system had other plans. No, thankfully I did not have breast cancer. I had my breasts checked many times. But I had breast implants, and they were ruining my health. My decisions caused this pain. My choices surrounding self-love created this. Did I just freaking shorten my life? Is it too late to reverse my symptoms and pain? Who can I blame for this? Me.

For the past decade, my breasts and the implants they contained would wake me up nightly. Daily, excruciating pain would radiate around my hard-encapsulated breast implants. And "excruciating" is not a word that is typically part of my vocabulary. I consulted four times with the surgeon who had put in my new silicone pair in 2014. My original implants were saline. The FDA approved silicone implants in 2006. My male surgeon suggested bigger and no longer saline but silicone. They are better now—safer, Vienne, the surgeon told me. (Well, that was a lie.)

My whole adult life, I have eaten organic food, taken all the right vitamins, exercised, and refined my organic diet to eradicate anything that caused inflammation, for my blood type or otherwise. I gave up wine and dark chocolate and reduced my coffee intake. It all helped for a while—until it didn't.

I enjoyed my large breasts for decades. They were huge for my petite frame. In my mind, they partly defined who I was. I had been a successful national-level bodybuilder for over two decades; I had enjoyed modeling for various projects and showed them off in my twenties and part of my thirties with just about everything I wore. It would have been impossible not to show them.

In 1993, I was twenty-five and reading the breast implant information the surgeon gave me. I distinctly remember lamenting to my twenty-five-year-old self. "God, I will be almost forty...maybe even *fifty* when these may need replacing, and who cares? By the time I am that old, I will not need to be sexy!" Three decades went by quickly.

So, the backstory on my 1993 fake breasts. It started in 1977 and fourth grade. I was tiny and athletic—a runner. I feared that I would be one of the girls who got fat upon hitting puberty and would lose all athletic ability. My father, my coach growing up, spoke about it often at the dinner table. Or is that just how I heard it? No one told me that gaining strength and muscle was a good thing. That I would be a better athlete if I fed my body. No one told me the difference between muscle and fat.

By fifth grade, all the girls in my class were developing breasts, and our tiny school's fourth-, fifth-, and sixth-grade boys noticed. Loudly and immaturely, for years. It was also the start of my interest in boys. So, when the boy I liked pointed at my chest in front of everyone and laughed and exclaimed in my face, "You are so flat, you have nothing!" "You look like a boy...!" it hurt. I remember crying. The boy's comments were not a chance incident. My chest became the subject of years of torment and flat jokes. Sex and a girl's body, particularly her breasts, were the subjects to talk about if you were an immature small-town boy wrestling with his out-of-control hormones. I assume it was the start of hating my body. Flat. As if it were some blight or parasite. Pancake-flat came next. As if just flat wasn't enough. I wanted to develop like the other girls. Mother Nature refused.

I figured if I bought a bra, it might magically edge my hormones into action. So, my mother took me to the local department store, and we went bra shopping. Nothing fit. Finally, the old woman helping us looked at me—and I will never forget this— said, "Honey, you are built like a boy...you do not have a chest yet." Come back when you grow some boobies." Great. A boy. Again! And who says "boobies?"

Later in my fifth-grade year, my mother found a yellow plaid underwear set. I loved it. It came with a bra equivalent to today's sports bra. Finally, something that fits me! I wore it to school proudly. Later that day, one of the sixth-grade girls noticed it under my light-colored shirt and pointed and laughed in front of the entire lunchroom, screeching, "Oh, my god, what is THAT? She then proceeded to mimic me—so much for my yellow plaid sports bra. I didn't wear it to school again. My natural breast size stayed at 29 AAA.

My senior year of high school arrived, and I still had not grown breasts or gotten my period. My mother took me to a group of gynecology specialists in Omaha, NE. The gyno specialists had no idea why I wasn't developing. My prognosis was that I had a tipped cervix and uterus and would never be able to have children. I was eighteen. So, I have no period or breasts. Now, I have a tipped cervix and uterus, and I will never have children. Not that I wanted them at the time, but wow. My doctors never talked about the fact that athletic girls often do not get their periods.

The following year, college brought joy and still no breasts. I moved away from the small town I had grown up in, vowing never to return. Between studies and work, I fell in love for the first time. My boyfriend didn't seem to mind my lack of breasts. I do remember my chest was always off-limits and embarrassing during sex.

Four years later, my boyfriend of four years and the love of my life gallantly and heartlessly dumped me to start law school and move to a neighboring city. My thinking was that my lack of cleavage was possibly a reason. A month later, my senior year of college started, and I was loving my life. My ex-dipshit boyfriend was history, and I was reveling in moving on with my bad self.

Stomach pain and nausea had been plaguing me for a few months. I blamed the stress on the ex-boyfriend debacle. So, before class on Thursday, I zipped into the student health urgent care on campus. My 100-pound ultra-athletic, tipped-cervix-and-uterus-hauling body revealed that I was not only pregnant but five months pregnant. I was in my senior year with seven months until graduation. I called up my now ex-boyfriend and gave him the news. He was mortified. I was mortified. Our parents were mortified. He was in law school, living with three other men. I had gotten over him and talked myself into the fact that I hated him. He had brutally dumped me. Long story short, we succumbed to family pressures and idiotically got married. Our daughter Kelsey was born four months later.

All of this is important, and while the previous paragraphs stand alone as lessons of learning and bad choices, they were all worth it on some level. Because in the days after my daughter was born, my milk came in, and my breasts grew. It was like my body finally roared and blossomed. It was apparent my pregnancy had opened floodgates of hormones. My tiny, non-existent breasts were suddenly 32DD—and I had enough milk to feed ten babies! I would breastfeed forever, and I did over the next few years. Two years later, my husband graduated from law school, and we moved to New York City.

My son was born a few years later, and I nursed him, not only because of the baby benefits but—hey, large breasts! I was holding my eight-month-old son when my supposedly wonderful, successful husband gallantly and heartlessly asked me for a divorce. My milk dried up instantly. No really. Instantly. No amount of prodding or meditating would make them larger or give my baby milk. My breasts, having deflated fast and furiously, were scarred by stretch marks, and I went right back to 32AAA. I was reeling from the high drama every divorce renders and trying to navigate my sudden life as a single parent. My solution was to fix the problem. I got breast implants. I loved them. But I was 25, and no one talked about any adverse side effects other than when I was old; they would have to be replaced or removed, and it seemed like a fair deal.

My breasts and I fled back to my college hometown of Minneapolis to raise two tiny children, return to school, and get on with the business of life as a single mom.

Fast forward decades and, having spent the past nine years and four visits to my surgeon complaining about painful breasts, I learned that I had capsular contractures. He also informed me if left untreated, they would get worse and possibly rupture the implant. It would never go away. (Capsular contracture is the continuous tightening of the breast implant scar tissue. It puts pressure on the breast implant, increasing the risk of rupture.) My only option was a full capsulectomy and either implant replacement or permanent removal. His recommendation was to have them replaced and go bigger (which I thought was weird). I went for consultations with three different doctors—females this time. I received the same prognosis, although all three female surgeons suggested I keep them out for at least a year to be potentially pain-free and to heal. At this point, I just wanted the pain gone—a decade of pain. I liked the idea of them, but in reality, they were killing me.

My current husband is a fantastic man who is not only the father of my younger children, but who has also stepped up to love all my children. An awesome partner. A grown-up. But he loved my breasts, too. He had never seen me without them. And let's face it, they were part of our sex life, at least in my mind. To say their removal brought up issues for me is an understatement.

And then, amid my breast kerfuffle, a girlfriend from Washington asked me during a Zoom call, "Hey, have you seen the new documentary called *Explant*?" My god. Did someone make a documentary on my nightmare? Yep. Damn. Her words horrified me. Fuck. I knew what it was going to uncover and say out loud. It wouldn't be the first time I had heard it. For years, the negative health information about breast implants made the rounds. Everything from silicone is bad—get saline; no, shells are still silicone; no, your implants are OK unless you are one of the unfortunate gits that had the bumpy implants; your immune system fights them and cannot fight other things, and the list goes on. I had heard about Breast Implant Illness (BII) in 2013; a friend died of it. She pleaded with me to have my implants removed, but I ignored her. I ignored the symptoms. I blamed the inflammation and pain on my genetics. It took me three weeks to finally watch the documentary.

I scheduled the appointment for a full double capsulectomy without replacement a day later. Both sets of my implants had been placed under my chest muscle, and my chest muscles had to be sewn back down to my ribs and chest cavity after the capsulectomy and removal. My heal time with no lifting would be two months.

The female surgeon I had chosen was skilled. She was kind and supportive and was a highly recommended surgeon for capsulectomy/en bloc breast removals without replacement.

And really, maybe no one would notice. Because, in reality, I had stopped showing my breasts off in my late thirties. At least on purpose. It just wasn't my thing anymore. I owned zero low-cut shirts. I looked for pictures on my Facebook and family photos to find a picture of my chest. Nope. None. When did that happen? When had I stopped showing my breasts? Somewhere between my single mom late sexy thirties and my late sexy fifties, I had changed. Part of this change had me dressing my body differently. They were not as important to me as I raised my children and created a thriving business. My breasts had ceased to matter, and I hadn't noticed until now.

The weekly women's Zoom group I participated in started discussing one of their typical crazy/fantastic assignments. Most of the assignment involved snapping a picture of ourselves in a red dress. Think mermaids and sexy. I found myself having an enormous aversion to showing my chest. There wasn't a minute in the day when my breasts weren't jabbing me with pain. I was the last to do the assignment. Late. I ordered this sexy, tight-fitting, super low-cut $10 red dress from Amazon and went with my 12-year-old daughter to the trees in our backyard where she helped me film a quick reel to music—Done. Watching the video reel shocked me. My breasts looked fake as hell, and they were not pretty. God, no wonder I covered them. The contracture had pulled my left breast up and over, and the other breast was peculiarly up near my clavicle. They were oddly lop-sided. How had I not seen this? I promptly took down the post. Okay. That was embarrassing.

*   *   *   *   *

I was wrapped tightly with an ace bandage when I woke from surgery. I had bloody, ooze-covered drains coming out of each breast. The implants, capsules, and tissue were removed from seven-inch-long incisions under each breast, not using the scars under my areolas, which was how my original implants had been inserted to keep me scar-free. I had to drain the squeeze bottles that hung from my now very flat ace-bandaged chest five times a day, measure the contents, and record the results—as if the whole procedure wasn't Frankensteinian enough. I could see no hint of a chest under the ace bandage. It had been a long time since I had seen my body without large breasts. It had also been a long time since I could lay my hand flat over my heart. I told myself my breasts had done their job. They were not supposed to be perfect. They had nursed six children for over ten years over the past three decades. They deserved medals.

It took me seven days to remove my bandages and look at myself. I stood in the bathroom mirror, staring at myself as I slowly unwrapped the bandages. They were worse than I could have imagined. I cried. I pulled the seventeen-inch per breast tube drains myself and clipped the stitches. The doctor had directed me to a YouTube video. It would have been fascinating if it hadn't been me.

My husband gave me a vast circle of space. He didn't know whether he should even touch me. To say I was sensitive about the removal was an understatement. I felt like that ten-year-old flat-chested girl all over again. Only this time, thank god, I had a tad more experience and significant life tools. I still cried. I still was ungodly insecure and self-conscious about them. I had no idea what size they were. It was the weirdest predicament. The memory of the plaid yellow sports bra came to mind. My daughter had started to develop within the past year, and we had found this cool online store for girls' bras. Thankfully, there wasn't a tall old lady with horn-rimmed glasses saying, "Honey, come back when you are less boyish and have boobies." So I went to this girls' bra site and ordered my new sports bras. I chose a black one with bits of yellow. The girl on the website modeling it was probably eleven years old. I took a deep breath and ordered nine more sports bras for 'tweens—six black, two purple, and one yellow—because my mind was telling me one would somehow not be enough.

The surgeon asked me if I wanted to keep my implants. Wildly, I said, "Of course." They arrived home with me post-op in a white hospital zip lock bag labeled 'medical waste', with my identity and information attached. The morning after my surgery, I made my way to the kitchen and found them lying on the dining room table. I figured I had to look at them. Why not? Everyone in the house was sleeping, and these massive, expensive bags of silicone had been with me for a decade and were the source of happiness, perfect breasts, sadness, and intense pain. One was leaking and dark yellow. The other was a normal color but left a silicone film on my hands. All kinds of emotions ran through my brain as I held them. First of all, they were heavy. No wonder I felt like a weight was off my chest! Secondly, they were gross and the complete opposite of sexy. Then, of course, my mind wandered to the dark and funny and thought of at least a hundred ways to bring humor and the implants into my and my husband's sex life. No. They would remain in their now sticky silicone-covered Ziploc baggie.

So, my morning implant musings led to my showing them to each child as they wandered into the kitchen over the next hour. My daughter was the first to enter the kitchen. She grimaced and promptly refused my efforts to get her to touch them. She responded, "Wow, I cannot believe those were in you…gross." Yep. My six-year-old wandered in next. He was fascinated and asked if he could take them to school for show and tell. It was bad enough that my son told his kindergarten teacher everything. He had informed me one morning at breakfast that he had shared with her that we all had blowing diarrhea. No, I think his poor teacher would appreciate the gesture if her room full of kindergartners were not allowed to ooh and ahh over my fake silicone breasts. Although I did chuckle at what the teacher's break room conversation would be if I allowed it. He shrugged and demanded to hold one, commenting he could make it part of a Lego city he was building. Double no.

My sixteen-year-old wandered in, followed by my twenty-one-year-old son, who had come back home half the time to help after my surgery. Both looked at me with horror when I showed them the implants. My silicone breasts in the Ziploc bag became the butt of every joke for the next week. So, I just left them on the table for weeks as a reminder to myself that I was no longer that insecure young woman who felt compelled to get them in the first place. Seeing them creepily all zipped up in their plastic bag felt empowering. I think they are presently taking up space next to the bird feeders in the broom closet.

So, here I am, fifty-seven and flat-chested. Thank god. It has now been three months since my removal. I am free of pain. Free of breasts. I have slowly been loving myself. I love that I can put my hand on my heart. I do it often.

Finally, there is no pain. My scars have healed to a dark red. I wear the 'tween sports bras that make me smile and remember the plaid yellow one of years past. After reading countless articles on dressing and shopping for a flat chest, I went on an enormously cathartic shopping spree for shirts, blazers, and dresses for the small-chested gal. Hell, there are flat-chested groups out there talking and praising every possible advantage. There are millions of us. Suddenly, I am very European. I am healing and have actually started to accentuate my pancake-flat chest. My chosen attire shows my actual chest and emphasizes its boyish flatness. So, many people have noticed, but they are unsure what has changed about me. Usually I get, "Wow, have you lost weight?" (Yeah, two-and-a-half pounds of slimy, leaky death). "No," I reply. Many people tell me how great I look. I am happy. I am grateful. I am proud to be flat-chested. The explant and full capsulectomy forced me to look at myself and to explore who I am, and damn it—what defines me! It dawned on me recently that I have learned to love myself. It sounds so simple. My core beliefs about myself had been scattered all over the place. It was up to me to decide what pieces to pick up.

There is this great picture of the actress Keira Knightly going into battle with a war cry in the 2004 movie King Arthur. I found it years ago on a Google search for female warriors. You will know it when you see it. That is how I see myself, a warrior finding her battle cry—pancake flat.

Vienne is a freelance studio artist and owner of Iron Bridge Art and Clay, located in the beautiful historic Mississippi River town of Wabasha, MN. She lives with her husband, Grant, and four of six children on the bluffs above Wabasha, MN, at her family's 100-acre organic farm, Surly Owl Farm. You will find her drawing, making soap, gardening, sewing witch cloaks, beekeeping, caring for farm animals, and growing pumpkins with her children in her free time.

CHAPTER 2

May 25th
By Tobias Forrest

The most effective way to learn something is probably by experiencing it. At the end of 1998, while everyone was just starting to worry about Y2K, I was a newly formed quadriplegic focused on learning how to "not walk." I was also a twenty-three-year-old fresh out of hospital rehab with a spinal cord injury after a life-altering experience. A few months prior, I was a former gymnast and recent college graduate getting ready to move from Flagstaff to Aspen. As a jewelry major who loved skiing, rock climbing, outdoor adventure, and danger, it was the perfect plan. I would make unique jewelry and sell it to rich tourists while getting white powder ski seasons and summers filled with extreme sports. But it also meant saying goodbye to a place I had called home for five years and my girlfriend of the past year and a half. So, we decided to take one last camping trip to the Mecca of Mother Nature, the Grand Canyon.

Havasupai Falls is indescribable because of its beauty, despite the harsh terrain surrounding it. Even the best poets couldn't do it justice if they were asked what a perfect oasis looked like. Deep in the Canyon, under layers of stone, time has created a Heaven on Earth. Even after years of human traffic and mistreatment, Nature is undeniably powerful there. I can't comprehend how valuable it must feel to the native Havasupai tribe who had to fight to sustain it after almost 800 years living there. But tourism infests even the most remote places, and although I consider myself a nature lover, I was just another visitor adding to the invading colony. Maybe we were all looking for a glimpse of something that would exist for millions of years after we were gone.

I've lived in some amazing places in almost ten states, from being born in Sausalito, to being raised on Maui, to currently residing in Southern California. Many of these areas have spots considered magical, breathtaking, gorgeous, and much more, but only a couple of them dare to compete with the contradicting beauty of Havasu Falls. Infinite drops of water coalesce into a single continuous body that is forced over the edge by gravity and converted into raw power. A destructive force that has torn into the Earth below, creating a deep pool of majestic water over thousands of years. The ferocity at its base ripples out into peaceful shallows before plunging over another ledge, which then becomes the second tier in a series of smaller waterfalls. The image is rivaled only by the energy from the green growth surrounding it and the pounding water generating an endless production of negative ions.

Looking up at a ninety-eight-foot cliff is intimidating but it is nothing compared to looking down from it. I know what you're thinking, "Holy shit! He broke his neck diving from a ten-story waterfall?" My ego wants to scream "Hell, yes!" but the reality is no, I absolutely did not. Although in my defense, I have leaped from plenty of cliffs, including jumping from eighty-five feet, backflipping from forty, and skiing from twenty. Plus, I also went cliff diving once in the middle of winter just after midnight in absolute darkness while completely naked. I can confirm that adrenaline is a real drug and being twenty-one and bulletproof is a real feeling. However, this was not a day that I needed to prove my lack of fear of death. Ironically, it was Memorial Day, the date our country honors all personnel who have died in service, including a grandfather I never got to meet. However, maybe all of that was about to change and I would get to introduce myself sooner than expected.

There are a lot of sayings like, "It's the little things;" "The devil's in the details;" and "Minutia is what matters." OK, I made up that last one but whatever—there are plenty of versions. Although this seems like a simple idea, it also seems like the absolute truth. As a jewelry major who worked at a jewelry store, I had a strong understanding of all things small—but that doesn't mean I always noticed them. Like many others, my accident was the result of a combination of little things that would become a huge, life-altering one. It started with a series of decisions followed by a series of actions influenced by a series of unforeseen circumstances. Much like a game of Jenga or a landslide, all it takes to come falling apart and cause destruction is one little piece in the wrong place. In my case, it was a brand-new camera that I carried into the Grand Canyon to capture a few last memories in one of nature's most amazing places.

I'm forty-eight years old, so I remember the times before cell phones when I never took photos. But we were celebrating a national holiday at the bottom of a national treasure surrounded by majestical water. Plus, this was the last trip with my girlfriend before we went our separate ways. So, I bought the best waterproof camera the gas station had to offer! I believe it could only take 24 photos so each one had to matter. Although I consider myself a pretty decent artist, I know absolutely nothing about photography. I definitely wasn't thoughtful enough to take a progression of photos showing the descent from the rim to our current paradise. That didn't matter to my girlfriend or me though, because we had an entire weekend for creating memories. After finally getting to the campsite with our crew, there was no hesitation to throw on swimsuits and head straight to the waterfall. And I knew I wasn't going to make a mistake because I had remembered to bring the best waterproof camera the gas station had to offer!

Directly behind the first waterfall is an incredible cave that was carved into the rock by God's architect. It is so perfectly placed that if you saw it in a movie, you might think it was a digital effect made for dramatic effect. Regardless, it is awesomely romantic and feels like you've been dropped into Middle Earth and the only thing missing is a unicorn. My girlfriend, my buddy and I were the first ones to make it to the water's edge. We quickly set down our gear and splashed into the fresh natural pool. We all swam straight to the cave and scaled the wall to reach its entrance. As we huddled inside this ancient rock, I looked through the liquid wall in front of us and saw the beauty of the Canyon from a new perspective. It was truly awesome, and I could only think one thing: why did I leave the camera on the shore? But there was no time to focus on that because more tourists were scaling the wall behind us. We were occupying the magical spot, and it was obviously time to vacate. I gave my buddy a quick smile and my girlfriend a quick kiss and dove straight into the center of thousands of pounds of falling water.

You're thinking, "Uh-oh, this is where it goes down," and I hate to disappoint you, but we're not there yet. After diving straight into the waterfall, the force pushed me past the whitewater and deep into the cold darkness. There was a soft light above and the quiet roar of the water but otherwise, I was weightless and felt alone for a moment. I wanted to see if I could swim to the bottom but chose to burst back to the surface and surprise my girlfriend. We played in the water a little before making our way to the shore. I grabbed our gear and scouted a nice rock closer to the other side so we could get a little alone time. The sun smiled on us as we admired our surroundings and reminisced about our time together. Although I was only 22, she was my first love and although breaking up seemed to make sense, I was completely doubting myself. I felt guilty for leaving and also for spending most of the day ahead of her on the trail. This was supposed to be a romantic trip to say goodbye with a special memory. I was ruining that and wanted to make it up to her by creating a moment together. But here's where I made my first little mistake: I told her how I felt.

I'm sure anyone who has ever been in a relationship has experienced having a polite argument about how great the other person is. This is basically what my girlfriend and I were doing on our rock. I had just revealed my guilt for being a trailblazer and not spending more time with her. I vowed that I would be a better boyfriend and the best partner she could ask for in our last few days together. Her rebuttal was that I was a great boyfriend and that this experience was for both of us. We would have plenty of opportunities to share, especially after the sun went down and we could have a little "together" time in the tent. Our affectionate dispute dissolved as more tourists arrived, including a couple of our companions. Our plan was to continue playing in the water and maybe find a couple more spots to jump from. My friends asked me to go with them, but I wasn't going to make the mistake of leaving my girlfriend's side. But she knew that I was feeling guilty and sacrificing my wild side, so she suggested something that I had been neglecting all day. She would take a photo of me with the best waterproof camera the gas station had to offer. It was the first and final photo that camera would ever take.

Choosing a place was no problem because there was a large boulder on the rocky side of the pool. We heard from other tourists that it was a good spot to jump from and it was deep enough. Unfortunately, another little thing became a big factor, El Niño had changed the water level. I hurried to the top of the rock and prepared myself for one of the smallest heights I had ever jumped from. It was only ten feet at most, so I was filled with confidence. I saw my girlfriend looking at me with her beautiful smile and the camera ready to go. I flashed her a quick grin before launching myself into the air. Normally I would've done a back or front flip but I knew it wouldn't look good on camera, so my ego helped me make the worst decision of the day. It was that little mistake that made all the difference... I chose to do a swan dive. Soaring in mid-air, I performed my best Jesus Christ pose before bringing my hands together to break the water's surface. I am positive that I had incredible form and that the photo could've made a great cover for Sports Illustrated or Men's Health, but the camera got thrown in the trash, so I never saw it.

However, I did see the sunlight flash off of the water as I entered it, expecting to feel the coolness rush over me as I dove deeper. Instead, I felt an instant and violent impact as my arms buckled and my head struck the solid bottom. Faster than a light switch, my body shut off and there was no getting back to the surface. There was no air in my lungs and no movement in my body, but I was fully conscious, floating face down in the bottom of paradise. It was just like earlier when I dove from the cave—soft light above me, complete weightlessness, and the feeling of being alone. But this time, no matter how hard I tried, I could not swim to safety. I could only sink further into the darkness, feeling only my face as it occasionally brushed against the bottom. I was fully aware of what happened and the resulting lack of communication between my brain and body. I was also aware that I had no oxygen, no way to move, and no time left. Just as panic began to consume me, I realized that this was the day I was going to die.

I refused to give up despite being consumed with terror as my body screamed to take that final breath. Every emotion coursed through me searching for a solution, but there was only one answer to my current situation and that was to accept it. There is a timeless moment when death grabs you; most may think it is filled with fear, but it is just the opposite—it is filled with love. I was no longer alone, cold and struggling to survive, because I felt the presence of greatness. I knew that God or Nature or whatever impossible word can be used to describe what creates us was there with me. My transition from physical form to spiritual entity was seamless and beautiful. The timeless moment continued as I understood that the beginning of my journey had just begun. There was no need for a body or oxygen or love because that's what I had become: absolute, pure love. I had the instant realization that even people who lived a life of profound suffering have also experienced absolute love at the very end of it. I felt complete, and the darkness was replaced with countless beams of indescribable light that created an interconnected web to everything, living or otherwise. I was part of this connection and being pulled towards the light, and I was filled with love for what was about to happen.

Butterflies probably don't dream about their lives as caterpillars; similarly, I've never met a person with a near-death experience who wanted to come back. I was no different, so when I returned to my body, breathing again and coming to consciousness, it was an absolute disappointment. The feeling of love was still there but so was the struggle to comprehend where I was and what was happening. There was some understanding as memories flooded back to me, but they were mixed in with visions of several people looking down at me. The sunlight occasionally blinded me, and I only heard voices as they decided the safest way to move my paralyzed body across the falls and onto the safety of the beach. I lapsed in and out of consciousness, waking up to the faces of strangers and apologizing for ruining their holiday before blacking out again. My makeshift rescue party placed me on the sand as I went back and forth between inaudible apologies and unconsciousness. They struggled to keep me alive as I caught glimpses of my reality between the flashes of light.

There was the scared but loving face of my girlfriend, my shocked buddy who had helped the doctor on vacation reset my neck and give me CPR, a kid who I think was the Doc's son who immobilized my neck for hours, plus all the other strangers who helped carry me. I can recall a helicopter that came but it didn't have the right medical equipment, so it had to fly away. Although I had initially felt no desire to be back in my body, I was now re-experiencing life and was obligated to continue the struggle to survive. Breathing was almost impossible because my lungs had been filled with water and my chest muscles no longer worked, so all I had was my diaphragm. Hours passed before the official evacuation helicopter with the necessary equipment finally arrived. They placed me on a gurney and rushed me off before I could whisper any gratitude to my group of saviors. The last thing I remember was looking up at the EMT and saying, "This is my first helicopter ride." Then I passed out again before they put a tube down my throat to keep me alive.

It has been 25 years since Havasupai Falls and there have been some incredible experiences since then. I have watched my nieces and nephews grow up calling me by my proudest title, "Uncle Toby;" I've whitewater rafted and had tons of adventures with my siblings, years of partying with my cousins and taking over entire restaurants with the size of our family, I've created tons of awesome new friends and done fun things like singing in a rock band, being in the Oscar choir, starring in a movie and being a guest star on television—plus the amazing opportunity to become part of the disabled community and meet the wonderful people within it. Most importantly, I've been able to continue to tell my parents and the other special people in my life how much they mean to me.

All of the little experiences that I had on May 25th were tiny lessons that were incredibly difficult. I could easily say that I trust my instincts better now and I know not to dive into untested waters, but there was a lesson greater than all of these small ones—I learned how to die. There's nothing that can prepare you for death other than to experience it; because of this, I feel that I also received a lesson on how to live. Basically, optimism is free, so have as much as you want! But that doesn't mean I'm not constantly reminded that my journey is not yet over and that I am only one timeless moment away from meeting my ancestors. I may never get to thank the strangers who saved me on Memorial Day, 1998, but if I could share one thing with them that I have learned the hard way, it is that we do not need to fear death because, in the end, we will become absolute love.

Tobias Forrest is an actor, writer, and singer who won the "Christopher Reeve Acting Award" for "Drauma," sang for the band Cityzen and "Oscars" choir plus voice over for several projects.

CHAPTER 3

Dorothy's Red Slippers and an Exorcism
On taking the long road to authenticity
By Kelly Sophia Grace

When I was a toddler, Mama and I had an argument. She said I couldn't be a girl because I had a penis. I shouted back, "Of course, little girls can have penises! I have one!" I made her cry. She went to a therapist who told her it was a phase and to let it play itself out, *but* it had to be a secret.

This happened in 1965, and in that era, it was probably the best advice we could have received.

There was never a moment in my life when I didn't know I was female, despite the pesky protrusion that suggested otherwise. The concept of being transgender (they called it transsexual back then) was not in the societal vocabulary. There were a couple of folks in the news who had undergone a "sex change," but they were mostly considered freaks and inherently "ungodly."

I was precocious and could read well at age three. I read Mama's *Cosmopolitan* magazines and the instructions in her box of tampons. I literally read those instructions every time I went to the bathroom. I didn't understand but I knew it was a part of being the woman I hoped to become.

Fortunately, Mama let me play with dolls and play dress up. A few times my dad would come home and catch me. He'd fly into a rage, yelling at both of us and sometimes punching a hole in the wall or breaking something. I learned to hate him. I believed that he hated me—the real me. He tried to make me do boy things, like baseball. I sabotaged all his efforts.

I was grateful when my brother was born. He was a rough and tumble, mischievous boy. My dad moved his hopes for a son toward him, which was fine by me. Then my sister was born. Mama's desire for a little girl to dress up and play with was finally fulfilled. Yes, I was jealous. I just disappeared into being as perfect and as invisible as possible.

Content Warning: Sexual Abuse of a Child plus Severe Spiritual Abuse

When I was four and five, I was put in an ultra-conservative Baptist kindergarten. Two men there, I don't recall their roles in the church, molested me on many occasions. They told me that what I was doing with them was shameful and that I couldn't tell anyone, especially my parents. I told my Mama I was afraid of the "Apple Head Man" (the bald one) and the "Banana Man." She would oblige me by looking under cars and under my bed to make sure they weren't waiting to pull me under.

I know now that these men observed my feminine spirit and thought I was gay—at age five.

In school, I made friends with the girls and had little interest in hanging out with the boys. I was teased and bullied over this. The more I was shamed for who I was the more I understood the need to keep my identity as a girl a secret.

My only solace was to disappear into books with a female protagonist. Books like *The Wizard of Oz*. In the second book of the Oz series, a little boy is magically transformed into Ozma, the Princess of Oz. I was transfixed by that, and decades later I'm wondering what was going on with L. Frank Baum that he would write about that experience.

I don't know how I survived puberty. I wanted to disappear. I would lay on my bed and cry and beg God to fix me. I'd lock the bathroom door and put on Mama's bra and panties. I'd put a plastic bowl over my genitals, so I'd be smooth like a Barbie. My fantasies were always about waking up from a coma and being female or finding some hidden zipper that allowed me to reveal my real genitals.

As much as I tried to hide my truth, the kids in middle school thought I was gay.

This got infinitely worse with my eighth-grade algebra teacher who was a flamboyantly gay male and would openly flirt with me in class. The other kids were unmerciful. One guy in particular, Donald, would hit me and kick me every day. Once he knocked out a tooth.

I knew something was up when I was fourteen and lying on my bed, crying and praying for God to fix my life. It was intense. Suddenly my spirit left my body, floated through the ceiling, into the sky, and eventually arrived in a huge room bathed in light. There was a being there that I assumed was God, but it was a feminine entity.

I stayed in that room for what seemed like hours—or even days—while the Being just loved me exactly as I was and am. No words were spoken. I laughed and cried. The event was beyond words. Because all I'd ever known was fundamentalist evangelicalism, I had no context to understand what had happened. I just knew it was real.

In that same year, my Mama made and gave me a pair of ruby slippers just like Dorothy's in the movie. She told everyone it was because I loved the *Wizard of Oz*, but secretly she told me it was so I'd know she loved me exactly as I was and that I could always come home.

I was never attracted to men. Generally, they had hurt me and couldn't be trusted. Even though I was secretly female, I was attracted to women, which does make me gay—but not in the way folks thought.

For the decades that followed, I simply survived. I played the role of a man as long as I could. Suffice it to say I had to keep my feminine identity a secret for most of the ensuing decades. It was that or poverty and maybe an early death, or so I believed at the time.

In my late twenties, I was a member of a smallish (100-member) Pentecostal church with all the usual accouterments: speaking in tongues, prophesies, and occasionally what seemed to be a bona fide miracle. To be clear, my membership there falls into the regrets category, although I did like that the pastor was a woman.

One Sunday a lady stood up and boldly announced that she had a "Word of the Lord." This was in Alabama, so imagine the term "Word of the Lord" being said slowly and with double the syllables. She was respected as a modern-day prophet, and this was a common and usually interesting occurrence. The pastor gave the OK for her to continue.

The "prophet" said she had a dream where she was a bride standing near the podium at a wedding at the church, observing another veiled bride in an elaborate gown walking down the aisle. The second bride reached the front, then lifted her veil. The second bride was ME! The prophet called out my name as the congregation gasped. Keep in mind everyone thought I was male back then, so my wearing a wedding dress was simply the most horrid thing ever.

The lady pastor turned red with anger and demanded that I come to the front. Yes, I know now that I should have shouted F.U. and run out, leaving that place forever. But no, I was sadly enmeshed in the cultic faith that was about to assault me.

My mind was spinning. It was true that I was secretly a transgender woman who had often fantasized about being a bride. It was also true that I was sexually attracted to women, so my dream wedding would indeed be just like the prophet described. What I didn't know was what was about to happen.

As I neared the front the team of deacons gathered behind me.

The lady pastor began to scream; then she pushed me so hard that I fell to the ground. The deacons pinned me down while the pastor wailed at the "demon of homosexuality" she said had taken me over. She was bent over, doing full arm swings with her Bible against my chest as her words and spit covered me. The whole congregation was yelling and praying in tongues, and this went on for fifteen minutes.

I began to vomit, which they all believed was the demon leaving my body. I was inconsolable, and I largely dissociated after that. I don't remember how I got home.

For the next three days, I was bedridden. My esophagus felt like I had regurgitated glass shards. I couldn't swallow. Even drinking water was painful. I have no idea why I was in so much pain, but I was told that the demon's fingernails caused this as it reluctantly came out.

The pastor came to my home and told me she'd made arrangements for me to go to a "sexual healing" conference that was coincidentally happening soon in a nearby town. The conference was for all kinds of sexual deviants, but particularly intended to make gay Christians become straight.

Everyone in the church, including the pastor, assumed I was gay — a man who was attracted to men. I wanted to explain that I was actually a woman who was attracted to women, but I decided that fact wouldn't help my situation.

Just in case this whole sequence was not yet bizarre enough, the featured speaker at the Sexual Healing Conference was Donna Douglas, the woman who played Elly May Clampett on the Beverly Hillbillies.

Yes, seriously.

After Donna's acting career, she went to the Pentecostal Christian Rhema Bible Training College, and after graduating, she toured as a gospel singer and inspirational speaker. I don't recall what made her a good fit for the "Pray Away the Gay" conference. I remember being delighted to meet her, but I don't recall anything she said.

Sadly, after all this, I returned to that same church and continued playing the role of a man. Like with any good cult-like religion, those people and that place were my whole world.

The only effect of the exorcism was to add substantially to the complex PTSD I'd developed over the dissonance between my soul and body.

My life moved at a snail's pace. Finding the courage to be on the outside who I always was on the inside required a series of major upheavals. I was married and had two step kids plus an adopted son. So I sabotaged my marriage while seeking a graceful exit.

Eventually, my wife asked for a divorce. I quickly drew up the documents (I was an attorney, so that was the easy part). I didn't have the courage to end things myself, although by then I had already moved away.

Next, I had to leave my religion, at least for the most part. That took far too long. A key complication of that was my role as co-pastor of a church.

Finally, I had to get away from my biological family. I moved 1,300 miles away. When I began posting about being transgender, my ultra-conservative family blocked me on social media. Sadly, my parents passed away, which was freeing. I didn't have the courage to transition while they were alive. Two of my cousins threatened to kill me if they saw me dressed as a woman. A handful of family members and friends continued to celebrate my quest to be my authentic self and gave me their support.

In 2019, at age 57, I began living full-time as my authentic feminine self. I've never been happier.

We come into this life with a quest to add depth and progress to our souls. However, in a universal irony, our circumstances often do not seem to be conducive to learning that lesson. We then spend much of our life seeking the authenticity our souls had prior to our entry into this physical realm.

I've found authenticity in how I present myself to the world. Now, I am focused on fully pressing into the spiritual component that I saw revealed in my out-of-body experience forty years ago. It makes sense now. I realized that when I met the Divine, it was me.

———————————

Kelly Sophia Grace is a former attorney, mediator, and pastor. She is now an author, artist, and life transitions coach, enjoying her best life in Santa Fe, New Mexico. Kellysophiagrace.com

CHAPTER 4

There is No Such Thing as Almost Honest
By Robert "Bobby" Plagmann

We all have a tenuous relationship with the truth from time to time. Everyone has something to share that sounds better with a little embellishment here or a little omission there. We have "mistakes" in our pasts. Many of us have had issues with mental health and/or addiction and have had to face the fear of answering questions about these struggles... We are not alone. There is a definite and debilitating social stigma facing those of us who have experienced these struggles. Society has largely adopted a zero-defect mentality based on nothing more than a fear of our collective propensities and generations of cultivated shame.

Shame creates the feeling that we must lie and hide our past. Shame tells us that our mistakes are a referendum on our personhood—that our inherent value is attached to our capacity for perfection. It is a fraudulent inner voice that tells us we are failing and irredeemable. This is just a story. And it just isn't true. Learning to find and share our truth is a shared human experience. I'm not talking about purity or perfection. There is room in every life for a harmless tall tale, fish story or two. I'm talking about the times when the truth puts you at a crossroads. The times when you know what the right answer is and for one reason or another saying or doing the right thing scares the shit out of you. Maybe you're afraid of the consequences. Or maybe you're afraid of being cast or seen in a light that is inconsistent with how you hope the world sees you. I've fought through hubris, countless different mindsets and mentalities, and jumped through every imaginable hoop to explain away or minimize my own dishonesty in these moments. And I am convinced that I have just barely started to map the landscape of my self-justifications.

Whether you call it a white lie, a fiblet, or a half truth, no matter what you call it, a rose by any other name still ends up smelling like shit.

The honesty dilemma is a real one. As Alfred Adler once said, "A lie would have no sense unless the truth were felt dangerous." It's true. I've run away from truth in every imaginable area of my life: truth about my body and my weight, truth about my grades, truth about my honesty and loyalty. I have made mistakes in all of the most important areas. I have made the disruptive choice in the places that are foundational to character. What is it that makes the truth so scary? We learn rather early and quickly that being honest upfront always saves us from fallout and cleanup. And yet, we continue to self-sabotage. And what's more, when the truth finally does surface, as it invariably will, whatever consequences we seek to avoid with the lie are still there waiting for us. When I look back on those moments where the truth mattered most, what I realize is that trying to slip away from the most accurate story of who I am and who I've been along the way only serves to kill me little by little. When I have been at my worst by my own choosing, I would often double down on the pain by trying to convince the world around me of a story I knew wasn't true. And every time I did, I fell farther and farther away from loving and accepting myself just as I am. Realizing this, accepting it as true, and saying it out loud helped me start to choose differently. I haven't arrived. There is no point in the journey where I magically evolve out of my humanity. The capacity to fear the truth and the temptation to divert myself away from facing it and integrating it into my life will always be real. Day by day, moment by moment, breath by breath—the more I endeavor to love myself, the more equipped I have become to face the fears around my story with courage. To give myself the best hope of being the best me. This is one chapter in the story of how I got here.

The best version of ourselves is always on the other side of struggle. I spent nearly two decades in the United States Marine Corps. I stepped on the yellow footprints at Parris Island, South Carolina on December 1st, 1999, and took my uniform off for the last time on December 1st, 2017. I enlisted first and made the rank of Corporal before being accepted into law school at the University of the Pacific McGeorge School of Law. I spent over a decade in the Marine Corps as an attorney. I of all folks should know that it isn't the crime that kills you, it's the cover-up. And it is this mentality that sets the stage for how life brought this lesson home to me in a visceral but also very loving way. On my way out of the Marine Corps, in the midst of my darkest period of shame, I told some lies. Bringing the truth behind those lies to light over the next several years helped to refine and brighten my heart and my life in unimaginable ways.

I quit a job in February 2023. It was the first time I had ever quit a job. Well, when I was 16, I quit a job at Dollar General because the manager kept pejoratively referring to women's hygiene products. He was such a creep. My entire adult life I had been a U.S. Marine. All of my paystubs, bosses, co-workers—all were part of the never-ending government machine. From age nineteen to age thirty-seven I wore the uniform of the United States. So, when I left the service in December of 2017, I had a lot of firsts to experience.

I was disenchanted with the legal profession. I had spent years as a military defense attorney representing clients accused of everything from attempted murder to grievous and dastardly sexual crimes. I also survived years of childhood sexual abuse. I had never taken the time or effort to accept that trauma or process and integrate it in a healthy way. Consequently, the years of representing child pornographers and pedophiles took a toll on me. Adding to that injury was the experience within the legal community that led to my departure from my beloved Corps. I was disgusted with the legal profession. It brought me no joy. I had to find something that did.

I never would have guessed that walking out of this job would lead to one of my greatest life lessons. I was working as a massage therapist for a chiropractor just outside of Richmond, Virginia. The clinic was situated in a strip mall and shared a plumbing matrix with several other businesses. One of those businesses was a restaurant that did a less-than-stellar job at maintaining its grease traps. Soon enough, most of the businesses that day found their plumbing overflowing into their spaces. It wasn't a minor overflow. I'm talking full-on feces on the floors flooding out into the halls. The employees did their best to clean it up, cordon off the bathrooms, and assure the patronage that there was nothing rotten in the state of Denmark… or Virginia, as it were. During lunch, I chatted up one of the clinicians at the practice about the untoward events the beleaguered staff was tending to. She told me that this had happened before, not many months prior. The toilets flooded, the sinks and bathrooms became unusable, and the clinic's owner was instructing clients and staff to cross the street to use the bathroom at a nearby Bojangles restaurant. I casually mentioned to her that that sounded like a violation of OSHA regulations. Medical facilities are required to have a functioning wash facility. Perhaps the best thing to do was close operations until the problem was resolved.

Word of my concerns made it back to the management. After lunch, I was in the waiting room of the clinic to discuss the next patient coming in with the doctor on duty. Instead of a conversation about a client, I was immediately met with "Hey Bobby, we don't have any OSHA violations, so you can stop telling people we do. OK, BUD?" It was just as snarky as I hope you're imagining it. I was mortified. The entire staff was present. There were patients in the clinic and family members of patients in the waiting room. I was humiliated. I was breaking down into tears. I asked the doctor if he would prefer to discuss this in the employee break room as this was the improper venue for the conversation. In the middle of speaking, he rolled his eyes and smirked hard. That was it. I'd had enough. In my triggered mind I had two choices. It was either to disarticulate him on the spot or quit. I chose the latter and was damn proud about it. It seemed like your everyday run-of-the-mill raging against the machine in the name of my values. I was disrespected. I stood my ground. I quit. And just as I was raising my hands to celebrate me: yay for enforcing boundaries, yay for speaking up for myself, fuck yeah…*Blammo!* A mistake from 2016 popped up to remind me that there is no such thing as "almost honest."

The clinic filed a complaint against my massage therapy license for "abandoning a patient." The outcome of that matter is still pending as I write this. While the complaint itself is baseless, it led the Virginia Department of Health Professions to my initial application for licensure in 2021. On that application, I failed to disclose my struggles with mental health and the effect those struggles had on my status as a member of the bar.

In 2016 I was an active-duty Marine. I was also struggling with addiction, an undiagnosed traumatic brain injury, and was staring down the barrel of the end of my career. For almost 18 years I had served in the Marine Corps. It was a childhood dream. One of the first ones I had. Like a lot of dreams, reality didn't always measure up. The Marine Corps prides itself on camaraderie. They sell it like crack on billboards and TV commercials that look more like video game teasers than a life in the military. I thought I was joining for a sense of purpose and belonging. I thought if I became a Marine and loved the Corps, it would love me back unconditionally. When push came to shove and the chips were down, the Corps ate me alive at my weakest.

In March of that year, I traveled down Interstate 95 from somewhere near Quantico, Virginia to my mother's house in an ironically landlocked town called Dolphin. I was a live wire of anxiety, depression, and hopelessness. I was heavily addicted to lawfully prescribed medication that the military kept throwing at me. When one didn't work, they'd try another. At one point I was taking 15 different medications, including a combination of opiates, benzodiazepines, mood stabilizers, ADHD prescriptions, and sleep medication. I was a zombie 24/7. I got to Mom's place and settled in for a weekend of house-sitting and visiting with my two dogs. I had to temporarily relocate my rescue pups, June Bug and Alcyon, once the Marine Corps started investigating my life in late 2015. A casual encounter with the wrong person and a false allegation was made against me that started a process that would lead to what felt like my complete undoing. The Marine Corps moved me from my master's in criminal law resident student seat at The Judge Advocate General's Legal Center and School on the Campus of UVA to their watchful eye in Quantico, Virginia. It all happened quickly, and in the midst of the haste and confusion I got myself a small apartment in northern Virginia and sent my dogs to live with mom while I waited out the storm that would decide my career.

My mom had plans to attend a music festival with her friends that weekend. I was being a dutiful son and came down to house-sit. It was the least I could do since my 65-year-old mother agreed without hesitation to spontaneously adopt my two large and excitable pit bulls. Once mom pulled out of the driveway, I don't remember much. I identified with the choices that brought me to that crossroads. I saw myself as no better than what I did when I was at my worst. That was the loneliest place I've ever been. In my experience with trauma and the military, I have seen that loneliness will bury a person quicker than anything else. We are not meant to do this life alone. When we can't see ourselves with love, we cannot believe that anyone else would, either. Sebastian Junger, in his book *Tribe* writes, "Human beings don't mind adversity. In fact, they thrive on it. What they cannot tolerate is being useless." At that point in my life, I felt both useless and totally alone. I fixated on my problem. What would I do without the Marine Corps? What would I do if I couldn't get clean? What would I do if nothing ever helped? Without much thinking or hesitation, I grabbed as many of my prescriptions as I could find, and I took them all.

I survived.

The next week the Marine Corps ordered me to a rehabilitation program.

I was sitting in a chair outside of our combat trauma discussion group in the Co-Occurring Outpatient Hospital in Fort Belvoir Virginia when I started filling out my application to the Arizona Bar. I was applying for admission on reciprocity. That means that as an admitted attorney in another jurisdiction, so long as everything in my life was according to Hoyle, I could practice in Arizona. The questions are straightforward. There isn't a lot of room to wiggle or work around them. I'm sitting in this rehab facility, wearing the uniform of this organization that is trying to rid itself of me, while my body is trying to rid itself of years of toxic drugs and chemicals and my brain is trying to cope with each new wave of reality.

Everything I couldn't feel and had been numb for so long was now ravenously tearing at my emotional body. I was in pieces. And yet, filling out that application gave me a faint glimmer of hope. Being an addict for so long had also conditioned me to lie. I started lying years ago to cover up my drinking. I lied about my prescription drug use to all of the important people in my life. I am not proud of those years. I didn't know how to cope. I didn't know who I was. I stepped away from everything I valued to try to keep the pain away.

So, when the Arizona Bar application asked, "Have you ever had any substance abuse or mental health issues that would impact your ability to practice law in this jurisdiction?" I wrote "no." Another question. A lip-biting moment of pause at this one: "Have you ever faced, or do you have any pending legal or administrative matter which may impact your ability to practice law in this jurisdiction?" Well, yeah. I've spent the last 18 years of my life in the Marine Corps, and in a matter of weeks, it could all be over. I was pending what's called a Board of Inquiry. It is a sterile administrative procedure sometimes used to discharge military officers who are accused of low-level misconduct. I rationalized, it's not a real lie after all. If things went well, it would be no big deal and Arizona would be none the wiser, I thought. I was wrong. I knew I was wrong. I couldn't bear to see the truth on paper. I didn't want it to be true anywhere outside of me. Covering up the parts of me that caused me pain continued to tear me apart.

Several months later I was sitting in a courtroom in Quantico, Virginia and it all came crashing down.

When I applied to be a massage therapist, I wasn't trying to be sneaky or deceitful. But when I came across a set of familiar questions on the application, I was overcome with an all too familiar feeling: shame. The questions are harmless enough, and I understand and agree with the need to have some kind of screening process before you allow someone into such an intimate and sensitive profession. And still, when I stared at the question "Have you ever had any action taken against any professional license," I answered no.

Here's the full truth. Shortly after I left the Marine Corps in 2017, I got a call from the Arizona State Bar. They were in possession of all of the documents and records from the Marine Corps that led to my exit. Though I was discharged under honorable conditions and was a 100% disabled veteran, the circumstances were less than ideal. At the board of Inquiry, a panel of senior officers decided that despite my mental health struggles, I had exhibited conduct less than what is expected of a military officer. I was no longer able to serve. Kicked out. Discharged because of the bad decisions I made during the struggle for my life.

Arizona knew it. I didn't tell them. They came for their pound of flesh. They offered me an easy way out. I could voluntarily surrender my license to practice and that would preclude any additional action against me. At the time I didn't have the kind of fight in me I'd need to stick up for myself and speak my piece. I also had no intention of moving to or practicing in Arizona, so I agreed. I surrendered my license and that was that. Or so I thought. I was (and am still) licensed to practice in Washington D.C. and New Jersey.

After corresponding with both of those jurisdictions I was issued a non-punitive reprimand by D.C. and no punishment from New Jersey. I kept my license alive and intact and went about the business of trying to figure out what the hell to do with my life after the military. In March of 2018, I took off for India. During my rehab at Fort Belvoir, I fell in love with yoga. At first it was terrifying; I wasn't able to sit with my thoughts and feelings, couldn't close my eyes, and didn't make it through the first class without leaving. And yet I knew there was something there for me. So I kept going back. I kept learning how to breathe. I kept hearing that there was a well of stillness within me, and in that well I'd find my healing. I took a chance and chose to believe in that. In doing so, I started to believe in myself.

One of my early teachers in the yogic practices recommended an ashram, or sacred teaching site, in northern India, where she and others had their own transformative experiences through deep learning about traditional Himalayan Kundalini Yoga and breathwork. I set out for India and Sattva Yoga Academy in Mohan Chatti, just north of Rishikesh. It didn't hurt that I'm a huge Beatles fan and anyone who knows anything about the Beatles knows Rishikesh is worth visiting if for no other reason than to say you had trodden the same holy ground as John, Paul, George, and Ringo during their spiritual zeniths. I spent nearly a year at the ashram off and on over the course of the next 18 months. I made several trips back and forth, each time more eager to return. In November 2018, I flew back home for the world premiere of the HBO documentary, *We Are Not Done Yet*. The film featured me and nine of my military companions. Produced by the actor and humanitarian Jeffrey Wright, the film delved into how we helped each other put our lives back together after the war through community, art, music, vulnerability, and family bonds—an alternative to the military's preferred mode of treatment: stuff pills down their throats until they're mission capable and fuck 'em if that doesn't work.

Shortly after the film's release and what would be my last visit to the ashram where my journey into self-discovery took root, I was hit with some shocking news. Several of the young women with whom I had attended these yoga trainings were looking for help holding the *Guru*, or spiritual teacher from the ashram accountable. Over the course of the next several months, more and more women came forward to tell their stories of physical, emotional, and sexual abuse at the hands of Anand Mehrotra and members of his staff, or *Gurukul*. Many of the teacher's students, both past and current, rallied around the women who came forward. We publicly campaigned to Yoga Alliance, law enforcement agencies, and anyone who would listen in an effort to bring the misconduct to light and to try to offer a modicum of healing to those affected.

Those closest to the sham teacher closed ranks to protect him. They smeared the women who came forward on social media. Their primary tactic was to shame and ridicule anyone who would speak out against their "enlightened master" and to disavow any possibility of wrongdoing. I found myself at the forefront of the efforts to bring years of abuse of myriad victims out from under the rug and into the light. In doing so, I caught the brunt of the efforts to shut us all up.

I received an email from the Washington D.C. Bar in the thick of the efforts. They had received an anonymous complaint from someone in the Sattva camp. An attorney who had been disbarred in Arizona was somehow involved in assisting women to promulgate false claims against their teacher. D.C. wasn't interested in what they had to say, save that I had been disbarred in another jurisdiction. When I voluntarily surrendered my license to Arizona,

I did not disclose that to the D.C. or New Jersey bars. They reached out to me and wanted to know why. I gave them my explanation and we litigated it for just about a year before Washington D.C. decided that my rationale wasn't satisfactory and temporarily suspended me from practicing in their jurisdiction as well. Wash, rinse, and repeat with New Jersey.

Though I hadn't yet been suspended in D.C. or Jersey when I applied for my massage therapy license, my attempts to defend myself were underway and the writing was on the wall. At the time of my application, I was a member in good standing of both the D.C. and New Jersey bars and had voluntarily surrendered my license in Arizona.

In my experience, the stories that I create around my fears are worse than the things I'm afraid of. And I've learned that I can never shame myself into changing any relationship. Not with my body, not with food, not with people, not with vices or habits that drag down my life or energy. I can only love myself into the next evolved version of me. Letting go of an old version and welcoming the new isn't about hating what I've been or what I've done. It is the acceptance of where I am today, inclusive of my past and not in spite of it. Practically speaking, everything that I have said and done is a part of who I am today. I have to love myself intentionally today. Some days are harder than others. It is a moment-to-moment, breath-to-breath undertaking. It is never somewhere that I can finally "arrive;" it will always require effort. So long as I am willing to change and grow, I will continue to face myself. It is easy to love the good things we do. But can I stand back and look at the lowest moments of my life when I was barely recognizable behind a facade of defense mechanisms and love that guy?

I revisit my worst moments over and over again sometimes, recognizing today that when I am at my darkest and lowest is when I need more love, not less. It's easy and almost instinctual to shy away from the hurt and pain we cause ourselves. As for my part, I can say that when I've seen that behavior in others it can trigger me into judgment and projection. There is a part within each of us, I believe, that is afraid of our own propensity for doing bad. For going against the grain of what our best selves are calling us to. I used to hate that cringing, sinking feeling I would get before or in the midst of a bad choice. Now I recognize it as my soul asking me to reconsider. To at least pause and think it through. Is this who I want to be? Is this the me that I am most proud of—the me that is flourishing and who I want most to share with the world and the ones that I love? As Steve Jobs would often say, "Embrace the pause," and consider the choice. There is a well of stillness between the trigger and the choice. In that well is where the difference is made.

When I read the questions on that massage therapy application, I was triggered into shame. Answering "no" where a "yes" was the truth wasn't about being sneaky. It wasn't about the people reading or processing the application. It wasn't even about fearing that the honest answer would keep me from being accepted. It was about my personal relationship with shame. Shame is a normal and shared human experience. Shame tells us that we are less than. That there is something wrong with us. Shame calls for a referendum on our personhood. On our right to exist. It corrupts our basic right to love ourselves as we are. In my life, shame has been an experience that I have done my best to avoid. When I see myself through the lens of shame, I will do anything to keep anyone else from seeing myself the way that I see myself. But shame is just a story. The truth is that nothing can take away our inherent value. We are born worthy. No action or inaction changes that. The journey to believing that truth is as unique and fantastic as each of us.

Through all of this, I learned that honesty is the highest form of self-care. Each time I cover for myself out of shame there is a tiny death involved. Self-care is not a luxury. It is the well from which all genuine kindness flows. All the real good that we do in the world comes from a place where we have taken care of ourselves. If we don't, if we aren't out to prioritize ourselves, eventually something will come for us—usually resentment. The kind of festering that boils up when we haven't had the courage to admit that we have needs. We want something in return. We want to be filled, fulfilled, prioritized, cared for. We want our service to mean something. We find that purpose in how we care for ourselves first. It's never in the response to what we give. If we do not fill our cup with self-love, we will have no love to give away. We greet the world with anger and frustration. And if nothing changes, then nothing ever changes.

Last year life gave me another chance to tell the truth under similar circumstances. I spent 2022 in community college. I took all the prerequisite courses I needed to apply to be a Physician Assistant. When I filled out my application to PA school, I saw a familiar set of questions. They wanted to know about my history with mental illness. They wanted to know if I had ever had any action taken against me for any professional license. They just wanted to know me. I felt the shame. I felt the trigger. And I told the truth anyway. In fact, I made it the basis for my application essays. And I answered each application question with the full truth. Finally, come what may, whether I was admitted or rejected, I wouldn't have to look over my shoulder to see who was coming up behind me for accountability. And I've gotta tell you, there is no freedom like dropping the weight of hiding from your truth. At that point I had already won. I was integrating this lesson learned the hard way and could feel my life changing every day because of it. I applied to twelve schools. I got into one. One is all it takes. During my interview for admission, I shed tears with one of the gentlemen who interviewed me. We talked about honesty. We talked about vulnerability. We talked about how learning these lessons the hard way and coming out the other side with a sense of self-love and self-respect was exactly what patients needed in the world of medicine. I was accepted. warts and all. Just as I am. Moreover, I received a 100% full scholarship. My cadre starts in January 2024.

It's not over when you think it's over. In the words of the great Ted Lasso, "I hope that all of us, or none of us, are judged by the actions of our weakest moments, but rather by the strength we show when and if we're given a second chance." As long as you're breathing you have a chance to make things right with yourself. Life happens in inhales and exhales. One at a time. And it only takes a moment to set things right with yourself. Struggles are not life punishing you. And no feeling you ever have arises with the intent of being pushed away. Shame is not a punishment. It is the voice of your soul speaking up against the story of failure. When the time comes, and fear tells us that the lie will save us, may we all see it for what it is and just tell the truth.

Robert "Bobby" Plagmann loves and appreciates being alive and his greatest joy comes from connecting with people. A survivor of multiple childhood and adult traumas, Bobby spent 18 years in the United States Marine Corps as part of his journey of self-discovery and belonging. Bobby strives to use a lifetime of lessons learned to be kinder to himself and the world around him. An accomplished attorney, military officer, licensed massage therapist, and semi-professional dharma bum, Bobby is currently studying to be a Physician Assistant at Elon University in North Carolina where he lives with his partner, Shaifali, and their two pit bulls, Baagh and Alcy.

CHAPTER 5

The Challenge *IS* The Revelation
By Jennifer McLean

I was ten days away from living in my car.

The eviction notice was on the door. I hadn't opened the door for four days because I had no gas to go anywhere and no money to get gas, or anything else, for that matter. This was it; at forty-five years old, after years of working way too hard in the agency business and "paying my dues," this is where it ends?

I opened the front door that faced due west to watch the sunset. I was awash in a wonderous display of oranges and purples bouncing off the streaks of clouds. The whole world took on these colors. Then, as I turned, I noticed something taped to my door, flapping in the orange twilight; it was an eviction notice.

CRAP!

This was now officially real. The notice had been there for four days; just ten days were left before my three cats and I were out. I was paralyzed by this moment; my future was completely unknown, and my legs went wobbly with instant fear and uncertainty. I couldn't help but think of how it just seemed completely unfair to experience such beauty in the face of this moment of abject terror.

How did I get here?

One year ago, I had absolutely had it. I was burned out, my soul crushed, and my energy level, past depleted. Being a highly sensitive neurodivergent, working in corporate America for most of my adult life was challenging at best. For some reason, my bosses and clients never trusted the deep creativity that I brought to the table. Whenever a client took the risk, it always paid off, but most wouldn't take the creative approach.

I was genuinely curious why so many needed to constantly play it safe. Considering my clients were always start-ups in the tech industry, the risk *was* the X factor. But when push came to shove, it was like they couldn't access that beautiful recess of intuition. I didn't know that it was something that didn't come naturally to them. I was a round peg in a square hole—meaning it looked like I fit in, but I really didn't. It was all just so darned confusing.

Since directly addressing intuition was a no-no, I would kind of cheat and use "business techniques" to help my clients access their intuition. I created a process where they had to write a story describing what the next five years of their company looked like using as many descriptive words as they could think of. This *forced* them into their imaginations and visualization.

Then, we would gather the best words from the executives in this "marketing workshop" and use those words to create the messaging for the company. That became the foundation of the brand, and they didn't have a clue that it was created from their visualizations, which linked directly to their intuition. Those moments were fun, but they were few and far between.

Working my way around the rules of patriarchy with dyslexia and ADHD was a unique experience, too. I didn't realize until years later that I saw things differently than most people I worked with (except the creatives at the agency). I didn't realize it at the time, but how I saw things was my greatest gift. My bosses and clients, on the other hand, just wanted the risk-free version that was uber-organized... and dull as a dishcloth. I wish I could go back and talk to that gifted young woman and let her know that her gut instincts were generally right. To tell her that eventually, she would know this and would be able to use those deeper understandings to create a multimillion-dollar business that helped millions of folks just like her discover their gifts and power.

I thought that the only pathway forward was to diligently work harder and longer, becoming more and more harried. I discovered that these colleagues never saw the possibilities I did until a project was brought all the way to fruition. And even then, they would be confused. "How did *she* do that?" I can't tell you how many times I heard, "You? YOU created a forty-million-dollar business?" And the amazing thing is that these men didn't even realize that specific question may have been seen as insulting.

Okay, well, that is a completely different conversation about female neurodivergent/highly sensitive souls in corporate America... ugh.

There I was, working my tooshie off for these unwilling, unappreciative clients and thinking there was something wrong with me. If I just worked more and did exactly what they asked (even if it was obviously not the correct strategy), this would get easier. It didn't.

My *leaving it all* happened with a particularly picky client. I didn't know it at the time, but it was the last client I would ever have to work with at the agency. This client was a small tech startup company that was not well known. And the category they played in was so nascent that no one had really focused on it. We had a big job ahead of us. We created this unique strategy of making up a category that hadn't existed until we said it did and then positioned this client as the leader of this category. We got some industry research companies on board with the idea that our client was a proof of concept for the new category, and then we took the story pitch straight to the most powerful magazine in business at the time, Forbes.

And by gosh, they bought it! A few months later, we got the cover story in one of the most important publications a company like our client can be in. I was ecstatic. *Now* they could see the relevance and importance of what we'd done.

NOPE!

I received an 8-page email that even though they were positioned as the leader of this brand-new category in this cover article, they wanted the whole thing to be only about them. This tiny little dinky company actually *complained* about this almost impossible achievement. You didn't have to kick me in the woohoo anymore to realize this was it; this was soul-crushing, and this would never change. I WAS DONE.

I printed the eight pages, plopped them on my boss's desk, and said: "I quit." They tried to convince me to stay for a few more months, but that was it for me. I was not going to allow my heart to get bashed any longer.

I then decided to become an Aflac insurance agent. It made sense in my little mind to shift to something safe and secure that delivered long-term commissions. In actuality, I just needed to tell myself that this was what I was doing so I could justify leaving my well-paying corporate job. It's amazing what we tell ourselves in order to give ourselves permission to leave behind the old, isn't it?

I went to the insurance licensing classes for several months and passed the insurance license test on the first go. Two weeks later I was an Aflac insurance salesman making cold calls. Two weeks into this Aflac gig, the dread started coming in, and it licked up my legs, then spread through my torso. I started having what I call the "clammy wobblies," thinking "This is my life now." The horror landed in my abdomen like a lead weight and stayed. It clogged my heart and closed my throat.

"NOOOOOOOO, I can't do this!" I screamed thirteen days later in my little apartment. "I can't live this small, uneventful, uncreative, safe life." In fewer than four months after leaving the agency job, I quit once again. I was now free, untethered, with nothing in particular to do next—one of the most thrilling *and* deeply terrifying moments of my life.

"What's next?" I thought. I took inventory. I'm really good at marketing communications. And I am a healer.

Back story: My extremely challenging childhood, which included sexual abuse, narcissism, and alcoholism, left me with severe PTSD. I spent many years during my twenties trying to understand how to recover from this. This took me on a journey of healing. I took a ton of trainings, workshops, and certification programs, which eventually led me to become an energy medicine healer. Over the years since then, I have taken on small practices with a few clients and worked with friends and family.

Now, I was on an obvious, clear path to actually pursuing this.

However, I did not believe that being a healer would generate the kind of money that I was used to. And my ambition had me thinking that I deserved to be *very* wealthy—something a healer would never allow me to be. Being a healer would have to be put on the back burner as a "maybe I can eventually semi-retire into a simpler life as a healer to supplement my retirement income" kind of thing. The irony of that short-sighted false belief will become evident shortly.

This back-burner moment did trigger the idea of using my marketing expertise to help market a friend's holistic product. This meant that I could promote the industry of healing without having to commit to my own practice. Perfect! This was my launch into online marketing. Now, I *knew* I was a marketing genius (ego much?) and that I could easily transfer my skills to the online world. This would be a breeze.

I got to work. I created an online funnel, but I knew better than the experts, and I created it my way. I was extremely confident that we could rake in thirty to fifty thousand dollars easily! I worked diligently for about six weeks in preparation: copywriting, getting the technology right, and identifying how to fulfill the copious orders. We were ready; it was time.

We launched this remarkable, amazing feat of marketing... and sold a grand total of $347.52.

This was not only disappointing, but I had also gone through my savings; I had put all my time, effort, and money into this. There were no future prospects, no income, no job, nothing. I was in big trouble.

Fast forward two months, and there I was, staring at the eviction notice in disbelief that it had come to this.

I discovered from this moment and more like it that when we are at the apparent bottom, that is actually where the magic happens.

This "dark night" moment forced me into a real state of being, a state where I stopped lying to myself and could no longer escape facing the reality and the consequences that I created. That may seem harsh, but this is the two-by-four moment that forced me into a change that I needed but couldn't yet see.

My pattern in these moments was to rail at God. "Why me? I have worked so hard for so long, and I deserve something better than this!" I've come to understand that this pattern is the moment of claiming victimhood. Something out there has "done me wrong," and I am just an innocent bystander. Another lie I told myself. But the truth was that I had to get to this place to activate what was next for me. And moving from victim to powerhouse manifestor and contributor *required* this moment.

After seeing the eviction notice, I went into the apartment in shock, flopped on the couch, and just stared ahead in disbelief. Thoughts swirled around in my head: Where was I going to go? What was I going to do? Would I get out of this? Would I be homeless?

And then I remembered that I was a healer. I had skills! I had a daily practice of energy medicine techniques that I used to help with stress and overwhelm that I had learned in my twenties. In my desperation, I was willing to do anything. And I was clearly guided to perform one of these techniques. I took an inner journey (kind of like a shamanic journey) to find out what I should do. This journey helped me discover that it wasn't ever about "doing;" it was actually about "being." This will become clear in just a minute.

I think because I was so scared, I took this moment very seriously. As a result, the energy medicine inner journey I embarked on was deeper than ever before. I felt I was being guided. There were energies there that wanted to show me some things. I was nudged to travel inside myself to a special chamber in what felt like a different dimension of being. Once in this chamber, I was astonished that I felt instantly better here. I felt safe; I felt alive. I felt detached from the terror that was there just moments ago.

It reminded me of a prayer that I performed daily as a teenager and young adult. I would often beg in prayer, "Please help me to know myself." Such a strange prayer for someone so young and confused by a challenging childhood. This chamber delivered the answer to that prayer. It helped me to have a sense of knowing who I was and that I was something *much more* than my circumstances. In this place, I was able to access a different state of being. I wasn't terrified, and because of that, I could more neutrally ask into this stillness of my soul about my situation. I asked, "What is happening? What is this about? What am I to know from this?"

Every so often in my life, during moments of "the dark night of the soul," I have heard what I call the "divine voice." Back then, I didn't tell many people about this except a few of my woo-woo friends. But here in this beautiful chamber of safety amongst some unique energies, including guides and angels, I heard "The Voice." It answered my questions with a depth of clarity and resonance that was unmistakable, delivering real truths. I knew it in my bones; I felt it in my viscera, and even my mind instantly quieted in the face of these truths.

The Voice said…

"You have been seeking the answers outside of yourself. You think that what you are praying for is some brass ring out there. And if you could just grab a hold of it, *then* your life would make sense. *Then* you would be safe. *Then* you would be healthy, wealthy, in a relationship, safe…

But you have missed something, Jennifer. *You* are the brass ring. *You* are that which you are seeking. *You* are the answer. You are the power, the grace, the intelligence, the creativity, the joy, the sadness, the open heart, the pain, the opportunity, the suffering, the happiness, the disappointment—you are all of it.

Trying to change your circumstances through pure will and pushing through an agenda of "making something happen" will not deliver to you what you think you desire. You *are* those circumstances; you are the journey within what is happening, and this journey is as it should be."

The Voice continued, "Thinking someone else has to change for you to be happy, better, or even okay will ensure that you are never happy. Thinking that your clients, your boss, and your family have to change for *your* peace of mind and thinking that is the only path to peace is false. Again, those answers fall outside of you, and your answers are here within. You are the only path to peace. Your power claimed and lived in is the only path forward; you are the answer, and your gifts are the way."

When the Voice ceased, in that moment I received a jolt, then a wave of the most profound and intimate energy surge I had ever experienced. It penetrated my heart and activated it. It unlocked this dormant part of me, like a piece of the power I never knew I had exploded into my conscious understanding. It activated my mind, my connection to spirit and soul, and neutralized my upsetting emotions. I was attuned to my power, which delivered the answer I needed most.

From that moment to this one, I have "re-cognized" that whenever I am seeking outside of myself for an answer, it's time to reconnect to the memory of my attuned power. In those moments of confusion, when I ask an unanswerable question like, "Why me?" or "Why now?" or "Why *not* now?" I can use those victim questions to remind me of that Voice and the message that activated my new power; then I can focus my full attention there.

That moment of activated power changed me, and like the Red Sea parting, my life moved in magical and wonderful ways. Within days of the Voice and the Attunement, I received a $3000 loan from someone at church who believed in me. It was a miracle!

Shortly after that, I was able to go back to working in marketing with clients, but this time as a freelancer, setting my own rates and working my own hours from home. At the time, I wasn't necessarily happy about what I thought was going backward—back into an industry I thought I wanted to leave behind. But as I look back, it is clear that it brought me good revenue and a measure of freedom and security to pursue something entirely new.

It gave me the financial freedom to become a healer. I decided, with this new attuned energy buoying me up, that I could simplify my life, downsize to a studio apartment, and finally devote myself full-time to being a healer. The message from the divine voice was to pursue my gifts, and healing was clearly a gift I had danced around my whole life.

I used my marketing experience to start my healing practice, I used a system of marketing I had created called Credibility Branding, and one of the tenets was to place yourself with other leaders in a market, and by proxy, you become a leader. Using this strategy, I created the very first online summit in the personal development space. Within eleven months, I would quit the freelance marketing gig. Within eighteen months, I had earned my first million dollars. I went on to be a force of transformation for millions, with over 500 shows and seventeen seasons, working with the best and brightest thought leaders and healers of our time.

And while that appears to be a story of magnificent triumph, which it is, the contraction and expansion of life continues…

Now, all these years later, I find myself in a position of wondering if I am going to be homeless again. Yep, as I write these words, I am in a moment where I can't pay the rent, and I am in arrears in a number of areas that might result in the repossession of my cars. However, this time is quite a different scenario. I am in the process of selling most of my company. I have the opportunity to be part of a roll up with other companies and to sell all to a large multinational media company. It is quite an exciting opportunity to take a lifetime of work and not only receive a big check but also have my programs now reach millions more.

However, the holding company overseeing the sale, which has been giving me direct distributions for the income coming from those products—well, they have stopped. They are claiming that they overdistributed funds to me. They cut me off cold with no recourse. And that was my only income.

It has been 2 months without my main income being distributed; I had already gone through my savings to invest in and ensure what they call the "exit" (which is the sale to the new entity) would be as good and profitable as possible. This exit was supposed to have happened 2 months ago, and I had timed it for that. So now I sit here writing these words with very little income to run the business, make payroll, and even pay for food and gas, let alone rent. But alas, life is what happens to you while you're busy making other plans, right?

I've come to understand that there are and will always be seasons of life. Just like winter moves into spring and summer moves into fall, I will move through the seasons of my life. And each season creates this new mulch of nourishing experiences that I get to evolve from. I am in a continuing evolutionary arc of change and improvement, and all I have to do is continue to see that.

What is different about this moment of potential homelessness is I *know* that this is all here for me, revealing what I am *ready* to heal through. And of course, I know at the end of this is the sale and the income that comes from that. However, the amount and timing are unknown, and there will likely be no income until the sale happens.

What I am learning from this current round of financial challenges is that my childhood set me up with a pattern of "terror and relief" (relief as in, "OMG, it's finally over"). And this is my chance to notice this pattern, heal it, and transform it into something different. Perhaps I couldn't see this pattern without the threat of homelessness once again.

It is also showing me how far I have come from all those years ago with the eviction notice on the door. This moment exposes that fear, but it is always short-lived. I've learned to trust my soul, to trust my soul's journey, and to trust the process implicitly. Perhaps this moment, in hindsight, might be my next book about resilience in the face of hardship.

I don't know what the future holds for me; I simply continue to seek equanimity, to be in good shape in the midst of it. And to use it to continue to attune to my power and gifts and share those insights with whoever is drawn to them. I now know that no matter what, attuning to my power and being in a state of trust—in a state of grace—continues to create the magic of what's next for me in my soul journey.

———————————

Jennifer McLean, author of several bestselling books, is an advanced, internationally acclaimed Energy Medicine Healer and Transformational Change Agent. Reaching millions of souls since 2008, she is the creator of the global phenomenon and healing accelerant: "The Spontaneous Transformation Technique (STT)," which delivers instant transformation, healing the unconscious and unresolved trauma from the body. With almost 1000 STT Practitioners in this unique system, it is quickly becoming a "go-to" for creating real change in extreme times.

CHAPTER 6

Let That Shit Go! No Seriously, You Gotta Let it Go
The road that led to my soul's purpose
By Rissy Lynn Smith

We all get into the nitty-gritty of life and take our punches like the next guy, but what happens when you bypass the grieving process by holding on to everything that comes your way after you lose your dad?

Well, I will tell you! You set yourself up for an implosion of astronomical proportions—one that you will either lose your shit over or from which you will learn to start letting out the collective steam.

Well, I ignored all the warnings of impending doom and lost my entire shit—so much so that I think those closest to me thought a mental evaluation was only a phone call away. It was not pretty. Well, from the outside (to those who did not know me) everything seemed in order. However, my insides looked like molten lava, just pouring into every orifice and looking for a place to exit.

I was walking through my days without being able to emote. I am a very expressive person; I wear my emotions like a comfortable robe. To the world, I had nothing.

Those close to me, now that I look back, were completely blindsided by my state of mind. They did not know how to reach me or tell me that they were available for me. It was like seeing your hero cry. Now I am not putting myself in the hero category; I am just trying to give you a little insight into how it compares to their love for me. No ego here, folks!

Here is the thing: you can have depression but still smile and pretend to laugh. You can have anxiety and still sound like you can breathe, and you can feel suicidal yet turn up every day to life, appearing completely normal. There were times that I would sit at my desk at work and play the soundtrack to "City of Angels" for the entire shift.

Hey, it was a graveyard, and I could get away with a lot of stuff, no one was looking for me! Okay?

In general, I am an extremely positive woman. No seriously, I am someone who always tries to find ways to make the light shine for everyone around me. You need it, I got it; you want it, it is yours. The problem with that is that you feel like no one sees when you are the one who is needy. Oh, did I mention that I am also one stubborn individual? You know, the one that tries to push her own needs into a bucket labeled, "Not Right Now!"

Here is my story.

It had been five months since my dad suffered a horrific death, one in which he was suffering immensely, and I had to decide to stop all life-saving measures. No guilt there, huh? Thanksgiving was coming up, which also happened to be my mother-in-law's birthday and my dad's favorite holiday.

One day—I think a week before Thanksgiving—my husband came into the house and informed me that I would be making dinner for everyone!

Hold on, did you just tell me what I was going to do? Yes, he really did!

My first words were, "are you insane?" because he knew. He knew how much it hurt that my dad had just asked me the year before if I would just make him Thanksgiving dinner, but I was too busy.

I was too busy! Full disclosure: the prior year, I had made every excuse not to make him dinner, because I wanted to make everyone else happy.

I just audibly took a deep breath because that memory still hurts. It has been twenty-seven years, but it will always be the day that the fuse was lit. I digress, where was I? Oh yes, planning a big dinner for his family.

Oh honey—do not worry, we are no longer attached to one another. But that is a story for another day! And no, this was not the final limit.

My husband stood there with this look of complete contempt all over his face, shocked that I would even consider refusing to do something for his mom. I stopped myself from saying the hurtful things that were going on in my head and tried to get him to understand that I was just not ready to entertain anyone on Thanksgiving. He refused to give in, and I spent hours that day making an elaborate full-course meal with all the trimmings.

That evening, everyone sat around the table eating and conversing in great spirits, even though my husband decided that he wanted to hang out with his friends instead of celebrating his mother's birthday. I mean, really? I could not eat one thing; I just kept pushing everything around on my plate. I laughed at the jokes and responded as appropriate for all the conversation going on, or if anyone asked me anything. It was going okay; I secretly patted myself on the back that I was making it through, right up until my husband's mom said she wished that I had invited my dad to her birthday party.

A little backstory: the day before my father had his stroke, my mother-in-law was diagnosed with advanced-stage Alzheimer's. Ba-dum-bump. I could not say anything about my dad having passed, because every time we mentioned it to her she would grieve for him. Like a robot, I said he was so sorry that he could not come. I got up from the table and walked into the kitchen. As I was standing at the kitchen sink, staring at the drain, my husband decided that was the time he wanted to come in to have some food. I was rocking back and forth; he stopped mid-sentence as he called my name. I was not answering. I just continued rocking.

Before I knew it, he had taken me out the front door and sat me down in a folding chair that he brought from inside the house. He forced me to sit down and said it was time to cry. He turned around and went back into the house, just as I heard him locking the wrought iron screen door.

I cried, I sobbed, I screamed, asking why I was left alone to do this, all by myself. I screamed at the sky until my tears stopped. I looked down at the lawn and noticed all the leaves piled near the tree, how they trailed across the yard toward where I was sitting. I was amazed by them—the different shapes and colors, and just the amounts of leaves that were there that I had not even noticed before.

As I was sitting there, all cried out and contemplating my thoughts, those same leaves started moving circularly. The wind had picked up out of nowhere, and the leaves began encircling me as I sat in the chair. I could hear the depth of the wind, the crackle of the leaves, and the smell of my dad's Old English cologne. Oh my God—he was here! My dad was here!

He was surrounding me as if in a hug, and I could hear him tell me how wonderful it was, how the spirits were in the wind that moved around us, how they were always close to us. How it felt to fly free. And I felt the love.

When I say that I "heard" him, it does not truly and adequately explain what was really happening. It was more like I knew and understood what was being said by my dad without him saying it.

And no, I do not normally converse with the dearly departed. The crazy thing is that when I thought about why I had been so completely upset, I realized that I had been waiting for my dad to appear in my dreams. You know something like, "Hey daughter, I am okay. I am not mad at you for the choice you made to stop the fight." I mean, anything would have been a solace to my poor lonely heart as I truly had been carrying around the guilt for ending his life with that one decision.

My dad Manny was nothing close to subtle. Instead of visiting my dreams, he dug deep and reached me a whole other way! Boom shakalaka—the gift of claircognizance shows her pretty head, right when you need her the most. What an amazing friend she is!

Now as I am experiencing this miracle, I hear my husband turning the lock on the door. Just as he walked out, the leaves fell, and it all stopped.

I wanted to scream "No, come back!" but I just knew that if I did, I would have to explain what had happened and knew he was going to tell me that I had finally lost it. But he fooled me; he walked right up to me with this look on his face, and I knew he saw what was happening. All that he could get out was, "What the Fuck was that?"

I just started laughing and it was not a little giggle that made your belly roll, but an outright guffaw! (Do people still say guffaw?) Anywho, I knew I was safe because he was just as out there on the limb as I was. So when I decided to share the experience with him, he had no choice but to sit there and listen.

Let me just say that the understanding that I was not alone—that I did not have to hide behind a smile, that I could truly be myself—led me to genuinely trust my intuition and start looking inside for guidance. To start listening and to understand that there was so much more to be experienced.

You know that saying, "It will all come out in the wash?" Well, consider me clean as a whistle after that encounter.

Now I do not want you to think that this was my first rodeo, nor the first time something woo-woo has happened to me. Nope! I have had clairvoyance, claircognizance, and clairsentience gifts since I could remember, but I pushed them way down and away because they made me different. Because no one would understand, and I just wanted to fit into the box that society had erected for me. Truly, when you push stuff down, you begin to think that it was all fantasy anyway—stuff better made for fiction.

The first instance that I can remember was when I was about six or seven years old. We were in our van on our way to pick my dad up from work—we, as in my mom, my brother, and myself. As we were on the freeway, driving next to Griffith Park, I got a vision of a lady who was so white that she was translucent. She told me that she was right there. She did not have clothes on, and I could see that the leaves were surrounding her. I told my mom that there was a lady on the side of the freeway in the trees who wanted to tell us where she was. My mom freaked out and told me not to say anything else about it ever again, to anybody.

The next day as we were approaching the same area and getting ready to exit the freeway, there were a bunch of flashing lights off to the side; we were being redirected to take the east exit instead of the west. My mom turned on the radio and looked for a news station. The station we tuned into was in the middle of announcing that the latest victim of a serial killer had been found in Griffith Park and to avoid the area. My mom turned to me and reminded me that I was not to say a word.

For a long time, trivial things would happen, but I would ignore them because I did not want anyone to think that I was a freak. After the incident with my dad, such things got even stronger for me.

For instance, this same husband and I were in a van driving through the mountains one foggy day, trying to reach the beach by way of a shortcut. Hey—I am in California, where you can go to the snow by day, beach by night, or even visit a lone desert highway. We were driving on a very narrow two-lane road where the cliffside was within arm's reach. As we continued higher, snow began to fall and visibility was close to zero. We kept going because we could not be too far from the other side. Plus, it was impossible to turn around safely. My husband was driving, and I could see that he was about to start panicking. I immediately reassured him that we were almost there, just to take it slow. Deep breaths, in and out, just hold on.

Not me though, you know—never let 'em see you sweat! I began to pray in earnest. I specifically asked that the clouds please be cleared from our view so that we could make it out of the fog. I remember feeling lightheaded but completely sure that we were going to be okay. No sooner did I finish asking, than the clouds disappeared from around us. They simply disappeared! Well—the clouds disappeared, but the rain started falling from my eyes like a waterfall. I was so grateful for the help.

Now you may not believe in any God or a benevolent being, but I can only tell you that I know that I am not alone in this life. Nuh uh—not me; I will know that!

But then that old self decided to creep on in. I kept telling myself that it was a coincidence; you just happened to be asking for help while you made it to a better weather pocket.

You would think that despite this, I would start looking into doing mediumship work—that the universe was showing me that it was there for me. That I had a unique opportunity to make a difference in the lives around me with this gift—or gifts, to be truthful. But no, I was too busy in my life trying to fit into that old comfortable box. Silly me!

One day in later years the universe got tired of putting out hints and outright pushed me. I was sitting there, contemplating my life and all the things that I did not feel adequately educated about or worthy enough of that limited me from doing anything in my life that made sense. I had just finished celebrating my fiftieth birthday and felt ashamed. Out of nowhere, the palms of my hands started to heat up like they were on fire, and there was nothing that I could do to stop it. I went to the bathroom and started to run icy water to cool them down. It would help for a little while, and then it would start up all over again.

I started to look at anything on the web that could describe what was happening; I got everything from thyroid issues to menopausal symptoms. I put my phone down because it was scaring me more than what I was going through. I picked up the remote and turned on the television. There was a commercial about a wellness center, and while I was not really paying attention to it, something they said grabbed my attention. A woman was talking about her soul journey into energy healing and how she had come to understand how she was meant to help humanity through healing trauma.

By the end of the commercial (or infomercial), I was so interested in what she was saying that it felt like she was talking directly to me. She was talking about a Reiki seminar that she was hosting, and how it had changed her life.

Ooh... another woo woo moment incoming, because it triggered memories of when people would ask me to put my hands on them. They asked me to lay my hands on them because I always made them feel better. For instance, someone would have a headache and ask me to rub their head and it would go away. A backache, a tummy ache, things like that.

So, what she was describing in front of me was something that I had always felt but never paid attention to.

I wanted to sign up for classes because it truly felt like that was what I was supposed to do. I made the decision to go on a journey for myself and ended up finding my purpose. Oh, and I learned that the heat in my hands was energy that needed to be released. Literally! Who knew the universe could speak so loudly?

I live my life in all my truths and can honestly say that I am my authentic self. I am no longer concerned with how I look or am perceived by others. What is paramount is that I found myself in the process. I make light of the circumstances, but the lessons that I learned were hard. The more that I reverted to ignoring myself, the harder the lessons became. Trust me, there were plenty of other lessons that occurred before my fiftieth birthday, but I continued to be stubborn. See, "truly stubborn" was a shield that I carried around. Finally, I realized that there was no reason to fight.

The incident with my father was significant because it was an event I could think back on and understand the messages that I was getting along the way, and how they were meant to open my eyes.

Today I write, I offer energy healing, I travel, and I make moves completely on intuition. I love myself completely and know that I have human flaws, but they are what make me a unique person. A unique human being.

Rissy Lynn Smith is a certified energy healer with a lifetimes' experience in care of others. She is currently pursuing certification in Substance Use Disorder Counseling and finishing her first novel.

CHAPTER 7

Reality Check
By Dr. Theresa L. Smith, D.C.

I was in the backyard watering with my daughter when I heard a neighbor yelling our names from the front yard. I knew he had mental problems; I'd dealt with him before. I had helped him and was kind and supportive. This time, it was different. He was yelling that he was going to kill my daughter and me. He was very high on drugs; it was his birthday, after all. So I went out front, wondering what the fuss was, because I knew this person.

He hit me so hard that I have no memory of it to this day. I remember nothing other than being in the backyard. I was hit so hard that I had a concussion, a torn retina, and broken facial bones and teeth. I went for a ride in an ambulance that I have no memory of, and I would want to remember such a ride. When they released me from the hospital, I had no idea where I was, why I was there, or who I was. That's right: they released me from the hospital, and I had amnesia. Thankfully, my daughter was with me. All I knew was that I wanted to find the person who had done this to me and beat him to a pulp. Anger was in every cell of my body, and I did go out into the street, screaming his name, but he was long gone, not to be found for six months.

During my recovery, a friend came to visit. She and I often enjoyed sharing philosophical thoughts, thinking about life and meaning. Being a spiritual person, she offered the possibility that maybe I was creating this post-attack anger and suffering for whatever reason. Either I was choosing to continue to suffer, or I was a victim. There was no in-between. When I denied creating anything about my situation, she told a story. She needed a new car bumper; shortly thereafter, she was involved in an accident in which her bumper ended up being replaced. She suggested that she had unconsciously "created" a situation that would remedy her bumper problem. I thought that was a pretty stupid line of thinking, involving someone else in a negative way to benefit yourself. I just couldn't agree. We parted ways; our friendship was broken by this disagreement. But she had raised some questions that I needed to have answered.

I could not accept, would not accept that I was responsible for my continued suffering. I had suffered a brutal attack that was not my fault. Could I possibly hate myself so much that I invited someone to break my face and teeth and cause a traumatic brain injury? Recovering from the brain injury made me unsure if I could remember what I needed to know to continue working as a chiropractor, and after I recovered, I never regained my memory of the attack. I had lived through traumatic experiences before, and now this. If I wasn't a victim or the creator of my suffering, I needed to figure out what was true; so, I embarked on a journey to discover the truth.

I have spent years searching my heart and mind and thousands of dollars in the process of seeking truth, and so far, I've found that the only thing we can control in life is how we respond. Unfortunately, our responses are often generated by beliefs, identities, and emotions, which trigger sudden reactions and outbursts. Our reality is littered with beliefs, emotions, and identities that were created from our conception until around the age of six or seven. Before that, we're not thinking for ourselves: it's all input from everyone we are around. We end up carrying those beliefs, emotions, and identities through the rest of our lives, and these childish points of view inform our responses to experiences, even when we're adults. Without properly healing these childish beliefs, emotions, and identities, we continue to respond with immature energy, leading to less-than-desirable outcomes.

For example, let's consider beliefs about money. I grew up in a poor family who had relatives with money. This led to a belief that I was not worthy to make money, and since I wasn't worthy, maybe if I helped people, that would make me worthy. I practiced chiropractic care for twenty-five years and never made much profit. I paid my bills, scraped by, invested in the business, and helped people, but I never earned the income that other chiropractors were earning. This belief that I wasn't worthy also impacted other areas of my life, such as relationships. This belief of unworthiness began when I was a child, but it continued to inform my unconscious beliefs as an adult.

The Power of Choice

As I continued my study of different modalities, I learned how the mind worked and how to create the life I desired. For me, it started with understanding my power to choose. I choose to live a life I love and to be the creative genius I am. My life is filled with joy, happiness, laughter, and abundance. I am blessed. That doesn't mean there aren't bumps in the road, but I now have the tools and insights to handle them. The power of choice helps me ask, "How is this an uncomfortable event for me?" I've learned how to be aware and to remove any negative energetic charge I might feel toward a difficult circumstance. I choose how I react; I choose what I do. I choose! I know how to intuitively ask what is next on the action list to reach my desired goal. I CHOOSE!

While many people agree we have a choice, few discern that our programming from childhood can cause us to choose out of fear or wounding. It's important when we feel a certain way to stop and ask ourselves, "Why am I feeling like this? What does this feeling say about what I believe about myself or others?" By slowing down our knee-jerk reactions, taking a few breaths, and asking ourselves questions, we can see clearly where our feelings come from and choose to respond from a better mindset.

Our beliefs, identities, and emotions end up creating a life of their own. I didn't want to be or feel unworthy, but the stories generated by these beliefs, identities, and emotions can take over our lives. Instead of being in the here and now, we end up being in the story we have created based on our interpretation of our situation through the lens of our prior programming. When we engage in the stories we tell ourselves, we end up perpetuating pathways in our brains to continue the programming we received as a child. Interpreting life through the lens of a six-year-old does not help us thrive. It is limited and often untrue, as I pointed out in my example about my money beliefs. We must recognize the stories we've created based on our childish programming and learn to respond from a positive mindset.

The Power of Focus

In my journey of self-discovery, I also learned the importance of focus. Whatever we focus on becomes our reality. When we focus on something, it's like we are zooming in with our camera lens – whatever we're focused on becomes huge! I now focus on my desired result, and it comes easily to me.

While I love teaching people how to reach goals, release traumas, and change prior programming from childhood beliefs, one of the most important reasons I went on this journey of self-discovery was to help people with illness or dis-ease. Based on my chiropractic training, I believed that if I aligned the spine, everything would work better. All those nerves connected to organs and glands would be running smoothly. But then I learned from Dr. Bruce Lipton, a renowned cell biologist, that ninety-five percent of the time, our subconscious beliefs are controlling our lives, and more than ninety percent of disease comes from our environment and programming during the first seven years of life. As a result, I considered that my chiropractic treatments would have limited benefit if people did not address their beliefs, identities, and emotions from childhood and the corresponding stories they were telling themselves about their illnesses.

I've seen that dis-ease can be used as a benefit, and if a dis-ease is benefiting you in some way, you'll have difficulty letting go of it. For example, if dis-ease gets people to feed, clothe, bathe, dress, and shop for you, that might be appealing to some people. At the very least, it requires people to pay attention to you, and oftentimes we can be starved for any kind of connection. In my case, I didn't want to be the dis-ease of my traumatic brain injury. I had to choose to apply this energy to a new story—a healthy and happy story.

We are not simply bodies. We are bodies, minds, and spirits, and we exude a certain energy whether we realize it or not. We won't see this energy, but we can feel it if we're paying attention. You can feel the anger in a room—or the joy. We pick up on this energy, and if we don't handle it properly, discharging the negative and engaging with the positive, we can develop symptoms of dis-ease. During the time I've been writing this, several of my buttons were pushed, and I ended up with shingles. Since shingles is the result of stress, I am still learning how to choose my focus and transform the negative energies that seek to connect with that old childhood programming.

Accept that Life Constantly Changes

Life happens, and nothing remains the same. Sometimes we're glad; who wants to be in the dentist's chair forever? Other times, we're sad that a happy event won't continue. What we choose to do with life's constant changes is up to us. I am choosing to be the creative force in my own life. I learned to do this from my journey that began with the attack in my front yard. I was told by a wise woman—my grandma—that learning never ends. That's because life is always changing, offering new challenges and joys. The world would undoubtedly be a better place if we were given a handbook on how the mind works so we could reach our desired goals, but that wouldn't require us to struggle to transform. Even a butterfly emerging from a chrysalis can't be helped or else it lacks the strength to fly; we must wrestle with the constant change that life brings.

Since life is constantly changing, that means you and I can change, too. We can change our thoughts, our beliefs, and our bodies by rewiring our brains to no longer respond negatively and refuse to engage in storytelling that is based on childish programming that no longer serves us. I changed the way I think, and I'm still changing today.

Take the First Step Toward Change

Let's take the first step toward changing our programming—becoming aware of how our thoughts make us feel. Try this exercise with me: think of a thought, either a good (expansive) thought or a bad (contractive) thought. As you think this thought, notice how it feels in your body. Does the thought create tension or ache, or does it feel like a warm glow? Thoughts create feelings, and either they make you feel good, or they make you feel bad. Thoughts have vibrations, so if they are expansive, your body feels them in a good way; if they are contractive, your body feels them in a bad way. As mentioned before, we exude energy; we are electrical in nature, and thoughts cause vibrations that are electrical in nature. Some thoughts carry high vibrations (expansive), and some carry low vibrations (contractive). If you're experiencing pain, tiredness, or fatigue, you are thoughts are emitting low vibrations, and your body doesn't function well on low vibrations or low electricity. The body and spirit need higher vibrations. The higher you vibrate, the more expansive you will feel, and the more you will receive what you desire.

Thinking back to the power of choice and focus, the clearer you are about your intentions and choices, the clearer the message will be to your entire being: body, mind, and spirit. When we send mixed signals, it's difficult for the body, mind, and spirit to interpret the signal. It's like giving conflicting directions to a driver: "turn left," "turn right," "stop," "go." The driver eventually becomes frustrated and stops. It's important not to become discouraged because it is a journey. Despite the years and money I spent, I am still on that journey. Rather than becoming discouraged, I keep reaching for the more expansive thought and the higher vibration. Notice the small positive changes – anything positive, expansive. Choose to focus on your desired reality, and you'll get there. Wherever your focus goes, that's your reality.

This doesn't mean that we won't have bad days, but we strive to turn toward expansiveness and higher vibrational thoughts in the way we process those less-than-perfect days. Whenever I am having a bad day, I allow myself a few minutes to pout and feel the grief, sadness, and disappointment, but then I turn the situation into laughter because laughter is the best medicine. It always makes me feel better.

We also need to pay attention to the company we keep. It is difficult to stay around a person of low vibration and not be affected by it. Some people wish to be fully immersed in their dis-ease or negative thoughts, and that is their choice. We can allow someone to be on the journey of their choice – that is unconditional love. However, enabling someone adds vibration and energy to that journey, which isn't good for either the caregiver or the companion. Finding a way to allow someone to remain in their low vibration without being affected or energetically attached is challenging. It's important to choose your companions wisely by noticing how you feel around certain people.

I was attacked in my own front yard and left with a concussion, broken facial bones, and teeth, as well as a torn retina. I don't remember the attack or the ambulance ride. What I do remember is the choice I made to recognize the childhood programming that made me interpret life's difficulties through an immature lens. I saw power in that choice and learned to focus on what I wanted, not on what I didn't want. I became aware of my thoughts and their vibrations, along with how they affected my body. And I accepted life's changeability, choosing to focus on the positive by making myself laugh and hanging out with people whose energy lifted me up. If I did it, I believe and know you can, too.

Dr. Theresa L. Smith, D.C.'s interest in the healing arts began when she was in her twenties. She has studied multiple techniques in the last forty years. Focusing on the cause, the true roots, is the most effective. Today, she offers a multidisciplinary approach focusing on the true roots of each patient's health problems – what is unique to their situation – and chooses the right treatment or approach that will make a lasting difference, utilizing techniques to rewire thought patterns, and body patterns to return the body to optimal health.

CHAPTER 8

Never Broken: Ending the Endless Search
By Kristen Marie

"Another course, Kristen? Seriously? Do you think you might have a problem?"

Wait, did I? I didn't think so. But I had to admit, my relationship with the world of self-help and spiritual development was.... well, complicated.

I had been excitedly sharing the details of an upcoming course with my friend, who was also into the world of spirituality and psychological growth. I was very selective about who I shared this part of myself with as most people in my life barely tolerated things like energy healing, non-duality, or psychic phenomena. However, my friend did. She was someone I felt safe sharing this part of me with. But then she hit me with her question. And it did feel like a smack. After all, she claimed to have experienced a spiritual awakening before we became friends. I put her on a pedestal and always felt like I was trying to catch up to her, trying to reach her level. I felt like she was better at life and had a deeper understanding of the world. And here I was – a mess. Not even a hot one at that.

What was wrong with me? At that time in my life, I could have unfurled my "scroll of defects:" PTSD, PMDD, TMJ, social anxiety, depression, deep insecurity, skin issues, digestive problems, fatigue, trouble sleeping, extreme shyness, crippling self-doubt, food sensitivities, and weight issues. Not to mention the Unholy Trinity of U's: chronic, deeply entrenched feelings of ugliness, unworthiness, and unlovability. And now I might need to add addiction to my list.

My myriad diagnoses and symptoms did not develop out of the blue. They were seeds planted in my early childhood, watered by almost two decades of abuse. Self-hate was taught to me, and I was a very good student. I learned to believe that I wasn't enough, that I was worthless and unlovable. It felt like there was something very wrong with me, and I knew exactly what it was: I was inherently bad. And I had proof. People told me so, although with much more colorful language like "ug" (short for ugly), "loser," "little bitch," and "fucking asshole." When you're in elementary school and you're told never to utter such foul language, yet an adult, a caregiver, routinely calls you these things then you must be bad. Really bad.

*   *   *   *   *

I stood, knee level, straining my neck to look up at their contorted faces, their hands gesturing wildly. The people I loved most in the world did not seem to love each other. They stood face to face, screaming. I had no idea what they were saying, but their rage felt like bubbles smashing against each other throughout my three-year-old little body. Please stop, please stop, please stop. I ran to the bathroom and grabbed the toilet plunger. Rushing back to them, I managed to wriggle myself between their legs waving the toilet plunger like a baton, hoping to create space – they can't hit if there's space.

*   *   *   *   *

My parents divorced when I was four. That's when my world fell apart for the first time. Suddenly and completely. Everything that I thought was solid and permanent – home, relationships, pets – evaporated. My mom, brother, and I moved to a different state. We left my dad and our house where my grandparents, whom I adored, lived right behind us. Our two dogs—my beloved four-legged siblings—were given away. Everything that felt safe and secure was gone, and I was left with a profound, crippling sadness.

*   *   *   *   *

"Can you tell me more about Kristen's heart condition?" the school nurse inquired.

Baffled, my mom asked, "What heart condition?"

"She's been telling her kindergarten teacher she has a heart condition, and we wanted to check with you to see if she's on any medication or needs accommodations. We want to make sure she's ok."

The term "heart condition" was something I picked up from my grandmother. She would broadcast her condition as a way to guilt people into behaving a certain way, especially around the holidays. But my five-year-old self wasn't trying to manipulate. I honestly believed I had a heart condition too. My heart was broken.

*   *   *   *   *

My world fell apart again when I was six. But rather than a sudden collapse like the divorce, it was a gradual devolution into hopelessness and despair. My mom met someone, and at the beginning of the relationship, things were fine. Frank seemed like a decent guy, and my mom, desperately wanting to rebuild a stable home life for her and us, moved forward with the relationship at a pace too fast to detect red flags. When I was six, they bought a house together, and we all moved in—a new family. We even got a dog, which made me so happy. On the surface, it seemed like this would start a bright new chapter—a return to stability. But it was as if the house was a portal, and once Frank crossed that threshold and we were all on the other side, he removed his "good guy" mask and let the monster out.

Although my mom and Frank never married, he lived with us for almost twenty years until he finally left us. Those years were filled with fits of rage, drunken spectacles, violence, and emotional and verbal abuse. He became the center of our universe. *What is his mood today? Is he drunk? Is something bothering him? What might he need so he doesn't escalate and spin out of control?* It became an impossible task of trying to soothe a raging bull who was always inflamed, always looking for someone to blame.

What made it even more confusing was when he did nice things. I felt like he hated us; he had said as much. But he would also take us to baseball games and concerts. We went sledding in the winter and hiking in the spring. In those moments, it felt like we could be a family. I would let my guard down, wishfully thinking this would be the start of a new era—the happy family era. I wanted to love him and for him to love us. I would have been so happy to forgive and forget anything in the past – if we could just start fresh from here on out. But the good times never lasted, and they occurred less and less as we got older. I would open up my heart only to be terrorized once again…

*   *   *   *   *

I was nine and unsure of what I did to set him off, but he was furious. I ran up to my bedroom and slammed the door. He was right behind me, yelling. He flung the door open, face red and eyes wild. I cowered in the corner of my room. He went to my dresser and grabbed a seashell sculpture that had an effigy of Jesus; it was a gift from my grandmother and meant a lot to me. He lifted the sculpture over his head and slammed it on my bedroom floor. The smashed pieces scattered everywhere. Frank yelled some obscenities and left my room.

In a state of shock, I went down to the kitchen and got the broom and dustpan. I went back up to my room. Frank was pacing in the hallway. I was crying as I swept up the mess. "I bet you're gonna tell your mother, huh? You're the cause of all the problems between us, you know that? Are you going to tell her what a monster I am? I guess I'm just a monster, right? If I leave, you guys will be out on the street. Then what's gonna happen to the dog…"

I couldn't bear to be the cause of losing everything. Not again. In hysterics, I found myself apologizing profusely. I felt horrible. "I'm so sorry. It's not you. You're not a monster. This is my fault. I'm the monster. I'm sorry. You didn't do anything wrong; it was me. Please don't leave. I won't tell mom."

*   *   *   *   *

Children *need* their caregivers; their very life depends on this relationship. Children don't have the capacity to perceive their parents and caregivers as flawed human beings who may be struggling with their own pain, trauma, or financial burdens—not to mention addiction or mental illness. In the face of ongoing abuse, children will often conclude that they are the bad ones; they are the cause of all the problems. This is an adaptive survival instinct. It is too overwhelming to realize that a caregiver, the person in charge of their survival, is dangerous and unpredictable. It can actually feel safer for a child to inhabit the belief of being "the bad one." Although this false belief brings a great deal of pain, it also brings a sense of order and control. The child now knows how to orient to their crazy, erratic world. They are bad. Believing this, even though it's untrue, provides a context for everything that happens to them—it helps them make sense of the chaos. And it also offers hope: if they are bad, maybe they can change and then everything will be ok.

This was how I came to see myself – the bad one. To atone for my badness and for causing all the ongoing problems at home, I tried to make up for it by being very, very good. At home, at school, and with friends, I took on the identity of the "excessively nice one." I tried not to have needs. I didn't speak up. I worked hard to meet everyone else's expectations. The word "no" was not part of my vocabulary. I took responsibility for other people's emotions, and I tried desperately to make them feel better. I became an expert at reading subtle emotional cues and did my best to meet a person's needs before they even realized they had a need. Disappointing someone felt like a matter of life or death to my young self. Because, in my experience, disappointing others, speaking up, or having needs could lead to violence.

As the years went by, the vast chasm between my inner experience and what I presented to the outside world felt unbearable. I watched in anguish as Frank continued to drain the vitality and joy from my mom, the person I loved more than anything in the world. She loved my brother and me too, fiercely. But her own terror of what Frank might do if we left, the lack of support and resources available to her (she didn't drive, which also made it feel harder to escape), the very real possibility of being homeless, and the way Frank continuously made her feel like she was nothing kept her feeling stuck and without options. So we all tried to make ourselves believe things weren't as bad as they really were, even though every day Frank stole our safety and murdered our self-esteem. And yet, I still put on a happy face to the outside world. By the time I reached high school, I fantasized about suicide almost daily, and yet someone commented, "Kristen, you're like a ray of sunshine." On the inside, however, I felt like a starless night sky.

By the age of seventeen, my life felt heavy and hopeless. It felt like a prison sentence, something I had to get through. Life was not about living—it was about enduring. I was desperate for something to change, but it felt like nothing ever would. And then a seemingly ordinary yet pivotal experience occurred in a bookstore…I bought a book. I'm not sure what drew my attention to this particular book. Maybe it was the sweet rainbow-colored heart on the cover. Or the title that promised the possibility of change. Or maybe it was fate—maybe the book actually found me. Whatever the reason, I bought the book and with it, unbeknownst to me in that moment, pure, unadulterated hope. A feeling I hadn't felt in years.

You Can Heal Your Life by Louise L. Hay is a book that examines the connection between the mind and body. It explores the way limiting beliefs negatively impact one's life and offers guidance on changing one's thinking to create positive changes in one's life. As I read through each chapter, hope blazed inside my being. I now had a roadmap for change. Perhaps, I could finally, *finally* be fixed! I could change my thoughts, and my life could improve. *I* could improve. I could be a better me—a me that wasn't so awful and bad. Louise was a shining example that change was possible, but her story wasn't unique. Others had also experienced these incredible life changes from her teachings. I dared to hope that maybe I could be one of them too.

I planned to devote all my energy to healing my life. Healing became my reason for existing, my purpose. I was going to get myself out of my pain and transform myself into something good and worthy. So I got to work. I reread Louise's chapters and highlighted every bit of wisdom. I created a schedule to work through the recommended exercises. I repeated affirmations over and over even though they felt like the furthest thing from the truth. *"I love and approve of myself, and I trust the process of life. I am safe. I love and approve of myself, and I trust the process of life. I am safe. I love and approve of myself, and I trust the process of life. I am safe."* Except I didn't, and I wasn't.

Although I believed in Louise's message, I had difficulty sticking to the relentless self-healing pace I had set for myself. I wanted to heal my life, to fix what I thought was broken inside me, but I had overestimated my bandwidth. I had just started college, was working a part-time job, and had entered into my first romantic relationship. My attention was divided. It was hard to heal my life when I was desperately trying to navigate it. In addition, I was still living at home with Frank. I wasn't actually safe, and the abuse was a much more powerful reinforcer of my negative self-image than my attempts to affirm otherwise.

At that time, I didn't realize that safety is of paramount importance; it's really hard to heal when your environment isn't safe, and your body doesn't feel safe. I didn't know that sometimes things can seem to get worse on the healing journey before they get better—that this is actually a part of the healing process and not an indication that you're doing something wrong. I didn't understand that sometimes a slow and steady approach can be much more impactful than great big sweeping changes, especially when there's been early childhood trauma. I didn't know any of this. All I knew was that I must not be working hard enough, that somehow, I was failing. It wasn't that the timing wasn't right. Or that maybe I needed more than positive affirmations. It was that I wasn't right. It was me. All me. The broken one. The bad one. The one who can't be fixed.

And yet, Louise's book had changed my life. She introduced me to the possibility of healing—that growth and change really are possible even if you've faced tremendous adversity. But maybe, even more importantly, she introduced me to the world of self-help. This new world had techniques and tools to improve *everything*. From relationships to body image to self-image to health to limiting beliefs to codependence to public speaking to…. the list went on and on. This was a world I wanted to inhabit: a place filled with wrongs that could be righted with just the right tool or technique. Everything that I thought was wrong with me had the potential to be fixed. Thus began my quest to find the holy grail of self-help.

I started with books. I read as much as I could on topics like personal growth, health, healing, and psychology. Each one ignited inside me a new feeling of hope: *Maybe this is the one. Maybe this book will have the exact thing I need to be ok. I have a good feeling about this one.* And I always did at the start. But no matter how much I read or learned or changed, I still, much to my disappointment, felt like me. I still felt broken and bad.

Undeterred, my search continued. I took an energy healing course as an elective in college, and that opened me up to a whole new dimension of possibilities: the world of metaphysics and spirituality. Through the years, I read and took courses on breathwork, sound healing, meditation, shamanism, consciousness studies, channeling, tarot, yoga, mantras, hypnosis, as well as a variety of energy healing modalities. These teachings also led to "aha!" moments and shifts but couldn't seem to transform the part of me that felt fundamentally bad and unworthy.

When I got right down to it, my incessant search was not necessarily about quieting my mind, thinking positive thoughts, setting boundaries, clearing my aura, learning how to be assertive, raising my vibration, or any other of the fascinating things that I was learning about. Sure, those were all great pursuits, but what I was really hoping for was that they would be the thing. And this thing would be the pathway for me to feel okay. To feel okay being me. To feel okay about life. To wake up in the morning and just feel…. okay. I wasn't searching for bliss or joy or even happiness – what I most wanted was a fundamental sense that I was okay just as I was. If I could wake up and not feel dread, if my body could relax its tension from armoring against life - that would feel like a miracle. That would be my form of bliss.

But I was continuously disappointed. Not in the teachings or with the teachers, but with myself. I felt like I just couldn't get "it." I felt like I must not be working hard enough. I would take a workshop, and it would always seem like other people would have these profound shifts, but not me. It's not that I didn't experience changes—I was learning and growing and making progress. It's just that these changes seemed mild compared to the life-changing experiences others seemed to be having. Unfortunately, I used this comparison to reinforce the belief that there must be something wrong with me. I had no awareness that healing unfolds in its own right time and not on a fixed schedule. It didn't cross my mind that some folks might potentially exaggerate their experiences to impress the teacher or make themselves seem "better" than others in the class. I had no idea that profound shifts often have to be integrated in order to have a lasting impact; a big experience at a weekend retreat doesn't necessarily mean permanent, lasting change in one's life.

Despite my growing fear that I would never find the okayness I was seeking, I did find inspiration, hope, and comfort from so many teachings, teachers, and therapists. But it eventually became hard to deny that my excitement for each new teaching was overshadowed by a sense of desperation—a deep longing for salvation…from myself. From the deep feelings of shame and unworthiness and pain that I carried within. With each new opportunity, there came with it a deep sense of urgency. I needed this. Like my life depended on this next new thing. I felt like a donkey forever chasing the carrot of okayness. It kept me moving forward and looking ahead, which I absolutely needed for a certain time in my life, but it was exhausting. Utterly exhausting.

Slowly, from a place of weariness, after having gone on the merry-go-round of self-help and spiritual bypass one too many hundreds of times, I came to the devastating, yet ultimately liberating realization: I could not outrun my pain. It was still there, patiently waiting to be met. Was I ready?

I took an honest look at my journey thus far. I had learned a lot of things about a lot of things. But this accumulation of information was also keeping me stuck. I was confusing learning with healing. Learning is certainly a part of healing, but it's only a part. I slowly recognized that all this learning served to occupy my mind while acting as a powerful distraction from my feelings. It was as if all my feelings of shame and brokenness and unworthiness were a gargantuan octopus lying quietly in the depths of the ocean, seemingly asleep. Not wanting to wake this creature, let alone acknowledge it, I kept studying all the beautiful, shiny fishes near the surface which kept me fascinated and engaged—and also helped me hope that maybe the octopus had moved on to a different ocean. But this beast would inevitably rise up, wrap me in tentacles of hurt, and threaten to take me down. My pattern up until this point had been to start descending into despair and then fiercely break free with everything I had, banish the octopus back to the deep, and then focus ever more intently on the surface fishes. But now, after many years, I was finally willing to face my pain.

Just as synchronously as *You Can Heal Your Life* appeared in my life so many years earlier thus commencing years of seeking, another book now emerged that marked the beginning of the end of my endless searching. It was not in a bookstore but at a party that I discovered this book. I almost didn't go since being in a crowd with lots of people I didn't know was a surefire way to increase my already high baseline anxiety to an almost unbearable level. But despite my fear, I had a strong inkling to attend. It was here that someone mentioned the book *The Presence Process*, by Michael Brown. She shared how it had transformed her life by teaching her how to feel her feelings—how to sit with all the discomfort, to face it and feel it. I was touched by her story and realized I had finally reached a point in my life where I was now ready to stop fixing and start feeling.

And so, I bought Michael's book. It didn't promise a quick fix. It didn't endorse a flashy trend. It was a guidebook on how to examine and work with triggers and then feel and integrate emotions, especially the big ones: fear, anger, and grief. I was nervous to take this on as it was unlike anything I had done so far. But I was ready. I began the intense ten-week process—one that took me through truly feeling and facing so many of the emotions I had spent my life running from. I was also examining the origins of these intense emotions as well as gaining clarity on how I defined love (love, for me, was equated with pain and loss). The process was immensely difficult and at times, overwhelming. Knowing what I now know about working with trauma and regulating the nervous system, it may have been better and more sustainable had I started by slowly and gently building up my capacity to ride the waves of intense emotions rather than white-knuckling it through turbulent feelings. Nonetheless, I found the process to be profound. After going through it several times, the chains that wrapped me in beliefs of brokenness and unworthiness began to loosen and fall. I wish I could say they disintegrated completely, but that was not the case. However, I was no longer bound so tightly by my beliefs. There were now other options—other ways to look at myself and the world.

My pattern of desperately seeking and searching outside myself (for answers that could only be found inside) was waning. And my sense of self was beginning to shift—not through fixing and improving but through understanding. I was coming to see myself through a more accurate and compassionate lens: I had experienced a great deal of trauma, and I adopted beliefs and behaviors to survive. I wasn't a broken and unworthy being. So much of what I thought needed to be fixed, what I deemed as abnormal and shameful about myself (beliefs and behaviors like hypervigilance, depression, procrastination, social anxiety, people pleasing, etc.) were actually a completely normal response to the trauma I endured. What I thought were my character flaws were actually survival responses. Yes, they caused me a great deal of pain and discomfort, but they kept me alive. They were absolutely necessary for a period of my life. Until they weren't.

But change can be challenging. The nervous system equates familiarity with safety, even if what's familiar is painful. Even positive change can seem like a threat, especially to a nervous system that's grown accustomed to chaos and hurt. This information helped me understand why my "guns-a-blazing" approach to self-help so often didn't produce the results I desperately longed for. It's not that I was a failure or that I wasn't trying hard enough, it's just that my body was trying to keep me safe. I wasn't actually doing anything wrong, and neither was my body.

Rather than working against my body by forcing change, I now work with it, gently and slowly, with breaks and time for rest. Through trauma-informed somatic practices, I am releasing stored survival stress that has been held inside my body for decades. Although Frank has long since been gone from my life, the stuck energies of all the screams I was never able to let out, all the anger I was never able to express, all the tears never sobbed, all the terror frozen inside, was causing my body to feel like I was still in danger—like I still wasn't safe, like something was wrong with me. So, I am working with my nervous system, not to fix it, but to rewire it. It was never broken; it did an amazing job of keeping me alive.

Looking back on my years of seeking and fixing, it can be tempting to believe I wasted my time. *Where was the direct route? Where were the signs that should have warned me of dead ends and one-way streets? Why wasn't there a blockade to signal that the road dropped off a cliff? Siri, for the love of God, tell me which way to go, please!!* But perhaps there were signs that I just didn't see. Maybe I needed all those detours. Or maybe, just maybe, they weren't detours at all. Perhaps they were paths I needed to take to help me recalibrate my internal compass so that I could find my way. Perhaps all the years of fixing and never getting fixed weren't a wasted effort at all but exactly what I needed to finally realize I was never broken.

Kristen Marie has a master's in psychology and a background in human resources, administrative support, and various healing modalities.

CHAPTER 9

On Honoring One's Authentic Self:
One Man's Journey On the Path to Self-Acceptance
By Robert Páez

"To stay young requires unceasing cultivation of one's ability to unlearn old falsehoods." –Robert A. Heinlein, from his novel, Time Enough for Love

"A good education can be expensive." –Unknown

One of the more sobering thoughts to occur to me when I was young was the realization that life was some sort of elaborate staging area, a "school" of sorts organized in such a way as to prompt, and even force, learning and personal growth. Obviously, the analogy wasn't exactly novel even then, but to a fourth grader stumbling upon the observation entirely on his own, it was truly mind-blowing.

I remember sharing my "discovery" with some close friends at the time and alternately laughing and cringing with them as we considered the implications. Most of us were eight or nine at the time and until that moment, like most kids, our primary focus when we were together was simply on having fun and exploring the world around us. At that age, the thought of even more schooling, let alone the possibility of a life of never-ending "lessons" was laughable, if not ridiculous. But of course, that was before the full implications of the analogy began sinking in.

I look back at that time and wonder if I didn't do a disservice to my mates by sharing my observation about life-as-a-school at so tender an age. For me, the analogy made perfect sense. I mean, the whole construct of preparation and testing, and then "grading" based on conduct and performance seemed to fit exactly with how I was experiencing the world at the time. Because I was being raised in a fairly strict, old-school Catholic household, I was okay with the whole cause-and-effect thing. I mean, by that point I'd already had my share of "action-reaction" experiences under the guidance of my discipline-minded father. But I could see that for some of my buds, the thought of living in some kind of inescapable learning institution, one in which every action had a corresponding consequence, may have been a total buzzkill.

Regrettably, some of my comrades took my observation more seriously than others and in random ways I couldn't understand at first, began showing their disappointment with me for having introduced them to so burdensome a concept. The net effect of all this was that I began to be shunned by some of my dearest friends simply for sharing something I felt was important for them to know—something I felt could be helpful to them as they took up their lives. Of course, it didn't help that my own family already considered me "odd" for being such a "serious child" and for being so insufferably curious about things that they, themselves, had yet to consider. In fairness to my family and friends though, it was pretty obvious to me as time went on that my contemplative nature, otherworldly experiences, and general outlook on things were considerably different from theirs. Though disturbing and terribly disappointing at times, I can see in retrospect that their reactions to me were to be expected. From their perspective, I really was an odd kid, I guess.

Needless to say, it was a painful and confusing time, especially for someone so young. It marked the beginning of what were to become countless occasions in my life where my choices boiled down to either withholding my truths to gain and/or maintain acceptance from others or expressing my true self without reservation, even in situations where I knew that doing so would likely result in my being misunderstood or ridiculed or labeled ("kook" and "weirdo" seemed to be the adjectives my bullying brothers preferred most). And as one might expect, there were many times when I was forced to simply "go it alone" for long periods in order to maintain my sense of self and avoid confrontation or unwanted controversy.

And so began what became for me a lifelong "schooling" in the practice of acknowledging and honoring my authentic self.

I expect that none of these early experiences will sound foreign to anyone. Pretty much everyone I've ever met has had to deal with similar episodes in their lives, sometimes later in life and sometimes, sadly, at even earlier ages than I did. And most, too, have had to make similar decisions about how to negotiate their way through increasingly more complicated situations and relationships. Some people might say, "Well, that's life; that's simply part of the 'maturation' process all humans must go through." But what I would say now, having spent a lifetime studying and exploring a number of orthodox and esoteric philosophies and belief systems, including those revealed through the course of my own life, is that so much of this shunning behavior simply isn't necessary. I say this because what I've come to understand is that what we call "peer pressure" is actually part of a larger societal norming process—an externally imposed domestication system designed to make us uniformly compliant and, to the extent possible, easier to manage and control.

Looking back, I can see how these early experiences with my family and mates resulted in my decision to begin editing my deepest thoughts and feelings, and at times even hiding them altogether. While the strategy was effective to a large degree in avoiding the rejection I was increasingly experiencing at home and school, it set me up to become in time, my own prosecutor, judge, and jury over the expression of my true self. It was the start of my practice of carrying around my own courtroom in my head, something I did for a good part of my early life. Pathetic as it seems now, I actually prided myself on not only running an efficient courtroom but on being a firm and sometimes overly harsh judge.

Ultimately, because I refused at some point to disown my deepest thoughts and feelings, I decided it would be better to simply keep my experiences and deeper observations to myself and choose on a case-by-case basis where and when to reveal them. While not a bad strategy for a young person to settle on, in time this practice only added to my estrangement from others, and even from myself, as it forced me to adopt alternate personas—other "false selves"—from which to operate when interacting with others. As I came to see, the pitfall to adopting these various personas was that I became almost too good at crafting and acting them out, to the point that a previously unknown part of me began emerging, one that wanted to believe that the more attractive and convincing of these were really me. I mean, yes, I knew these alternate selves were largely fake, for sure, but some of them were so impressive and so easy to slip into that learning to keep track of them and keeping them distinct from my genuine self-became, in time, a major preoccupation— and even a chore—all its own.

To place the foregoing in context it might be helpful to share something I learned in a human development course I took in college. It's something that's helped me better understand human nature in general, and my own children in particular when their times came. It seems that child psychologists regard the adoption of alternate personas by teens and pre-teens as a natural, and even necessary, phenomenon. It's how self-identity begins to take shape in one's early years and it occurs through an extended period of active comparison and contrast. In other words, this phase of human development provides a young person with their first opportunity to consciously take up and experiment with alternate ways of being and expressing. It's believed that this is done by all young people to test how—and who—they might be in the larger world they're encountering. Of course, at that early stage of our development, we can't possibly know the dangers of over-identifying with our "creations;" it's simply a fun, natural thing to do. For many of us, experimenting with alternate personas when young is a lot like trying on new clothing—some of them fit beautifully, some are just okay, and some are better off being tossed into the back of the closet or given away as soon as possible.

I became reacquainted with this phenomenon years later during my apprenticeship in a shamanic tradition I took up in my late thirties. The concept of "masks" as an embodiment of false personas is a significant one in the Toltec tradition, as unveiling how we come to adopt and use masks opens the door to a more honest review of one's personal history. Such a review, referred to by the Toltecs as The Inventory, is one of two cornerstone practices in their teachings (the other being The Recapitulation, which follows directly from The Inventory). The immense value of The Inventory is that, if done properly, it provides us the opportunity to view past events with a more mature, more objective set of eyes and in this way, begin the process of detaching ourselves from the emotionally charged stories we've told ourselves about pivotal past events. Ultimately, that detachment, completed through The Recapitulation, doesn't in and of itself relieve us of our tendencies toward further story-making, but it does return to us the energy trapped in these past events, including, mercifully, the emotional and psychic energy bound to our past traumas. And it's that retrieved energy—our own energy—that can be used to empower us toward a more conscious and purposeful future.

A great example of this in my life was how these personas, or masks, played out around the issues of romance and dating. I mentioned before that I was kind of a serious kid. I generally preferred my own company over that of my peers or my large, boisterous family. My nature and practice in my early years involved reading (a lot), reflecting (a lot), and theorizing (a lot) about what "was" (as far as I could tell at the time, anyway) and what "could be." I asked so many questions around these inclinations that some of my sibs would sometimes call me "What If," since I used to start a lot of my questions exactly like that (in truth, this continues to be a core part of me— I'm still asking "what if" questions).

When it came to girls, I was awkward and unsure and generally lost at sea most of the time. This was partly because most of my early ideas about the opposite sex came from hero-heroine type stories I'd picked up from books, movies, and popular culture, and partly because my original role models for intimacy were two incredible people caught up in an impossibly tumultuous love affair. Through my parents' eyes and my own tentative ventures, I learned a painful and difficult lesson early on, namely, that love doesn't always abide, and that there are some pairings that, while beautiful and even magical, especially at their start, in a practical sense should probably never be.

These understandings should have been lesson enough for anyone paying attention. And yet, unwittingly, my own marriage was actually a recreation of my parents' own fateful union. What surprises me, even now, is how few of my early life lessons, and how little of my acquired knowledge and best wishes I was able to bring to bear in the events playing out at the end of my marriage. It's become a trite expression now, but the entire experience really was like watching a massive train wreck happening in slow motion.

Without question, the disintegration of my marriage was by far one of the most devastating events of my life. What made it all the more painful was that it started at about the same time I began feeling I'd finally achieved what I'd been secretly longing for all my life. Being a devoted husband and father and building a future with a love and faith I'd previously never allowed myself to experience was so incredibly fulfilling that I was sure at the time that I was as happy as any person could ever be. I was actually living that "white picket fence" dream I'd doubted was even real, let alone possible for someone like me.

There are lots of reasons—and rationalizations—to explain how my ex and I arrived at such a desperate place in our marriage. No question, the multiple sleights and irritations we'd accumulated over the years certainly added to the massive estrangement we came to at the end. But ultimately, our failing was related to something far more fundamental. And far more revealing.

You see, the defining factor in our marriage's demise wasn't the petty annoyances we'd been harboring against one another for so long. I understood fully that these were things all couples had to accept or resolve in order to be successful. No, in our case it was the fact that we couldn't see our way past the hall of mirrors we'd created for ourselves from the beginning. Neither of us could see that from the start, from our earliest coming together, we'd presented versions of ourselves that we couldn't help but fall in love with, but which were largely just projections of what we wanted the other to see.

In other words, though we couldn't have possibly seen it for what it was at the time, we'd built our relationship on beautiful illusions we'd crafted for one another—illusions we'd hoped we could grow into and be sustained by the other over the course of our marriage, but which were destined for dissolution from the start.

It turns out my ex and I were rather good at creating and maintaining our projections. This was chiefly because we were both well practiced at it by the time we'd met and also because we'd found in one another the "perfect" person to enchant with our hopeful but undeniably false selves. More significantly, when the time came, we failed to find a way to admit to ourselves that we'd not only set one another up, but we'd set ourselves up as well. And as I came to see toward the end of my marriage, it was those self-deceptions—those innocent, well-intentioned, but in the end, utterly false selves—that compounded our estrangement and led inexorably to the collapse of our house of cards.

And still, for me, there was even more to 'fess up to.

It took some time to understand, but eventually I came to accept that I'd committed a grave "sin" against myself. I did this by failing to acknowledge that the various personas I'd adopted and had been projecting to my ex (and pretty much everyone else I knew at the time) were created not simply to make myself more appealing, but more importantly, to shield myself from an important truth—one that I'd been trying to minimize and at times even ignore at important moments of my life. And that truth was that because I was indeed very different from most other people, I was "destined" to always feel disconnected and apart from them. In my case, my projections weren't meant to make me appear more than I actually was (as is usually the case with most people), they were meant to make me appear less. And this was because I wanted to "fit in." I wanted to fall within some acceptable portion of that bell-shaped curve that defines typical human thought and behavior. I wanted to live that "white picket fence" life. I wanted to be someone who others thought of as a "regular guy" and not someone who challenged people's sensibilities and triggered avoidance responses simply because I was being who I actually was.

But even more than this, driven by an unacknowledged "something" deep inside me, I wanted to challenge The Fates. I wanted to prove that by exercising my free will I could overcome what my fears and presumed "destiny" were telling me. I wanted to prove through my marriage that we— all of us— could be captains of our fate. Masters of our destiny.

Obviously, that experiment, as noble and heroically waged as it was, didn't exactly turn out the way I intended, for it seemed that the more I allowed my genuine self to be present and fully engaged in my relationship with my wife, the more distant and detached she became. It was as though my commitment to continue evolving violated some unspoken pact we'd established, one that dictated that we were to remain steadfast in the projections we'd begun with each other when we first met. I didn't know it at the time, but this pact was something my ex, and apparently many others, was deeply wedded to— even more so than she was to me personally. This was pretty confusing to me, as throughout this period I was sharing with her my joy and excitement—and gratitude—for being able to deepen and reclaim my commitment to expressing my true self. What I didn't know, however, was that my ex had stopped supporting my personal growth goals long before.

Things came to an irreversible climax when, one night, while sleeping next to her in our bed, she witnessed me engaged in a fairly dramatic paranormal act. Apparently, while lying there motionless and sleeping, I "detached" from my physical body, and in my energetic form (my "dream body," as the Toltecs call it), I slipped out into the night through our closed bedroom window. According to my wife, before exiting I stopped momentarily to smile sweetly at her and even blow her a kiss. Understandably, this shocked and terrified my wife quite badly; so badly, in fact, that she refused to talk to me about it for three days.

I knew upon waking the morning after the event that something was distinctly "off" in the household. My wife had abandoned her customary morning routine entirely and wouldn't make eye contact with me when I rose and found her in the kitchen. When I approached and attempted to kiss her good morning (which was part of my morning routine), she literally recoiled from me and held her hand up in front of her as if to say, "Please don't come near me." Startled, I tried immediately to get her to share what was troubling her so, but she refused to talk and just paced the floor with her eyes cast down.

After some long moments of anxious waiting, I turned to what I thought was playful banter to see if I could lighten her mood. "Wait, did you catch me talking in my sleep again last night? Is that it? Was I having some kind of sexy dream?" I asked good-naturedly. Those remarks, however, registered absolutely no reaction, no response at all. Her non-reaction made it clear that something deeply disturbing had occurred the night before and so I pressed even further in an attempt to have her reveal what had happened. But still she refused to talk.

At some point she relented and with her eyes still downcast, said in an almost pained voice, "Yes, yes, Roberto, something did happen but... I don't... I can't talk about it yet. I'm still trying to understand."

"But, sweetie," I said, "I don't understand either. I can see how freaked out you are and you've got me really worried. Is it something about me? Something I did, something I said to hurt you? Please let me know and please let me help. I know we can figure this out together."

"No," she said quickly. "I just need time to think it through."

This went on for three straight days and when she finally found a way to speak about what she'd witnessed, she began with words I'll never forget. Earlier that third day she had one of her friends take the boys for the evening and when I returned from work, I found her sitting on the living room sofa staring solemnly ahead. Upon closing the front door, she quickly stood up, turned to me, looked me dead in the eye, and in a cold, almost defiant voice, asked, "I just need to know, Roberto... who are you? What are you?" The way she said that, as though we'd never shared a tender moment together or engaged in so many loving and sincere exchanges, broke my heart as I knew in an instant that whatever had happened, whatever she'd witnessed that night, had set in motion an irreconcilable divide between us. It was as though she was regarding me now as a stranger, or worse—as some kind of monster.

She went on to explain in detail what she witnessed that night, interjecting repeatedly that these kinds of things simply didn't happen in her world, that she was the daughter of an engineer, and those kinds of things were not only not possible; they simply could not be. And yet, here she was, poor thing, struggling to reconcile what she'd been brought up to believe with what she'd seen with her own two eyes only days before. Hearing her words was painful enough, but witnessing her in the throes of such extreme cognitive dissonance only deepened the sense of anguish and confusion I was feeling.

I tried hard to explain what might have triggered the event that night, suggesting that it could be related to the lucid dreaming practices I was doing at the time. I suggested as well that while rarely reported, what she witnessed that night could well be something more natural, more common than most people knew. But she refused to consider any of this.

What made the episode more desperate for me was not being able to explain how or why this ability had revealed itself in me. In truth, I was as amazed as she was by what she'd witnessed. I knew that such things were possible, of course. I'd heard and read accounts of similar experiences before. I'd even experienced my own extraordinary occurrences, including some profound, life-altering ones I had yet to reveal to her. But until her recounting, I was unaware that I was capable of manifesting something like that myself.

And so began the slow downward spiral that led to our separation and divorce. Not surprisingly, we were never the same after this event. My ex couldn't accept that her husband was far more different than she could have imagined and that the ways he was different were well beyond her comprehension and comfort level. My lifelong dilemma had raised its head again, only this time in a manner far more dramatic and consequential than anything I'd ever experienced before.

As one might imagine, those moments of disclosure by my ex are forever etched in my mind. They signaled the end of a beautiful dream, one my heart was deeply, deeply attached to. Those moments and the countless moments that ensued signified the end of whatever hopes I might have had of securing a lasting relationship with another "normal" soul. To say I felt wrecked at the time would be a monumental understatement. To this day, there are no words to describe how devastated and broken I felt in those moments.

It took time, a great deal of time, to get over the ordeal and its subsequent impact on so many aspects of my life. But eventually, I did. I did this by re-examining how I came to be so incredibly attached to my dream (hint: it began very early in my childhood). And I did it by consciously detaching from the emotional trauma that losing that dream triggered in me (hint #2: that, too, had its origins in my formative years). I did it also by surrendering to the fact that I was indeed a different kind of human and that it would do no good to pretend otherwise. I did it by remembering finally that it was my dream, my energetic contribution to our partnership that fueled the opportunity for so much joy and fulfillment in the early part of our marriage. And I did it by allowing myself to recognize fully that it was, without question, a very beautiful dream and that both its intent and energetic content were worthy and still alive in me. And I did it by embracing in the end that these realizations freed me to take the next steps in my life and begin celebrating the extraordinary lessons this part of my journey had given me.

Of course, my recovery didn't happen all at once. It required both aid and inspiration from a number of sources, over a number of years to complete. Foremost among these was the great love I had for my then still-young sons. My concern for their well-being and my determination to limit the emotional and psychic impact the divorce was likely to have on their lives served as both fuel and grounding for me during those difficult times. The augmented strength, courage and resiliency I derived from that love were, of course, invaluable to me at the time and the empowerment I gained as a result continues to be a source of countless blessings in my life.

I was also benefited tremendously from the life-affirming principles and practices I'd come to embrace through my studies in the Toltec tradition. The transformative tools available through this ancient tradition are nothing short of amazing and my commitment to deepening my understanding and practice in this tradition made it possible for me to maintain my integrity even as I struggled through some incredibly challenging moments.

Finally, and thankfully, I was also benefited from the counsel I received from the remarkable Toltec master, don Miguel A. Ruiz, who after bestowing a special title upon me at an open ceremony one Easter, told me that in the future I must choose someone "of my own kind" if I was to ever be truly happy in a relationship. Don Miguel was right, of course; however, as I've come to appreciate, incorporating that knowledge into my life, while making my subsequent passage far less complicated, has yet to make the possibility of finding such "a one" more achievable. After all, I remain a bit different from most people in this world, and perhaps even more so after living through this episode of my life.

I'm reminded of all this when I think of my ex's final words to me before our separation. In fact, they still echo in my head from time to time. "You know, Roberto," she said, "I think some people just aren't meant to be married." At the time, I wanted to believe she was talking about herself. But over time it became abundantly clear that she was referring to me. And in fairness to her upbringing and expectations, I would have to say she was right. Kind of.

Getting back to the life-as-a-school analogy, it's impossible to predict what one's "final grades" will be as our lessons are infinitely varied and the testing we undergo for each is unique, progressive and seemingly forever ongoing. Still, I want to believe that if sincerity of effort counts for something, my overall performance on this one important lesson, perhaps the most fundamental of all life lessons, will be gauged to be at least passable (even if a little slow to complete). And given that the school is known for being incredibly rigorous, if not brutal sometimes, perhaps that's not a small thing for one to have accomplished in the end. Yes?

*   *   *   *   *

To expand on the above, what follows is an excerpt from a story I'm writing about the exploits and challenges faced by three seemingly disparate characters, each struggling to bridge distinctly different yet intricately intertwined life paths. The passage foreshadows a pivotal choice point the youngest of the protagonists will soon be facing in his apprenticeship to his wise and remarkably gifted grandmother. Though dramatized for the purpose of storytelling, the passage mirrors in an idealized way my own struggles to remain true to my authentic self even as I engage the "practical" world and work to maintain a sense of balance and completeness with what I know myself to be.

*   *   *   *   *

Abe

Among the various groups of people Abe had met so far, the calm and genuinely compassionate ones were his favorite. Abe seemed to know instinctively that they, like himself, had come to the realization that everyone was "crazy" in one form or another. The wisest of these, he observed, seemed to have accepted completely the ridiculous state humans were in and not only openly acknowledged the fact, but were often in complete amusement at the absurdity of it all.

The wisest of the wise, like his Abuela (his grandmother), had the added dimension of knowing why things were as they were. And this knowledge, like a razor, had cut through every doubt, every fear, every illusion she'd ever had, leaving her in the end with a startling sobriety and an indescribable sense of peace (and, Abe marveled, an extraordinary capacity for irony).

For Abe, to witness the calm wisdom of his grandmother, to know her unconditional love and her indomitable spirit, was to know without question that he, too, wanted these things in his life. And this, it turns out, was a good thing, since, as his grandmother pointed out to him when the time came, his destiny as successor in the lineage they shared was apparently already set.

"Someday," she said on his tenth birthday, "it'll be you who carries on these traditions, Abel. You are to be the next curandero (healer) in the family. Do you know what this means?"

"Well, in a way, I guess, but not really, 'buelita," he replied sincerely. "I mean, if you're saying that I'll be the one to gather the plants and treat people when they come for help and pray for them like you do when they're too sick to visit, then, yes, I guess I understand that that's what I'm supposed to do."

And here he paused a moment and then continued.

"But, 'buelita, how will I do it? I don't know anything and, for sure, I don't know how to heal anyone."

"Well, no," his grandmother said softly, taking his hand and looking into his eyes, "of course you don't know all the things you need to know, at least not yet. But you already know somewhere deep inside, don't you, that this is meant for you. You already know, as I know, that it's "your way" to want to make things right for yourself and others. And this, mijito (my child), more than knowledge, more than acknowledgment from others, is what your life is to be about."

"Someday," she continued, "you will know all the things I know and more, and when you do, you will be a great healer, greater than me. With the aid of las *plantitas* and with your thoughts, prayers, and soothing touch, you will heal many. I know, because I've already seen it in my dreams. And I also know because of the signs and blessings that accompanied your *nacimiento* (your birth)."

"You see, Abel, you came into the world a certain kind of flower, and the task of those of us caring for you is to provide you with the right kind of soil and water and the right combination of sun and shade so that you might grow as God intended. That's why your parents sent you to live with me—so that I could prepare you for what is to be."

"Though you already know you're different from others, what you don't know yet is that you're a rare and necessary human. You were meant by God to live in his garden, and by your example, give strength and courage to the other *floresitas*—the flowers who are weaker than you but who are also His children."

"Pero, 'buelita," Abe objected, "how can I give strength to others when I, myself, am not strong? My friends say I'm a fool and that the things I believe in are old-fashioned and stupid. They make fun of my ideas and they laugh at my dreams. They say things that make me feel ashamed and so alone sometimes." Abe lowered his eyes for a moment after saying this, swallowing his emotions and allowing the water in his eyes to recede.

When he looked up again it was to see his abuela smiling sweetly at him. He returned her gaze but then closed his eyes again, hesitating for a moment with the burden of what he felt he must say next. He paused a moment longer and said finally, "And 'buelita... they say... they all say... that you're a witch."

He looked at her with deep questioning eyes, not sure how she would respond to what he'd just shared, not sure that she could see his hurt and the anger he had for those who would brand his dear grandmother this way.

She, too, hesitated a moment, staring ahead motionless as the significance of his words and feelings set in. And then, slowly, her smile returned, her smile turning into a knowing grin and then a chuckle and then a full-throated, all-out avalanche of a laugh that shook her weathered shoulders and drew deepening streams of tears from her eyes.

"Ay Dios, ay Dios!" (Oh God, oh God!) she kept blurting, in between laughing and quaking and catching her breath. "Ay Dios mio, nunca se acaba" (Oh my God, it never ends), she sighed after calming down a bit.

She began slowly composing herself again, still chuckling occasionally to herself. And then, seeing the puzzled look in Abe's eyes, she came and stood before him, gently placing her hands on his shoulders. Looking into his eyes reassuringly, she smiled slightly, enigmatically, like an aged, sun-drenched Mona Lisa. "*Escúchame bien, mijito,*" (listen to me carefully, my child) she said, her eyes more solemn now but twinkling still.

"People will always try to condemn what they don't understand. They understand so little and fear so much that it's inevitable. It's simply that way with humans. Always has been. But you mustn't pay attention to such things. *En verdad, (in truth)* they're the foolish ones for not accepting the things that God places right before them." She paused awhile, looking deeply into Abe's eyes, letting her words set in.

"Do you understand what I'm trying to tell you, Abel?" she asked at last.

Still a bit overwhelmed by her response, by the hilarity she'd broken into at having been called a witch, Abe smiled hesitantly, almost sheepishly, and then said, "Yes, 'buelita, I think so."

His grandmother continued, more serious now, "I know it's hard for you to understand right now, and it's perfectly alright that this should be, but *te juro (I promise you),* someday you'll see how this was all meant to be. You are who you are, and I am what I am and our task is to be just that, just the best 'us' we can be. It doesn't matter what others think about it. What others think of you is their business. But what you think of yourself…," and here she paused for dramatic effect, "well, now… that's your business."

"Do you not see, mijito?" she asked.

"I think so," Abe said, somewhat seriously.

"Try to understand, Abel. It's not really us who chooses our path; it's God, and He's already chosen you for this work. You can say He chose you a long time ago. You may want to resist and there may be times when you'll want to abandon your destiny, if for no other reason than to be more like others but understand that you'll never be able to escape His wishes for you. One way or another, He will bring you to understand the gift He offers by having you serve others in His name. It's His way. And it's a blessing."

"Hopefully," she continued, *"you will see this early on and, like me, surrender yourself fully to His will. You could choose to do otherwise, of course, but it'll simply make for a difficult journey, one that I would not wish for you, mi amor. And in any case, in the end, you'll just wind up surrendering anyway, like your bisabuelo (great-grandfather) don Gonzalo, who spent his whole life trying to ignore his calling only to fall back into God's arms after losing his sight as a mature man. He went on to become a renowned and much-loved healer, as you know, but he also lamented for the rest of his days his foolishness for not having taken up his path from the start."*

"Do you think that could happen to me, 'buelita?" Abe asked seriously.

"No," his grandmother replied quickly. *"You have me to guide you and I don't intend to let that happen. And besides,"* she said slyly, *"it's not likely you'll ever go blind. No, mijito, with my reganadas (scolding's) it's much more likely you'll choose to go deaf!"*

And with that, she put her hands to her ears and widened her eyes wildly as if in surprise. And Abe, thoroughly pleased with her antics, joined her in laughing uproariously for several minutes.

Roberto Páez's professional background includes having worked as a grant writer, educational programs analyst and director, and conflict management specialist. Since retiring from active employment in 2016 Roberto has dedicated his time to writing, teaching and hosting live music events in and around Sacramento, CA. Roberto is currently working on his first novel.

CHAPTER 10

Midnight on the Jersey Turnpike:
A Journey from Pain to Insight
By Claudia Micco

The last thing I remember before the car collided with the tree was the surge of adrenaline and my thoughts echoing, "Oh, shit, I knew it!" An eerie silence swiftly followed this, then darkness. Pain coursed through my body as paramedics worked to free me from the wreckage. It felt as though I floated outside my own being. It was just before midnight on that fateful Saturday. Suddenly, the joyous revelry of the night abruptly stopped. Cruising in a Camaro while Van Halen blared, "Running With The Devil" was drowned out by the deafening collision of metal and nature. If only I had trusted my instincts... But it was too late to undo the events that would haunt me for the rest of my days.

On a warm summer night, the five of us were in full swing, partying and seeking adventure. We decided to hop into my friend's car for a night of cruising. In the back seat, I lay sprawled across my boyfriend's lap, half of my body wedged awkwardly between the front and the back. It began as an ordinary evening, and school was out until September. My friend Cathy and I were immersed in mischief, tagging along with the boys. We were all piled in the car with a few cases of beer and a decent amount of weed. However, an unsettling feeling washed over me that night. Though I had wanted to leave on numerous occasions, I found myself persuaded by their assurances that my unease was nothing more than paranoia.

I remember at one point during the night, it was dark, and we were up in the mountains, sitting around a picnic table. Everybody was drinking, but I just couldn't bring myself to consume anything, and I told my friends I wanted to go home—but not with my friend Jim at the wheel. My requests went unheard, and I was beginning to panic. It took them about twenty minutes to convince me to return to the car. Jim insisted on driving at breakneck speed throughout the night. I was terrified and digging my fingernails into my boyfriend's arm. I tried to maintain a brave face because I knew everybody thought I was acting like a crazy person.

I was no innocent child, and maybe I was a little crazy or just too outspoken for a young girl. I always had a curious nature; by the time I was in fourth grade, I'd already been smoking and taking risks that got me kicked out of the Brownie troops of northern New Jersey. I went to my first rock concert at twelve years old. I ran away from home at thirteen. I wanted to be free to do as I pleased and never really gave in to peer pressure. As the instigator, I usually tried to convince people to do things they shouldn't do. I would be the first to light up a joint and ignite the party. Yet, that night, I was resolute in my decision to abstain from alcohol and drugs despite carrying a stash of Black Beauties, an illegal amphetamine, and low-grade Mexican weed in my purse, intended for sale the next day. Squeezed into the confines of a gorgeous metallic blue Camaro, everyone but me was intoxicated and reveling in the effects of alcohol and marijuana.

Throughout the night, I begged them relentlessly to slow down. "Please, let me out of this car! We're going to crash if you don't stop!" However, my pleas were met with boisterous laughter, leaving me perched precariously on my boyfriend's lap, consumed by uncertainty. Even at the tender age of fifteen, it felt like the longest night of my life.

The consequences of our actions are only fully realized once we face them head-on. In this instance, I was heading down a treacherous path that landed me in a hospital bed. Perhaps this was the only way I would avoid the toxic path I was heading down.

That fateful night became a catalyst for profound change, imparting upon me the first of many valuable lessons. It taught me to hold steadfast to my instincts, even in the face of ridicule from others. It shouldn't have taken a gruesome accident for me to comprehend the potency of that lesson.

I had only been dating Alvaro, my boyfriend, for a few weeks. That particular night, our plans involved a venture to Garrett Mountain, followed by a drive along the New Jersey Turnpike. In 1981, seatbelt laws were nonexistent, and organizations such as Mothers Against Drunk Driving (MADD) were still in their early stages, which caused us to dismiss their messages without a second thought. Little did I realize that my choices that evening would inadvertently contribute to the foundation of MADD's success and become a rallying cry for mothers everywhere.

In retrospect, it may seem preposterous, but the act of drinking and toking weed in the car paled in comparison to what ensued later. Jim abruptly steered us off course, leading us directly into a massive oak tree! Although none of us had bothered to fasten our seatbelts, I emerged as the sole individual subjected to significant injuries—ones that necessitated hospitalization. The impact hurled me through the car, my head colliding with the windshield and my hip fracturing against the seat—a stroke of luck that ultimately saved my life.

I endured a significant amount of time in the emergency room, the memories hazy and blurred due to the intense pain that engulfed me. I frequently drifted in and out of consciousness, the sensation of hovering above my own body persisting. Eventually, the initial emergency procedures were complete and I was led to a room where I was trapped for approximately five weeks. My leg was suspended in traction by a metal bar inserted into my lower leg, and tubes were protruding from various places. A peculiar assortment of unpleasantness surrounded me.

As summer took its fledgling steps, little did I anticipate the two surgeries that awaited me, targeting my hip and thigh and subsequently adorning my body with unsightly, prominent scars and a future plagued by persistent pain. Thankfully, at that time, my head, neck, and shoulders were relatively unscathed compared to my leg. The medical team prioritized averting internal bleeding in my hip—a weighty concern that overshadowed the rest.

Amongst the chaos and trauma, a peculiar sense of happiness endured within me, gratitude for the circumstances not being more dire, perhaps. Hints of optimism colored my perspective, potentially influenced by the regular shots of Demerol administered into my unaffected thigh which intermittently provided respite from the torment.

During my hospital stay, I shared a room with a young woman of around seventeen years old who battled a severe eating disorder. Night after night, she would succumb to tearful episodes, refusing to eat despite the desperate pleas of the medical staff. I witnessed her skeletal frame— her fragile body consisting of nothing but skin and bones. Standing tall at 5'8", she weighed a mere 80 pounds. Despite her struggles, an unexpected bond blossomed between us, forging a deep friendship.

In comparison to her harrowing ordeal, I felt fortunate. My room became a hub of lively gatherings as my energetic friends managed to surpass the restricted visitor limit imposed by the nursing staff. The party atmosphere persisted, providing a semblance of normalcy amidst the chaos. Regrettably, Heather's parents remained her sole visitors as she continued to starve herself into a downward spiral. It was disheartening to witness her deteriorating condition, a plight that should have warranted transfer to a specialized psychiatric care unit months earlier. Through our conversations, I gained profound insight into the intricate relationship between the mind and body as Heather vividly articulated the war waged within her own psyche.

After enduring five weeks of immobility, the use of bedpans, and relying upon sponge baths, my first surgery was finally scheduled. The procedure involved an incision on the backside of my hip, through which a fourteen-inch surgical steel rod would be inserted after removing the bone marrow. As described by my orthopedic surgeon, this innovative technique was pretty new at the time. They would employ a hammer to forcefully secure the rod in place, an option that presented itself as preferable to the alternative: spending six months encased in a body cast, a less than glamorous prospect for me.

From a young age, I possessed an innate curiosity about the human body. Thus, as I prepared for surgery, a mix of fear and fascination permeated my emotions. I still had a long journey ahead of me. After a few weeks passed, the police returned my purse to me. To my surprise, all traces of the Black Beauties and Mexican dirt weed had vanished. No charges were filed against me either. It was then that I fully grasped how perilously close I had come to finding myself entangled in a truly dire situation.

My parents remained blissfully unaware of the presence of drugs in my purse. They harbored deep suspicions regarding my friends and our indulgence in partying despite my commitment to refrain from promiscuity and theft. The havoc wrought by my older sibling, a heroin addict with schizoid personality disorder, cast a long shadow over our family. From a young age, I witnessed the chaos and trauma it unleashed, the perpetual presence of law enforcement at our doorstep, and the harrowing fights that teetered on the precipice of fatality. The toll it exacted upon my parents etched itself into my memory, forging an indelible resolve to never succumb to such destructive paths. The memory seared within me, serving as a poignant reminder of the consequences that awaited should I turn a blind eye to the wake-up call presented by my accident.

As I lay in the hospital, determined to recover fully, I knew that a 180-degree turn in my life was still a work in progress. At fifteen years old, I couldn't quite let go of my rebellious nature. I had a thirst for partying, boys, and fun that still needed to be quenched. But before I could dive back into the world of wild teenage hormone-induced adventures, I had to undergo physical therapy and learn how to walk again.

The journey to rehabilitation was not an easy one. After my first surgery, my doctor told me I would need another six to eight weeks of physical therapy. My summer plans were shattered, but I remained optimistic. After all, I had a hot Puerto Rican boyfriend eagerly awaiting my return, hinting at steamy make-out sessions and the possibility of reaching second or third base.

Determined to be the best patient my doctor had ever seen, I embraced each physical therapy session with enthusiasm. I vividly recall lying on the massage table, enduring the precise and painful movements given by my therapist, Lillian. She was intelligent and fit, and I wanted to be her star patient. Her unwavering encouragement sparked an interest within me. I tried to understand every movement's rationale and role in helping me recover. It became clear that this was the pathway to regaining my mobility and independence, and I was willing to do whatever it took.

Finally, the day came when I was released from the hospital. Although I couldn't yet walk on my own, I had become proficient in using crutches. This meant I was back on the scene, ready to dive back into the world of lively gatherings and raging with my friends. My parents even granted me the freedom to have people over in our backyard during the Indian summer. I was young and entangled in a new romance that would eventually dissolve into ex-territory, but not before he took my virginity and self-worth. I was devastated to discover he was cheating on me the whole time I was recovering, a dismal outcome that added insult to injury.

In spite of Alvaro breaking my heart, I remained resolute during my healing and physical therapy and never missed a session. I found myself utterly captivated by the process. I asked countless questions at every session, eager to understand which muscles we were targeting and why. I'm sure Lillian grew tired of my relentless curiosity, but I couldn't help my insatiable thirst for knowledge. Little did she know what a profound impact she would have on my life going forward. Little did I know that those physical therapy sessions would serve as the catalyst for the profound turnaround I had always yearned for.

About eighteen months later, I underwent a second surgery, and this time, I was determined to walk out of the hospital on my own two feet. And I did just that. At that moment, my fascination with exercise and aerobics began to take hold.

At seventeen years old, I was still too young to join a health club legally. However, that didn't stop me. I borrowed my sister's driver's license and pretended to be twenty, which allowed me to join Women's World. This female-only health club offered aerobic dance classes, chrome dumbbells, those old-fashioned massage rolling machines, and, of course, all the equipment was upholstered in pink. Regardless of the decor, the moment I walked into that club, my world transformed. With Madonna's music blaring through the speakers, I joyfully jumped and danced, feeling renewed strength and healing. I was healed, unstoppable, and hungry to understand how the human body worked.

One day after an invigorating class, I approached the instructor and asked her how I could become an aerobics instructor myself. At that time, there were no official certifications. You just needed to look good in a leotard and be energetic. She told me that all I had to do was create a routine and audition. She recognized my potential and believed I had what it took to become an instructor. However, I soon realized my true age would be discovered if I applied for the job.

As luck would have it, one of my friends, Candy, who was two years my senior, had just opened a small ladies' health club with her parents' blessing. I told her how much I loved aerobics, and she offered me a path forward. In those days, formal training was scarce, but with my passion, a stunning fuchsia leotard, and undeniable enthusiasm, she was willing to provide me with the necessary training and guidance. I would work part-time for $3.35 an hour and have free use of the gym and tanning bed. At the time it was a dream come true for a Jersey girl.

As I embarked on this new journey, I quickly realized that traditional methods of instruction were lacking. Yet, armed with determination and a small amount of natural talent, I thrived. I was tanned and I looked great in that leotard, but it wasn't enough. I didn't know what I wanted to learn, but I knew I wanted to learn more.

I had set my sights on making a living as an aerobics instructor. The time had come for me to venture out of my parents' house, as they had always said, "When you're 18, you can get out if you don't like our rules." And so, at 18, I seized the opportunity to spread my wings and follow my intuition. Guided by an inner compass, I stumbled upon a small ad in the back of Shape magazine that caught my attention: "Come to Maui and transform yourself." At that moment, I made a long-distance call and requested a brochure. While everyone around me called me crazy—even my high school guidance counselor dismissed aerobics as a "passing fad." I refused to let their doubts discourage me.

I defiantly thought, "Screw these people; I am getting out of here!" Six months later, armed with the money I had received from my accident, I boarded a plane destined for Maui. I had never been on a plane before but was excited to escape the city and its temptations. My destination? A rigorous and transformative eight-week training program nestled in the heart of the jungle. There, I immersed myself in a comprehensive curriculum that encompassed not only aerobic dance but also tai chi, yoga, weight training, and much more. Those eight weeks became a period of mind-body bliss, where I honed my skills and deepened my understanding of the interconnectedness between physical and mental well-being. I was working to graduate with an actual certification and the confidence to teach others the methods that transformed me.

However, as the program drew to a close, the realization washed over me that I had to return to New Jersey. A wave of unhappiness engulfed me, and I spent the entire fourteen-hour plane ride home in tears. Back in those days, you could smoke on an airplane, and the first thing I did was ask my seatmate for a cigarette. I had an uneasy feeling I might get back into my old habits. I had no idea what I was going to do. While I felt confident with my newfound education and expertise, my spirit longed for much more than New Jersey could offer.

Intrigued by stories of San Francisco's health-conscious atmosphere and eager to take advantage of its free college classes, I obeyed my inner voice and followed a man who would eventually become my ex-husband to the West Coast. Although I had never been to California before, I trusted my instincts once again. Despite the warnings and dissuasions from friends and family, I knew I had to take the leap. I was well aware that it wouldn't be easy, especially given my lack of traditional dance training; the fitness field on the West Coast was fiercely competitive.

Immersed in my passion for dance and fitness, I eagerly took every available class and received private training from my coworker, who was an Alvin Ailey Dancer. Through dedication and hard work, I ascended the ranks, managed the studios for three Golds Gyms, and eventually became one of the top teachers in the Bay Area. I was living my vision professionally. However, personally, this period coincided with the height of the devastating AIDS crisis, and the toll it took on my close friends was heart-wrenching.

Weekly memorial services became the norm, a painful reminder of the fragility of life. I watched the inhumane treatment of those I loved so dearly. It all seemed to happen so quickly. One day, I'd be having lunch or dancing at a disco with a seemingly healthy young friend, and soon after, I'd be crying, numb at their funeral service, wondering what the hell was happening. The loss hit me hard, particularly when my best friend and roommate succumbed to the disease.

There was little support from outsiders and the world at large; they were afraid of the word AIDS and gay people. In our dwindling community, we cared for each other with little knowledge of what we were dealing with. We were all ostracized and outcast, gay or not—guilt by association. We even had death threats on our phone machine from one of my family members, and a visit to our house with a baseball bat. The weight of grief and the constant reminders became too much to bear in San Francisco. Despite being at the top of my game in a competitive industry, I reached a crossroads that demanded yet another leap of faith.

I was in such a vulnerable state, feeling so lost and depressed that I tried desperately to grasp onto my intuition to lead me forward. I wrote long, detailed dream journals, smoked enough pot to make Snoop Dogg blush, and pushed myself to exercise obsessively, all in the pursuit of discovering the next chapter of my life. Meanwhile, I had to go on with my daily duties, like teaching classes full of adoring students who looked up to me, while pretending that I was okay. I felt so drained from faking optimism that at the end of my days, I would sink into a hole of exhaustion and isolation.

In my quiet moments, all sorts of doubts crept into my mind. My best friend was dead, and a failed marriage was behind me. I felt hopeless; I was lost in despair and sadness. Maybe this whole move was a mistake. Was I a fool for having gone against my parents' wishes when they wanted me to take on a safe life with a stable job at the post office? Did I even have any unique talents or abilities worth exploring anymore? Would I ever be able to successfully motivate and inspire crowds of students in the classroom now that I felt like such a phony?

All these conflicting questions and moods pulled me in different directions as I desperately sought clarity. Everywhere I looked, there were mysteries and obstacles that threatened to keep me from taking the next step. It seemed impossible to move forward.

Just as I considered giving it all up and returning home, a remarkable opportunity fell into my lap: a teaching position at a world-renowned spa in Mexico. It was the perfect escape, a chance to rejuvenate my spirit and trust my intuition again. I seized the opportunity without hesitation, knowing deep within that it was the right move. Once again, I was met with objections from friends and family, and once again, I said, "fuck it." I sold everything I had, packed up my Ford Escort, and drove to Mexico.

From that moment forward, my intuition became my guiding force, leading me down a path of endless adventures. I traveled across the world, teaching and sharing my knowledge in various countries, immersing myself in different cultures. From living in Europe to traversing continents, my life became a tapestry of experiences I wouldn't trade for anything.

Looking back on my journey, I realize that my accident and subsequent trials were not mere accidents or random misfortunes. They were catalysts for transformation, forcing me to trust my intuition and follow the path that was meant for me.

Through all the challenges, losses, and doubts, I have emerged stronger, more resilient, and unapologetically true to myself. In each mistake, there was truth, love, and a desire to do it right next time.

––––––––––––––––––––––

Claudia Micco, a thirty-five + year industry veteran, is an internationally recognized fitness trainer, podcast host, and influential educator. Inspired by a traumatic car accident in her teens, she explored the body's healing potential. With diverse certifications, Claudia focuses on the mind-body connection. Her HypnoFitness program, rooted in hypnosis and NLP, empowers individuals to achieve holistic well-being. www.claudiamicco.com

CHAPTER 11

Now, Let's Talk About the Kids
By Allisum Sturges

I accept responsibility for being the grand original cause of all the circumstances in my life that I would identify as "challenging." Because my awareness level was much lower in my earlier years, I stumbled through much of my lifetime believing other people's choices or "situations" were the causes of my challenging life circumstances, as many of us do.

One bleak and chilly day in November 2006 found me living back at my parents' house after signing the final documents for a divorce I started but did not want to finish. My ex-husband, as I had to get used to calling him, was the petitioner, but I initiated the entire matter in the first place. There is a world of evidence substantiating his right to warrant a divorce from me, but that is another topic for another time. Now, let's talk about the kids.

A thirteen-year-old boy by the name of David and a four-year-old girl by the name of Ember found themselves in the crossfire of a vitriolic divorce and bitter custody battle that divided two formerly very close families and dragged everyone involved through a painful and destructive process that would last many years.

David and Ember each had their ways of managing the situation. David was outspoken, "calling a spade a spade" as he utilized frank honesty and candid language to express his identification of the wrongs of each "player" and had no problem telling each of us to our faces what our mistakes were, often in front of whoever may be listening. To this day David maintains this communication style, and I often find myself changing the subject whenever "the past' is brought up, as it will always guarantee feelings of embarrassment on my part. But I would not change him for the world.

Ember, on the other hand, managed the situation also by being outspoken, but her expressions were outrageous and hilarious declarations of a precocious character as she utilized charm to please and subdue the adults around her. Ember's communication style has grown over the years to resemble a more "politically correct" tone, but that "wild child" is still there, as evidenced by her Instagram posts that are not meant for me to see.

The prospect of losing custody of my children was unbearable to me; as the divorce was settled, the ongoing custody battle had just begun. My ex was out for blood. He wanted full custody and monitored visitation only for me, for the least amount of time possible, forever. And if he could manage to "out" me entirely for the rest of our days, that was the endgame goal. He had also found an accomplice to partner with to bolster his position. A girlfriend who started out as "the babysitter" who soon became "the fiancée," who made it her life's purpose to "protect my daughter" from me. I am not certain if she meant to include my son in this "purpose" as well. She seemed to focus more on my daughter. Not having her own children, and not wanting any, she adopted her own brothers, taking custody of them from a mother who had substance abuse problems. I became the representation of her mother, as substance abuse issues were the exact nature of my afflictions at the time and one of the main reasons for my divorce and subsequent custody battle. It was personal to her, and in her soul, she and my daughter were one. Although I could understand her position, I knew I was in for a ride.

For my ex, it was a family matter in addition to being a personal matter. He grew up in an alcoholic home of four children and harbored his own issues with alcohol. Born to older parents who grew up during the Depression, money was a point of conflict always and there was lots of dysfunction in the household. Boundaries were not healthy, and relationships were enmeshed, especially between my ex and his sisters. Codependency reigned supreme. So not only did he have "the fiancée," he also had three more accomplices in his sisters. It was me against him and the four women. Actually, in a broader sense, it was their family against ours, with the kids in the middle. My ex was shell-shocked from growing up with dysfunction related to rampant alcoholism, so by the time he encountered my similar issues, his patience had worn thin. The day he met "the babysitter turned fiancée" was the day all hope of our reconciliation died.

116

My background had its share of dysfunction and substance abuse as well. My parents were twenty-three years old when I was born in 1970. Growing up in the 1970s and 1980s with baby boomer parents working full-time in the music industry provided a setting that gifted lots of freedom to me and my several "fostered" cousins, and many opportunities to develop my growing fascination with getting high. I worked from age eleven as an actress in multiple popular prime-time television shows of the day, so that was another reason I was able to garner more freedom to do as I wished. I had my own money. My parents were young and spirited and loved me unconditionally no matter what I did. There were rules but they were lax, and the focus was on having fun and doing what you loved in life. I had an amazing opportunity to develop myself artistically growing up, but I took it down another road. I was an addict by the time I was sixteen years old, and that road led to many years of pain and loss.

David and Ember were surrounded by dysfunction and substance abuse on all sides, and the battle was on. Our lives centered around the ensuing drama of the day. From my ex and his fiancée's reconnaissance missions staking out my parents' house to catch me taking the kids to school late while on my way to work, to the inclusion of all of the staff at each kid's school being looped into the polarizing situation as they took one side or another, to the police department becoming involved at times, it was one thing after another for the kids to deal with. Public affrays at the kids' schools during and after student performances, conflicts at cheer, soccer, and baseball, confrontations between different family members separately, court dates swallowing up hours of time and energy fighting over every detail—all provided an extremely contentious and stressful environment for the kids. The adults were out of control. The events of normal family life often went from tense to all-out verbal melees with multiple parties engaged. This went on for a couple of years. What were these kids to do?

I was aware that something had to change. I could have listed in great detail (and still can) every nuance of every mistake my ex and his fiancée made, every mistake everyone in their family made, and every error engaged in by anyone who had anything to do with the situation. I abhorred what seemed to me to be "the fiancée's" obsession with annihilating me and destroying my relationships with my children, and at the vengeance in my ex's soul. My daughter was especially impressionable, but my son felt the pressure to turn against me as well. Having to receive negative messages about their mom on a daily basis, in my view, was "abusive" to them both, no matter how justified the senders of these messages believed they were in maintaining their loathing and active opposition to me.

I was not going to let them replace me, no matter how hard they tried. I vowed to fight to the end to keep intact the relationships that mattered more than anything in the world to me—my close connections with my children. Beyond the custody issue, it was their love and their understanding of my love for them that was most at stake here, and no one was going to take that away from them or me. The long list of my own past mistakes rang in my ears like bells that never ceased. I replayed them over and over in my mind, guilt-ridden and despondent at my failure to be the mom I had always dreamed of being.

Reeling daily from feelings of grief and fear, I was committed to the process of rebuilding my life from the ground up, but I still had a long way to go. I found myself constantly defending myself and having to go through hell to sustain a relationship with my daughter. My son had long left my ex's household after an ugly fight in their home and was with me full-time. This was initiated when my ex and "the fiancée" asked him to leave, with the declaration, "If it is between you or her staying, you are going to have to go," spoken by my ex, who had adopted him when he was eight years old. My son experienced this as a heartbreaking and deep betrayal by the only father he had known, as his natural father was not around to be there for him during those years. My daughter was with us a few days a week, and we tried to make the best of it. There was no peace and it looked like that was how things would be indefinitely. What was more unsettling were the continuous daily errors of judgment and perception on both sides that perpetuated the ongoing feud that colored the childhoods of two precious people who did not deserve to grow up with all this strife. My heart ached for David and Ember. I knew something had to change, but I did not know what or how.

The answer arrived just as my heart was opened to it. One day, during one of my Sunday house-cleaning missions, I encountered a little white diary. It was no doubt one my mom had given to my daughter, either in an Easter basket or for Valentine's Day. It was on a little white table in my daughter's room surrounded by bottles of glitter, coloring books, stickers, and colored pens. I stopped for a bit to look through it. I had put this little diary back on the table or in the dresser drawer many times, but today was different. Although I was in the middle of deep cleaning the entire house, I felt the instinct to read through this little book. There were random words spelled or misspelled on various pages, along with funny little pictures of who knows what.

I continued on and came upon a pink heart carefully drawn on a page toward the middle of the book. Written within the borders of the little drawn pink heart were 3 words: Mommy, Daddy, and KK. My heart stopped. There it was, my daughter's heart, holding the names of the parents she loved. All three of them. In that moment everything inside of me shifted. I felt as if my heart had been opened and a spear of guilt and awareness lodged deep into my chest. I was wrong— and had been wrong all along. In one moment, every complaint I held against my ex and the fiancée (and everyone else involved) vanished into the clear realization that the major change needed was inside of myself.

In that moment of awareness, I resolved to make things right. I would no longer divide my daughter's heart by being at odds with the other two parents, but instead, I decided to become "one" with them, no matter what it took. The only thing that mattered to me at that point was repairing the damage "I" had done to everyone. I decided to honor my daughter's right to love whoever she loved. As for my son, I understood that I had played a part in his losing the only Dad he had known, and I had to make that right again. I realized my children needed to grow up in a supportive environment with parents who put their differences aside to work together to support and nurture them. And so, my new morale was born.

My making these stark changes in attitude and behavior so suddenly was confusing and uncomfortable for everyone. The fiancée (KK) was suspicious for at least a year, always waiting for me to snap out of it. My ex was equally cautious as I gave in to his requests regarding custody of Ember, as long as my visits with her remained uninterrupted. What mattered was the quality of the time I spent with my kids, not so much the quantity. They were more interested in spending time with friends anyway, and I had a lot of work to do. From that day forward, I refrained from vilifying my ex and the fiancée in my mind, in my words, in my actions, and moreover, in my own heart and soul. I learned to be grateful for the love present in my kids' lives, and for there being people beyond myself to love and care for them.

I learned to free my kids' hearts to receive and give love to whoever they felt they wanted to, without feeling that they had to choose between us or maintain loyalty to one side or the other. I embraced the relief of "humility" and the willingness to see where I am "in the wrong" whenever I feel angry, hurt, jealous, offended, threatened, or fearful. It is an ongoing work in progress but worth the effort. I found that I had not lost anything, but rather gained everything, as I let go and let things be, trusting all events to unfold in the course that is best for everyone involved.

Thankfully, all our paths were forever changed for the better with that one initial decision within one of us. One decision can change the course for all involved. Since then, for every holiday, birthday, sports or school performance event, community event, on to the graduations and everything else life has to offer, we celebrate together as one family. It is not always perfect, but it is usually great fun. I cannot see a better way to demonstrate my love for my kids than making sure that every family memory they have had since then is a happy one, filled with light hearts and the knowledge they are loved above all else!

Allisun Sturges grew up in an entertainment industry family, spending her childhood and young adulthood in some of the most prominent luxury neighborhoods in Los Angeles, growing up with and learning from many well-known and talented entertainers, comedians and musical and theatrical artists. By age eleven and into her young adulthood she was a working actress in multiple prime time television comedy shows, doing commercial, print and voice over work for large media companies. She found particular success in the mortgage industry and began to realize that her love of remarkable properties, beginning in her childhood, could be integrated into a successful career in real estate.

CHAPTER 12

Close Encounters With the Bear Kind
By Mary Adams

I was born in Los Angeles to parents that were camping enthusiasts. We took amazing trips to magical places: deep caves underground, crystal clear lakes, and tall mountain peaks all over the United States. I recently came across a black-and-white photo that my father took with his Old Minolta in Sequoia National Forest in 1968. My young mom was holding me tenderly in front of a backdrop of giant trees; I was about six months old. I grew up in the mountains on the weekends and during vacations, and it ignited a feeling of being home in nature.

I have a well-developed travel mentality and am blessed with wanderlust and a long bucket list of places I must see while I am still roaming this earth. So many memories come to mind of horseback riding in my mom's lap, hiking to waterfalls, camping in our tent, and attending all the wonderful park programs and events that were offered. I have always had a fantasy of working part-time as a ranger in the National Park Service system when I retire. My only exposure to vvwild animals as a young child consisted of educational TV shows, Wild Country Safari Park in California, and the Los Angeles Zoo. I had been taught to have profound respect for all animals, and I remember having the deep impression that everything was harmless and safe, not knowing that in controlled environments with cages, triple-plated glass enclosures, and viewing platforms, it all was simply an illusion. My innocent mind was filled with endearing fairy tales like "The Jungle Book," with the sweet, wise bear Baloo. I was brainwashed to believe that cuddly, cute, overly friendly animals roamed the forest.

I guess you could say we have a family totem "animal." Over the years, we have cultivated many tales and dangerous lessons on camping trips that have been attended by uninvited guests: bears. It is funny to look back and think about all the attempts we made to secure our campsites, hide and hang our food, or clean up thoroughly to avoid a visit. But no matter what measures we took, inevitably the bears would sneak in to inspect our campsites for crumbs. The truth is these were dangerous, frightening moments with highly intelligent, adapted wild animals with strong instincts to survive and eat anything smaller and weaker.

A bear's level of intelligence is quite evolved; they have a thinking process beyond that of most wildlife. There are thousands of videos on YouTube Showing bears opening car doors, casually letting themselves into houses, and doing as they please. They are the bandits of the animal kingdom and are much smarter than we give them credit for. I have this notion that bears have been taught, either through their DNA or some other instinctual knowledge, how to ruin a good camping trip. During dozens of bear encounters, they have broken into my car, shredded several of my tents, stolen my food, and chased me on hikes for wholesome fun. I have learned to always be aware of my surroundings and be ready to defend myself at a moment's notice.

It still amazes me how bears have transitioned from wild predators to opportunists in tourist locations. I was in Yosemite National Forest recently, boondocking in a parking lot, snacking on some lunch, and hoping for an afternoon nap after hiking to Bridal Veil Falls. While sipping on a warm cup of coffee and going through my photos from the day, I detected movement out of the corner of my eye. I looked up to see a bear strolling up right next to my rig. He was looking right at me, and I was afraid he was preparing to make a visit. I was parked in front of the village restaurant, and he quickly passed by, as he was on a different mission. That 300-pound bear made a beeline right down the middle aisle of the crowded tables full of tourists and straight for the trash can. In most national parks, there are safety latches to keep wildlife out of the bins, but this bear was a seasoned professional as he casually unclasped the brass clasp on the dumpster lid. He had a look of excitement as he gingerly started sorting through the contents of fresh table scraps. As he picked out his midday snack, he would taste a tiny nibble as if he were sampling an expensive cheese in a gourmet deli.

The audience of tourists stood around him; some moved back and even left to find a safer place farther away. There were gasps and chatter as they gawked and talked in their native tongues. Some of the other diners were busy at work getting those prize-winning vacation photos with which to wow their friends on social media. It all seemed innocent to the bystanders having their moment of connection with nature. But then again, a few years prior I had seen a bear rip off a car door because dinner was waiting in the ice chest in the back seat. I have learned the hard way that to expect a wild animal to be civil among humans can be a deadly mistake. The best advice I can give is to back away slowly and take your chance to get to safety while you have it.

My father often shares the story of my first bear experience in Big Bear National Forest when I was an infant. He was returning from the communal bath house on the trail back to our cabin in the woods. It was getting a bit chilly as the sun began to set and he was enjoying the beauty of the moon and the colors of the sky. Shaken from his trance, he was greeted along the path by a mother bear and her two cubs. He stopped cold to assess the situation and looked ahead to see how far he had to run to the safety of our cabin. As he looked over, he caught a quick glimpse of my mom holding me up to the window as we both started waving joyfully, smiling, laughing, and chanting for *"Dad-dy!"* He said his only thought at that moment was that he was about to get mauled, and my mom and I had a front-seat view of what was about to happen. My pop started waving his arms and yelling at the bears, dancing around, and I giggled and laughed thinking my dad was being funny for my benefit. The cubs were startled and ran away into the thicket of the forest, with the mother bear chasing close behind.

One of the first memories and most frightening experiences of my life was while camping with my family when I was about four years old. We had a 1972 Chevrolet Station Wagon, with the infamous wood paneling on the exterior. This vehicle was bigger than anything I had ever seen on the road; you could fit a dozen passengers in it with its three rows of stiff black vinyl bench seats—the kind that would cause a third-degree burn on your legs in the summer. My little brother and I loved that vehicle, especially the electric back tailgate window. We went everywhere in this boat; it was ideal for camping and storing our gear and had the added convenience of our custom-built pullout kitchen in the very back, which included a kitchen sink crafted by my dad.

It was early morning, and we were on the main road driving through Sequoia National Forest. I remember the huge trees and the morning sun rising through them, creating strange shadows that glistened with hues of gold. The eight-track was playing John Denver, as we all sang along: "Country roads… Take me home … to the place…I belong…" Suddenly, my Dad hollered and pointed to the side of the road. "Kids, Look over there … it's a bear!" It was the strangest sight I had ever seen. A humongous brown bear was on the side of the road, and my childlike mind made up a story that he must be hitchhiking for a ride. Suddenly, my dad pulled over, jolting the station wagon quickly to the side of the road, dirt and gravel flying as we came to a screeching halt. I have never seen my father move so fast in his life as he did at that moment.

Within seconds, he turned and grabbed his camera gear, hollering at my mom to "stay in the car!" Before we knew what was happening, he disappeared around the back of the wagon, running toward the bear. We were stunned and unsure of what was happening or what to do. My mom was yelling my dad's name and my little brother and I had escaped out of our car seats to look through the big back window. It was exciting to see my first bear! They certainly looked different than they did on the TV show with Grizzly Adams. My dad was poised and postured like a National Geographic photographer capturing a prize-winning shot. And then, unexpectedly, the bear took off running at full speed, headed straight for our vehicle, with my dad standing there holding his camera.

This animal was moving at lightning speed; before we could even scream, this beast was just feet away from us with my father trailing far behind. The huge bear stopped and assessed our vehicle, sniffing through the window that was cracked open just a little at the top for ventilation. He then reached up with a giant paw as big as my head and started clawing at the rear door to find a way to break in. He was sniffing around with that huge nose and his large mouth full of razor-sharp teeth were chomping as if he was ready for a snack.

I remember being frozen in fear as this 300-pound creature paused and stared straight at me, eye to eye. The hungry bear then forced its thin black nails into that crack of the rear electric window. My dad immediately sprang into action, ran back to us at full speed, and leaped into the driver's seat like a superhero jumping in to save us. He started the station wagon and pushed the button to close the rear window. But the bear's strength was no match for the little motor. With a heavy thud, that bear had pushed the large glass barrier completely down. He stuck his head into our camp kitchen in the back and began to crawl into the vehicle. My brother and I started screaming, " I see his ears!" "I see his teeth!" I had a deep sense that this bear was going to eat my brother and me for breakfast, and I understood I was a little girl who had no defense against this monster.

In an instant, my father took off, tires spinning from the fast acceleration, figuring it would startle the bear and he would abort his mission. But he watched the review mirror in horror; the bear had its hind legs on the back bumper and the top half of its body still in the car. My dad started driving erratically, fishtailing the vehicle while the bear was getting tossed about. So off we went in the station wagon, the bear taking a long joyride on the back—paws on the roof, feet on the bumper, and looking like he was riding a surfboard. It must have been a hilarious sight for cars passing by; our hitchhiker had no intent on ending his mission. After a few minutes of driving along, my dad honking his horn wildly and all of us screaming; the bear lost his grip, jumped off, and ran into the forest. This story has become a family heirloom, as my father still enjoys bragging about the photos he took that day.

My most recent bear encounter happened in 2021. I had set off on a solo grand adventure road and camping trip. The itinerary had been planned for months and went through five states and nine national parks, covering over 7,000 miles (about twice the width of the United States), driven over the course of more than three weeks. About halfway through my trip, I needed supplies desperately as I had used the last of my rations, and my gas was running low. Kings Canyon National Park had opened back up but was still partially shut down due to COVID-19, so gas stations were closed, and food supplies were hard to find. I finally found a park ranger who told me I would have to make the fifty-mile trek out of the park and head into Fresno, CA, to restock, get gas, and grab a hot meal. So, I decided I would head down to the city and then to my next destination, Sequoia National Forest, a few days early. I thought I had allotted plenty of time for my quick stop, but as things went, everything took longer than I had anticipated; traffic was an issue and getting lost cost me some time.

With a full belly and my GPS set for my recently reserved campsite for the night, I headed into the forest. As the sun started to set, I was well on my way and maneuvering the curvy and dangerous road, freshly slick from a recent rain shower. When it got dark, my high beams were not bright enough to see far ahead of me. It had gotten foggy on my trek up the mountainside, so I took it slow and stayed laser-focused on the road. I found myself gripping the steering wheel hard and holding my breath. I have ample respect for these forestry roads and know how to look for animals and hazards; one small mistake or distraction could cost me my life.

After a few hours of driving, I finally saw the sign for the campground, took my right turn onto the dirt road, and went ahead up the hill.

According to my GPS, I was right on top of where I needed to be, and yet there was no campground to be seen anywhere. As I stopped to check my online map, my cell phone service cut out and it was just me, my paper map, and the dirt road. I wished I had printed out an itinerary with maps and information ahead of time to avoid this type of situation. Everything indicated I was where I needed to be, so I decided to continue on the dirt road as I was certain I would find the entrance. I saw campfires and tents to my right—what a relief! I had found my resting spot for the night. The road soon got rocky and uneven, and I had to switch into 4-wheel drive mode as I could feel a bit of slip in the dirt beneath me. There were limbs and uncut brush in the road. Up and up I went, on a steep incline. This was my first indication that something had gone terribly wrong with my navigation. I was prepared to stay at a rough campsite, but my reservations had included electricity, water, and a bath house for the first hot shower in days. My disappointment was growing at the false advertisement for my three-day retreat and campsite. So I kept going, as there was nowhere to turn around. The brush was now scraping my vehicle on the driver's side and the road had narrowed, with no turn-offs.

I had to stop at least half a dozen times within a two-hour period just to catch my breath, as the panic attacks and uncertainty were growing within me. I had to get my mind straight and focused, say a prayer, and hope for the best. There was no choice but to continue to move forward up this mountain. Not a person, a house, or a car was in sight. A few times the road had gotten so narrow that, using the side mirrors, I could see that I barely had enough room to stay on the road. The brush and downed trees on the driver's side of my SUV were screeching as they scratched and dragged along my car. At one point I put it in park and switched over to the passenger side to get a better look with my big flashlight. The drop was thousands of feet down, with no guardrail.

After three hours, I finally hit a clearing on the right. I carefully maneuvered myself off the dirt road into a pasture. It was midnight and I had had enough of this day; I needed to sleep and wait for daylight. It was time to set up camp, so I jumped out of my rig onto the soft dirt and headed to the back hatch to grab my wintry weather gear as it was already thirty-six degrees—the forecast was calling for a twenty-eight-degree low before sunup. I had not used the bathroom in over six hours, and the time was now. My camp bucket was deeply packed. So, I put on my big coat, shut the back hatch, and leaned on the bumper for leverage to do my personal business.

The sky was full of stars with no moon, and the Milky Way galaxy was showing off in a big way. Looking up at the giant redwood trees, I caught a glimpse of the twinkling stars shining through the limbs and I wondered if this is where the idea of Christmas tree lights came from. Every moment of this detour was suddenly worth it. This is what I came for; it was a holy moment that brought tears to my eyes. In gratitude, I was relieved to know that I was finally done for the night and could rest until sunrise and find my way to safety. I started laughing loudly, as it was such a spiritual moment for me, and I configured the title, "My cosmic bathroom experience."

I was suddenly taken out of my deep trance when I heard a rustle in the bushes, and at that moment, I realized that I was not alone. I quickly assessed my best next move, as I was in a compromising position with my pants below my knees. Now I knew I was far from civilization, so I highly doubted it was another human; it was pitch black so there was no need for embarrassment. Maybe someone had found me, and I could get off this mountain and into that hot shower that I had been dreaming of for days! But there was no flashlight or any human-type noises. I was at the back of my rig with only a flashlight and a roll of toilet paper to defend myself from whatever was out there. In my rush to get my heavy coat and relieve my bladder, I left my only means of protection, my twelve-inch hunting knife, at the front of the vehicle.

I froze in place, hoping that whatever kind of creature it was, it would lose interest in me and move on. The comedian in my head thought maybe it would retreat since I had just marked my territory. I was deeply hoping that a raccoon had stumbled across me, or maybe a herd of deer. And then I heard a noise that chilled me to the bone—a deep guttural grunt, about twenty feet away from me and in the same area where I heard the limbs bending and leaves crunching. I knew at once a bear had found me; I know that sound so well. I froze to attention and knew that if I didn't get out of there quickly, I was going to become dinner. I had no gun; I had no real protection. And I realized that a big enough bear could rip both me and my vehicle up like a tin can. My ice chest was full of fresh food and boxed emergency rations, and

I knew the bear could smell it. I had one chance to get into my SUV without getting attacked… or worse.

I stayed still and slowly shuffled while crouching, creeping myself closer to the driver's side rear door. I then slithered on my back, getting up to my feet from the ground slowly, simultaneously pulling up my jeans in one swift movement. It was now or never, so I took a deep breath, pressed the alarm's panic button to stun the bear with the flashing lights and loud noise, jumped into my rig, and started her up with a loud roar of the engine. I started honking the horn and was ready to drive off and escape if that became necessary. I began to realize that heading back down that trail road in the dark could be more dangerous than coming up. No one knew where I was—heck, *I* didn't know where I was, so the bears and I needed to coexist until sunup. I felt like a monkey in a cage and hoped for the best until morning.

After resting for a bit and catching my breath, I worked up the courage to open my moonroof and shine my spotlight to see where I was, taking a better look at the situation. I was parked in a huge high Sierra meadow, and there was a little stream nearby; I could hear it gurgling in the distance. I soon realized that not only had a bear found me, or I had found it, but there was an entire pack of bears surrounding my site for the night, foraging and smelling about. I had landed in their pasture, and they had probably never seen a human before, this far out in the woods. I was like an alien in a spaceship that just landed in front of their home.

Thankfully, the rest of the night was uneventful, and I woke up early after a restless night. Upon first light, I finally got to see where I had landed. The view from the top of a mountain was like nothing I had ever seen—fresh snow on the mountains in the distance, with the icy remains of a cold spring night in its last few days of winter. It was obvious I was on a private forestry road used for maintenance and fires. In the morning, I discovered fresh bear tracks and scat surrounding my vehicle. There were no bears in sight, and I figured they were sleeping in after keeping watch over me all night. The drive down was mind-blowing, and I took my time as it was steep and slippery on the unmaintained road. When I saw how close I had come to the side of the cliff most of the way up, I was already on the way back down, within inches of the side and hanging on the edge of that road from the driver's seat, praying each inch of the way and calculating every next little movement. Thankfully, I lived through that whole ordeal, and I crept out of a gate that had been accidentally left open—with a sign that said, "Do not enter," hidden by the brush. I felt like a hero when I finally found the campground entrance—ten feet from where the GPS had said it was… but on the opposite side of the road.

Each of my trips and encounters has taught me important lessons about safety, resilience, and smart thinking. Traveling alone as a woman can be considered dangerous, and I have been told that I am taking unnecessary chances with my life, yet I have experienced my existence from a broader place, hitting the road alone on a magical journey to discover a new part of myself. I have added many safety measures to better prepare for unexpected needs and emergencies during my trips. I now preplan as much as I can, including a full notebook of possible itineraries and printed maps with lists of points of interest and emergency needs. You never know when you will be without heat, shelter, or in a potentially harmful situation, such as a breakdown. I have a plan for the worst-case scenario, so I can be that good "Girl Scout" and be ready for anything. After so many frightening encounters with bears, I now religiously carry bear spray and my knife when camping, no matter where I am in the forest. Those bears don't get another chance to take me by surprise and I don't get caught unarmed. My next investment is a personal locator beacon with a satellite messenger that I can use to send an SOS signal when I am out of cell range in an emergency.

My takeaway: After all these years and visits from bears, I have realized that they are curious and mostly timid animals, but they will act aggressively during the summer if they are hungry or in the middle of breeding season. Even though I have had some close calls, they have not stopped me from traveling through bear country—although tent camping is a no-go, and you should learn to always expect them for a visit, making sure you are never caught unprepared for an escape.

———————————————————

Mary Adams is a dreamer and a teacher who is passionate about empowering others to their highest potential. She is owner of "Infinity Global Creations" Established in 2008 - Working with best selling authors, rising stars and famous musicians, to expand their marketing, products and social media globally. infinityglobalcreations.com

CHAPTER 13

Dream
By Wayne D. Carter

In the fall of 2017, I experienced a series of dreams that profoundly altered the course of my life.

Previously, I had been quite skeptical about the significance of dreams, dismissing them as absurd figments of the imagination. For instance, how could one seriously consider a dream where the dreamer finds himself flying over a Swiss lake frozen in time and dotted with pristine 1970s muscle cars, while clad only in underwear and yet impervious to the cold?

However, as I delved deeper into understanding how dreams manifest in our world, I began to see the necessity of having a firm grasp of this knowledge to truly appreciate the revelations presented to me.

These were no ordinary dreams; they were vivid, all-encompassing experiences that spanned the entire night, only dissipating with the arrival of dawn.

From an esoteric standpoint, dreams are much more than mere nightly wanderings of our resting minds; they are mystical bridges connecting our conscious thoughts to the profound depths of our subconscious.

They weave into the rich, enigmatic tapestry of our souls, serving as channels through which the universe imparts cryptic truths and hidden wisdom. In this boundless realm, unfettered by the constraints of time and space, dreams allow our spirits to transcend the banalities of waking life, journeying through astral planes and exploring ancient archetypes and symbols.

This passage through the dreamscape is considered an integral part of spiritual awakening and self-discovery. Each dream is a cryptic oracle, mirroring our deepest fears and desires—an unending quest to unravel the mysteries of existence.

Thus, dreams are venerated as sacred gateways to higher consciousness, offering esoteric insights and guiding our souls on their eternal journey toward enlightenment. These extraordinary dreams of mine were not just a series of nocturnal escapades; they were transformative experiences that reshaped my understanding of reality and my place within it.

At the very inception of this dreamlike voyage, within the confines of a space ensconced in walls of tan stucco, a room where an unglazed window offered a panoramic view of the night sky's celestial ballet, the intricate process of dream creation began, deeply rooted in the complex interplay of neurochemical signals within the brain.

As the mind embarked on a journey through the enigmatic realm of Rapid Eye Movement (REM) sleep, my sensory gateways, wide open yet introspective, cast doubt upon the authenticity of the unfolding spectacle: a nocturnal canvas where beams of laser light, evoking images akin to a fantastical light display, gave life to ethereal vignettes depicting various people and events. These transient images, a vivid testament to the subconscious mind's interaction with a cascade of neural impulses, vibrated with a sound that seemed to fill the ether, yet remained impervious to my attempts at initiating dialogue.

In this otherworldly domain, the cerebral cortex, a master weaver of dreams, intricately fused together fragments of memories and a spectrum of emotions, spinning tales where the lines between reality and illusion blurred and intertwined.

This dream's landscape was further enriched by the arrival of a formidable yet benign figure, a silent overseer who appeared to be the guardian of this threshold space. From a neurological standpoint, this entity symbolized an archetype, an emblematic construct of my inner psyche, seamlessly woven into the very fabric of the dream.

As the room spun gently, as if suspended in time and space, my hesitance to blink reflected my fear of missing even the smallest detail of this mesmerizing adventure, a clear indication of the dream state's remarkable ability to captivate with its vividness and clarity.

Simultaneously, a conversation unfolded subtly in the background, featuring the gentle, soothing voice of a woman engaging with a man whose tone carried a more clinical and pragmatic timbre. They were in deep contemplation regarding my navigation and interaction within this extraordinary phantasmagoria.

This auditory element in the dream highlighted the brain's remarkable capacity to integrate and synthesize external stimuli, weaving them seamlessly into the ongoing narrative of the dream.

The dream's concluding chapter was heralded by a gradual shift in the sky's palette, transitioning from a deep, star-filled indigo to the gentle yellow hues of early dawn. This shift, accompanied by the angelic melodies of unseen young female voices, symbolized not only the end of this inaugural act in the elaborate theatre of dreams but also denoted the brain's gradual emergence from the profound depths of REM sleep, moving toward a state of waking consciousness.

In the subsequent chapter of this recurring nocturnal narrative, the dream's motif persisted with striking familiarity—the same earthen stucco walls, the identical window serving as a portal to the cosmos.

However, a notable deviation manifested within this familiar dreamscape: the room was now inhabited by figures garbed in white suits, their attire reminiscent of scientists in a sterile laboratory.

Adorned with respirators and latex gloves, they epitomized a fusion of clinical sterility and methodical precision. Propelled by an amalgam of curiosity and an inherent spirit of defiance, I found myself rising to confront the verisimilitude of this enigmatic environment.

This act of mobility set off a domino effect within the confines of the room. A side table lost its balance, precipitating the descent of various objects; a lamp, a book, a cellphone, and a pocketknife clattered in a cacophonous symphony upon the floor. Amid this disarray, a voice, distinctly masculine in timbre, resonated with a cautionary note, addressing me by name: "Wayne, take it easy."

The palpable reality of his words juxtaposed bizarrely against the backdrop of what was ostensibly a dream, a paradox that stirred within me a profound sense of bewilderment.

As the room maintained its celestial gyration, it served as a metaphor for the inexorable passage of time in a dimension where the very concept of time appeared to lose its conventional significance.

The recurrence of this dream, a phenomenon deeply entrenched in the complexities of human psychology and neurobiology, can be attributed to various factors. From a psychological standpoint, recurring dreams often reflect unresolved conflicts or ongoing stressors in one's waking life.

These dreams can act as a subconscious mechanism for processing emotions or grappling with situations that remain unsettled in reality. Biologically, the phenomenon of recurring dreams is intertwined with the functionality of our memory systems, particularly the hippocampus and amygdala, structures in the brain integral to emotion regulation and memory formation.

During the REM phase of sleep, where dreaming predominantly occurs, these areas of the brain are highly active. They replay and sometimes amplify emotional experiences from our waking hours, weaving them into the tapestry of our dreams. This repetitive process can lead to the recurrence of specific themes or narratives in our dreams, as the brain attempts to make sense of, or reconcile, these emotional experiences.

Additionally, neuroscientific research suggests that the repetition of dreams could be linked to the brain's neural pathways and the way memories are consolidated. During sleep, particularly in the REM stage, the brain is thought to consolidate and organize memories from the day.

If certain experiences, thoughts, or emotions are particularly intense or unresolved, they might be replayed more frequently in dreams as the brain works through them. This can result in the same dream occurring multiple times, as the brain processes and attempts to integrate these experiences into our long-term memory.

In the context of this dream, the appearance of figures in white suits, embodying scientific rigor and precision, could symbolize a subconscious grappling with themes of control, uncertainty, and the quest for understanding in the face of the inexplicable.

The dream's recurring nature, coupled with its vivid and tangible details, underscores the profound impact of our subconscious mind in shaping our nocturnal experiences, reflecting deeper layers of our psyche and the unresolved puzzles of our waking life.

Approximately two weeks subsequent to my initial encounter, the dynamics of human interaction and the neurochemical underpinnings of love became evident through a peculiar episode. As morning light permeated my abode, a woman in business attire approached, her persistence evident as she returned every couple of hours, rhythmically knocking and attempting to slide a paper through the door.

From behind sheer curtains, I observed the diurnal passage of light and shadows, pondering the nature of my consciousness and the reality of my experiences. As afternoon transitioned into evening, a cadre of individuals clad in white converged upon my lawn. Among them, a slender man with circular spectacles, exuding an air of tranquility, gestured invitingly from a distance.

Despite the apparent gentleness radiating from this assembly, my instinctual response was reticence, a manifestation of the brain's amygdala reacting to unfamiliar stimuli, potentially perceived as a threat. This standoff continued for over an hour, an intricate dance of invitation and refusal, highlighting the complexities of human social interaction and the innate wariness toward unaccustomed expressions of affection.

As the evening hues melded from vivid orange to a dusky amalgamation of brown and orange, the man, embodying a serene disposition, proclaimed, "Love is the answer" before departing. This declaration triggered a profound emotional response within me, catalyzed by the release of oxytocin, a hormone associated with bonding and emotional connection. His departure, coupled with his words, elicited a cascade of introspection and regret, underscoring the paradox of human nature's simultaneous yearning for and fear of genuine affection. My tears, a physical manifestation of this internal conflict, marked a moment of realization about the complexities of accepting love, a powerful force that often challenges our deeply ingrained instincts of self-preservation and skepticism.

In a somnolent state, I found myself enveloped in a dream, a surreal tableau set within a vast, dimly lit, multilevel room, its architecture allowing a glimpse into a lower classroom level. Recognizable figures in my life, Vince and Chalice, were present, engaging in a ritual of smudging various objects and areas, including seats, an altar, and a fountain-centered pool, their actions steeped in solemnity.

As they approached, my attempts at communication, first with Vince and then Chalice, were met with silence, their indifference to my calls starkly contrasting with the familiarity I associated with them. Confusion reigned in my mind, questions swirling as to why I was lying immobile on a table, draped in a black blanket, and why my attempts at connection were unacknowledged. This scenario, a vivid representation of my psyche, mirrors the brain's complex processing of emotions and memories during REM sleep, where dreams are most vivid and often reflective of our deepest fears and desires.

The dream progressed; the room remained dim except for the illuminated classroom below. The entrance of friends and family into this somber setting intensified the feeling of disconnect. Despite my desire to engage, my body remained motionless, a poignant reminder of the disconnect sometimes experienced in dreams where the brain's prefrontal cortex, responsible for logical thinking and voluntary movement, is less active. The heartbreaking realization that my beloved dog, Soulo, was also motionless, symbolized by the black blanket, brought the harrowing truth to light: this was my memorial.

The neuroscientific explanation for such vivid and emotionally charged dreams lies in the brain's limbic system, particularly the amygdala, which plays a key role in processing emotions. During REM sleep, the amygdala is highly active, often leading to intense emotional experiences in dreams. The dream's progression, marked by my silent cries and apologies, unheeded by the mournful attendees sharing stories, mirrored the brain's attempt to process complex emotions like guilt, regret, and the need for closure.

The dream's closure came with a hauntingly beautiful serenade by two young women standing in water, followed by a descent into silence and darkness. The transition from this dream world to waking reality was abrupt, marked by sunlight and the tangible feel of a wall, juxtaposing the dream's ethereal quality with the starkness of reality. This moment of awakening, coupled with the two-dimensional appearance of the sunlit window, underscored the brain's gradual return to full consciousness and the disorientation often felt upon leaving the vivid world of dreams.

In a state of existential contemplation, I reached out to Vince, seeking validation of my reality. His response, a simple declaration of his whereabouts, served as a grounding truth, pulling me back from the brink of the metaphysical abyss explored in my dream. This dream, a profound exploration of the concept of mortality and the longing for connection, underscored the intricate ways in which our brain weaves together memories, fears, and desires, creating narratives that, while surreal, speak to the core of our human experience.

As the chapter of my life marked by these transcendent dreams draws to a close, I find myself profoundly transformed. The lessons gleaned from these nocturnal odysseys have not only reshaped my perception of reality but also deeply ingrained within me a newfound wisdom that transcends the ordinary boundaries of consciousness. These dreams, ethereal in their essence, have served as celestial guides, leading me through a labyrinth of self-discovery and spiritual enlightenment.

One of the most significant lessons I learned is the impermanence of our perceived reality. In the dream world, the laws of physics and time dissolve, revealing a universe where anything is possible. This revelation has taught me to embrace the fluidity of life, understanding that change is the only constant. I've learned to view challenges not as insurmountable obstacles, but as transformative opportunities, guiding me toward personal growth and evolution.

Another profound insight from these dreams is the interconnectedness of all things. In the dreamscape, boundaries between the self and the other blur, reminding me that we are all part of a greater, interconnected cosmic tapestry. This has instilled in me a deeper empathy toward others and a sense of unity with the world around me. It has also fostered a greater appreciation for the natural world, understanding that we are not separate from nature, but an integral part of it.

These dreams also illuminated the depths of my subconscious fears and desires, allowing me to confront and understand them. By facing these inner shadows, I have been able to heal past traumas and let go of deep-seated fears. This process of introspection and healing has been instrumental in cultivating inner peace and emotional resilience. I have emerged more self-aware, with a clearer understanding of my purpose and a stronger sense of self.

Moreover, these dreams have unlocked a wellspring of creativity within me. The fantastical landscapes and surreal scenarios I experienced have inspired a newfound artistic expression, enabling me to channel these visions into creative endeavors. This has not only been a source of personal fulfillment but has also allowed me to connect with others on a profound level, sharing pieces of my inner world through my art.

Perhaps the most transformative aspect of these dreams has been the spiritual awakening they have sparked. They have opened my eyes to the vastness of the universe and the mysteries that lie beyond our physical realm. This spiritual journey has led me to explore various philosophical and mystical traditions, enriching my understanding of the world and my place in it.

In summary, these dreams have been a crucible for transformation, a series of nocturnal teachings that have profoundly altered my trajectory. They have taught me to embrace change, fostered a deep sense of interconnectedness, facilitated personal healing, ignited creativity, and sparked a spiritual awakening. As I step forward into the next chapter of my life, I carry these lessons with me, grateful for the profound impact they have had on my journey. The dreams may have faded with the morning light, but their legacy endures, a guiding star in the vast expanse of my life's odyssey.

Wayne Carter is a distinguished dream healer, combining psychology and traditional medicine in his work. His enthralling publications delve into the enigmatic territories of the subconscious mind. Renowned for their profound depth and insight, his books decipher the mysteries of dreams, merging scientific understanding with creative narratives.

CHAPTER 14

Is Love Really a Battlefield?
How I (eventually) learned it doesn't have to be
By Marie Benard

Relationships have been one of the most challenging and rewarding areas of learning (and re-learning!) in my life. I grew up in foster care and experienced almost every "Adverse Childhood Experience" on the list. I moved out on my own at age fifteen and never felt any sense of safety or belonging for most of my life. That history and lack of access to what represented a healthy relationship made it hard for me to create safe and mutually fulfilling relationships. I learned a lot of hard lessons along the way, but I'm happy to say that things are going really well in the present. I've not only experienced and maintained some incredible relationships, but I've built up the self-assurance that I'll be okay even if certain relationships don't last forever. As a person who has struggled with abandonment issues my entire life, that's incredible. That's freedom. I wish everyone could learn this through their family of origin because it took me several decades and a lot of therapy to sort out.

If you're anything like me, you've probably had to learn some of the same lessons more than once! How frustrating is that!!? Fun times. That frustration has been a source for something else I've had to learn the hard way: self-compassion. Yes, I've co-created some unhealthy, even abusive, relationships over the years. But do you know what I didn't do? I didn't regress to the same depths of unhealthiness as the time before. I was doing the best I could with the resources I had at the time, which were pretty lacking in most cases. Every time I went through that cycle, I did a little better the next time. I repeated a lot of similar mistakes, but each experience illuminated a new level of nuance and understanding.

Out of the frying pan, and into the fire...

Let's talk about my first boyfriend—quite a prize for an impressionable, attention-starved kid. He was a ripe 32 when I was just 14. The staff at the group home where I lived warned me, "he only wants you for one thing." What they didn't do was spend any 1:1 time with me, give me a hug, or parent me in any real way. I got my affection, life advice, and pep talks from him. He had a knack for dropping chilling threats to keep me under his control, like saying he knew a place where nobody would ever find my body. Yep, that was my initiation into the world of romance. Yuck.

I was always on the hunt for a person who could give me all the love and support I needed and craved so much; there are quite a few dating traumas I'm not including in this dating drama highlight reel.

Second try for the win?

Next up, I fell for the classic love-bombing strategy. This guy came from a wealthy family and acted like he worshipped the ground I walked on. Here I was, little me from the wrong side of the tracks. I'd grown up in poverty and even had to couch surf due to homelessness during several periods of my life. Finding a man I was totally into, who didn't have to worry about money and who treated me well was like a dream come true—until the fairy tale took a sharp left turn. From admiration to disdain, it was like a soap opera, but with more heartbreak. It was still better than the first relationship! At least it was age-appropriate, and he paid for dates!

I'm no psychiatrist, but he demonstrated more than enough traits for a diagnosis of Narcissistic Personality Disorder. With decades of hindsight, rather than labeling him a "narcissist," I realize that if I had acquired better skills, that relationship might have gone differently. As hard as I tried and as abusive as he was toward me (and others), I now understand that it didn't occur in a vacuum. I'm not blaming myself, but the grown version of me can take responsibility for my younger self not knowing how to navigate that relationship more effectively. I know that his accusations that it was all my fault—that I was the cause of his abuse—weren't accurate. Regardless of blame, we brought out the worst in each other. I wish I had mustered the strength to leave him sooner. I literally had to leave town for several months to break the addictive cycle, including my hopes that things could go back to how they were at the start.

Back in the days of Mr. I-Don't-Call-Him-Narcissist, I actually read that book, *The Rules*. Holy hell was I trying hard and failing miserably! I'd forgotten about that until just now. If you haven't read the book, it's basically a guide to manipulating, confusing, and making a man jealous in hopes that he'll propose. I think the intent behind the book was to help women have boundaries and maintain their standards in relationships. It's not written in a way that facilitates that growth. Instead, it taught me arbitrary "rules" that served to manipulate, deprive, punish, and prevent effective communication. What could possibly go wrong!? I followed it so well! I took all the advice. No wonder that dude ended up hating me. Yikes!

Fast forward a few years...

I'm over the really scary guys by this point. Twice seemed to be enough to avoid the red flags I learned to spot thanks to *that* hard lesson.

Can you see how every fresh hell was a little better than the one before it? This time around, I had yet to learn this: take time to get to know someone before getting too emotionally invested. This will be a common theme moving forward. With this new guy, we got physical pretty quickly. But as soon as he started to develop real feelings—no more sex for me! It appeared that as he got to know me as a whole person rather than just focusing on physical aspects, he saw me more as a little sister than a potential life partner. This was very confusing because he treated me quite well, gave me lots of affection, and wanted me to act like his girlfriend, but didn't want sex—nor did he want to let me go. He had his own stuff going on and did a lot that hurt and confused me.

It took a couple of years to get clear on what was going on and to set my boundaries accordingly. Here's the silver lining—he cared about me, genuinely. We've remained friends all these years. He wasn't abusive; he encouraged me to get therapy in a compassionate way. Speaking of boundaries, I want to make it clear that I'm sharing our story with his consent. He gave me an incredible gift: he was the first real constant in my life. He actually *helped me,* whereas previous parties mostly used me. He is one of two people I consider family in my life, despite the rocky moments. Our friendship was worth the pain, and it's a bond I cherish.

Getting professional help...

I had seen counselors and therapists in the past, but the free services were very time-limited, and... to put it mildly, some of the clinicians I met seemed to need therapy even more than I did! Not exactly therapeutic. I would've *loved* to have had a safe and trusted therapist, but where was that money going to come from? I didn't have many healthy role models growing up and was having a hard time navigating life. Even the charities that offered sliding-scale prices were too high for me to afford at the time. My ex-boyfriend-turned-friend offered to cover those reduced prices if I went through the process of applying for them. So I did. And I got *really* lucky. It turned out I was eligible to get *free* therapy, because of the abuse I experienced in foster care.

Let's take a moment to acknowledge the privilege this twist of fate brought into my life. I'm fully aware of the countless folks out there who are left longing for mental health and life skills help, trapped in a system that seems to shrug off their needs. It's infuriating how little support makes it to the people who need it the most. This was a genuine gift, a lifeline in a sea of uncertainty, and I don't take a single second of it for granted.

It took a long time to find the right kind of therapy and the right therapeutic relationship. My first therapist was lovely. Then she moved out of the country—after working for months on healing my abandonment wounds! Ironic much? The next therapist was also kind and supportive, but I spent years going through the same cycles, without any long-term progress. She didn't offer the type of therapy or guidance I needed in order to make lasting changes. The struggle is real! Therapy wasn't a magic fix, even though I was trying *so* hard. During this period, I was reading a lot of self-help and new-age material, hoping to find the *thing* that would make my life better! It was a painful process.

I kept working, exploring, and strategizing how to grow into the kind of person who was... lovable? That's a sad thing to admit. I know we're all worthy of love, no matter what. It's not something anyone should have to earn or strive for. It's a basic freakin' human need. No matter what mistakes any of us have made: WE. ARE. ENOUGH. Part of the problem is that my inherent enough-ness didn't guarantee that people would treat me as such. If that little kid inside doesn't get the love and nurturing required to grow into a secure adult, she's gonna put up with a lot of bullshit that keeps reinforcing her unhealthy beliefs—the key belief being that she'll never be safe and she'll never be enough. Invalidation, lies, and abuse were normalized in my childhood. How was I supposed to spot the warning signs that more bullshit was coming around the corner?

On a decent track and back to dating...

I finally got into therapy that was more goal-driven and skills-based (as opposed to complaining about my life for an hour each week). I started getting back into shape after having regained the 80 pounds I lost at a higher point in my life. Apart from a few sporadic coffee dates arranged online, I hadn't really dated in *years*. I was 80 pounds overweight and had no confidence. Since I was in therapy which helped me work more strategically on building skills and resilience, I decided to go out with the *first* guy who asked me out and didn't give off creepy axe murderer vibes. Those were literally my *only* criteria for the first few people I met, just to build up some confidence around meeting new people.

Casting a wide net and having a lot of first and second dates just for the practice was pretty fun! There was no fear of screwing it up or worries about whether or not he liked me. I got to practice all the things I was learning in therapy and from online "relationship experts." It was a time of experimentation, learning, lots of mistakes, and a lot of fine-tuning. Overall, that period of my life was healthiest when I wasn't sleeping with anyone. When my focus was connecting and getting to know people, making friends, and building my confidence, I was a lot happier. At that point, I hadn't yet learned this lesson: no sex outside of a committed relationship, and no exclusive relationship with anyone who isn't *already capable* of consistently meeting my basic relationship needs.

I knew I got easily attached, but my sex drive was also at its peak. I'd already been mostly celibate for years and didn't want that for myself. I was just as scared about getting sexual again as I was about dating. I hadn't intended to get attached to the next guy. I never in a million years saw a future with him, which is why I thought he'd be a safe choice. Nope, not for this girl! I fell for him and it was pretty stressful and unpleasant. You'd think by my early 30s I would have already known this about myself, but I guess I needed a few more emotional hits before I *really* learned the hard way. We were sleeping together for about a year. He genuinely cared about me but he was so emotionally unavailable and careless with my heart.

Picking up the pace...

This next period is full of growth and lessons, but they're all so intricately tied that they kind of all needed to be learned simultaneously. A lot of mistakes were made. The pain didn't dissipate but it didn't knock me down and set me back quite as hard as before. I kept trying!

My therapist was coaching me to use these experiences to practice my skills—and practice I did. I got really skilled at communicating my needs and wants, thanks to DBT's Interpersonal Effectiveness Skills and the work of Alison Armstrong. In addition to communication skills, I was also trying to learn not to make rash decisions like breaking up or quitting my job when I'm upset. Even though it was almost always the right decision, the emotionality of it only made me doubt myself in hindsight.

Cue the next lesson in the bloopers reel: trust my gut. Go slow, see what he's really like over time. I needed to cut my losses earlier and more frequently. Unfortunately, this has been one of my longest-standing missteps: investing too much, when it was obvious from day one we weren't a good match. As any good poker player knows, if you have a bad hand from the start, fold. Don't keep trying to make it work with a crap hand.

I've learned (and am still learning) that slowing things down and paying attention to *how I feel about myself in relation to him,* is a better way to approach dating. My previous approach was to be constantly checking, "Does he like me? Where is this going? Am I pleasing him?" Gross. I learned to lean back a little instead of trying to "fix" all the yucky feelings happening inside of me. Most people who care at all about their partner's feelings will try to make adjustments in early dating, especially if they're really attracted. The problem with men who are really attracted is that they are blinded by the attraction such that they don't consider if they can sustainably meet the needs of this new partner they're head-over-heels for.

There's a fine line between gently letting him know what makes me happy ("Gerbera daisies are my favorite flower!") and having to beg for what I need (and still not getting it). It's exhausting and ineffective. Begging or demanding usually leads to a couple days of best behavior, then back to me feeling unhappy. Those sporadic moments when I felt calm and connected would fuel hope for the future! We'd keep going through this cycle of effort, then deprivation. Another name for that is intermittent reinforcement, which is one of the best ways to develop a bad habit. Nobody would stay in a relationship that was all bad, all the time, and never met any of their needs. If only it could be so simple and clear-cut.

I don't blame the guys who got into this dance with me over the years. We were doing the best each of us knew how to do. None of us had ill intent, but that didn't stop it from being incredibly painful. Part of this was down to the guys not walking away, and largely my responsibility. One of my best and worst qualities is that I have a hard time giving up on people and walking away. Loyalty and commitment are great when the situation is healthy. I'm getting better at completely walking away when that's not the case, or at least maintaining firm boundaries if they're still somewhere in my social circle.

I *eventually* learned from online relationship guru Alison Armstrong that a person's capacity to meet my needs isn't a reflection of me or their feelings for me. So much pain was spent on the question, "If you love me so much, why won't you do this for me?" Whether it was a decision or a lack of capacity didn't really matter. My needs weren't being met. Period.

Alison Armstrong also taught me something that she calls "listening to learn." Rather than listening in order to see what we agree on, I listen intently to him. I listen for what he wants, values, enjoys providing, and doesn't want to provide. Instead of filling in all the blanks and telling him to be the person *he'll pretend to be in order to please me* for a few weeks, I listen to what's true for him. I "know" this and have great success with listening to learn, but I need to remember to do it more frequently. It requires daily practice. It's almost a form of mindfulness training. I need to keep practicing because, as you can probably tell from reading here... I'm a talker! I *learn* so much more when I shut the hell up and *listen*. Ask, listen, reflect, listen. Less talk, more listening. I need this tattooed on the inside of my eyelids to help me remember.

My knight in... beige Dockers?

Once upon a time, after searching far and wide... I miraculously met this new guy who seemed like he was everything I'd been dreaming of! He was cute and came from a stable family that liked me. He had a stable career, the sweetest dog, and owned his home. The thing I most wanted out of a relationship (aside from the sex and companionship), was safety and stability. It didn't get more stable than *this* guy. My one worry was that life with him would be really boring. You might think "Oooh, she's attracted to danger and

145

drama." Nope. Not a lick. When I say I was worried life would be boring, I mean... like a chore. I remember shopping with him at Costco. While that can sometimes be stressful, Costco is a ridiculous wonderland of fun and unusual stuff to look at, taste, and debate about the need for a lifetime supply! What a deal! With him, it was so dull. I felt like I couldn't be my playful and silly self because we had seriously dull shopping work to do. While I did see this as a red flag, I also didn't have the self-confidence in my intuition... I worried I was having this feeling because there was something wrong with me. That if I wasn't enthralled with this man, I must have some kind of character defect.

Prince Beige Dockers started out *really* into me. This is where I got hooked and missed the previous lessons about leaning back and slowing things down. It felt good! He was talking about me moving in. He quickly introduced me to his family and they *loved* me. I got really focused on all the ways I could make him happy and please him. It seemed like a lovely, albeit beige, fairy tale.

One red flag, in hindsight, was his communication style. It was very... covert. I remember when he tried to give me his house key only two weeks into our relationship. Part of me felt excited that he trusted me that much. But the way he gave it to me was so casual, it felt like he was loaning it to me for the day, like a temporary house guest. It was so confusing because his intent wasn't clear. Trying to get clarity felt like pulling teeth. He seemed to have an expectation that I could simply read his mind, and that he could read mine. He made so many assumptions without checking with me and seemed to expect me to be able to accurately assume his thoughts and feelings, too. How emotionally exhausting!

Suddenly, he started expressing jealousy over things most people would find endearing or positive in a relationship—like when his little niece wanted me to read her a bedtime story, and how his dog would compete with him for my attention. One minute he was full steam ahead for our relationship. Then he suddenly dumped me, in a really awful way. I grieved that relationship *hard*. It wasn't so much that I missed *him*. I grieved what a life with him represented: belonging, a loving family, a stable home, and security. He treated me very unfairly and it hurt me so much.

I don't know if I'd say that I've forgiven him for what he did to me, because he *should* have known better than to do what he did. I also recognize that, if I had the skills I have now, I would've put the brakes on that relationship and not gotten caught up in him talking about marriage and moving our relationship forward so quickly. I would have had the communication skills to get clarity on a lot of things, and to have stronger boundaries with him. I would have understood what I later learned from Alison Armstrong, that he was "charmed and enchanted" with me and made promises he hadn't thought much about. He just said things that felt warm, fuzzy, and romantic in the moment, with no regard for how much it would hurt when he turned on a dime and ripped it all away from me. I had to learn how to pace new relationships and recognize that all the future talk was just lovely-sounding verbal diarrhea.

I learned from dating coach Evan Marc Katz to "ignore the positive and believe the negative." He teaches that the positive stuff we want to see is mostly the manifestation of wishful thinking and best behavior. Consistent and congruent behavior *over time* is more likely to be genuine. It doesn't mean Prince Dockers was intentionally trying to screw me over. He was just blissfully negligent with my feelings. Maybe it would've worked between us if I knew then what I know now and had paced the relationship more slowly and waited longer before agreeing to couplehood and sex. I don't think I'd be as whole and interesting a person if that path had worked out, though. He cared a lot about what other people think. Consequently, he was disingenuous. If things had worked out with us, it likely would have left me feeling stifled, hushed, muted, and miserable.

Last but not least...

My most recent and longest-lasting romantic relationship has been a major source of learning (and frustration, fear, and all of the feels...). I wanted for so long to find someone to marry, who could take care of me as much as I would take care of him. As I get older, and as I see women my age getting divorced or staying in unsatisfying but tolerable marriages because it's not worth the hassle of divorce, I'm rethinking what I want. Does that sense of family, belonging and security need to come from one person? Is trying to find all that from one person even fair or realistic?

I'm not sure how to label my current relationship. (He's read and approves of this message, by the way.) At times, we've been "partners" or "boyfriend and girlfriend" and at other times we've been "just friends." We broke up several years ago and were maintaining a mutually supportive friendship. Then things shifted at the start of the pandemic. With the amazing work of Dr. Stan Tatkin, creator of a Psycho-biological Approach to Couples Therapy (PACT), we've learned how to build what he calls a "secure-functioning" relationship. This has been a source of tremendous growth and healing for both of us. As much as we love each other, I don't realistically see our relationship progressing toward anything akin to marriage. But I don't know how either of us would have survived the pandemic without the other. We have both been free to date other people these past few years but haven't really wanted to.

Over the years, our relationship has provided the support and motivation to do a lot more for myself. Knowing that he's not in a position to support or be an equal partner financially forced me to invest more time and effort in creating my own financial independence. As the cost of living rises, it often feels like I'm treading water. But if I hadn't worked this hard, I would've sunk long ago. If I was still holding out hope that some man would swoop in and save me, I don't know if I'd be doing the meaningful work I'm doing now.

We have both had the opportunity to work on our boundaries and communication skills, as well as our attachment issues. We still make mistakes. Agreements still occasionally get broken, but we're able to work through it and cope, both individually and as a team. When I start to think about the future with him, all of my fears rise to the surface. I still crave the security and stability that he's not currently in a position to provide. This forces me to stay mindful of the present and remind myself that I am safe right now. My needs are met right now. I am meeting my financial needs and a lot of my emotional needs. We both have a stable friendship in which we're able to share our fears, our successes, our hopes, and our aspirations. We provide mutual support, care, and love. I don't know what the future holds. I know from experience that if he meets a new partner, it's possible he'll choose to end our friendship. Neither of us plans for that, but I don't have to learn *that* lesson the hard way again. I know the risks, and how likely that is to happen, despite his promises to the contrary. As difficult as that would be, I now know I can survive, regardless of the choices he makes.

Twenty years ago, if I'd magically found a partner who could give me everything I thought I needed, I don't think I would have been forced to grow as much as I have. I don't think I'd have the incredible friends, supporters, and colleagues who are in my corner now. I don't think I would have so skillfully been able to transform the post-traumatic stress in my life into post-traumatic *growth*. Prior to this relationship and the forced growth as a result of my choices, I didn't think I'd have as much meaning in my life.

I still want to experience a sense of family and a greater sense of belonging. I'm still working on building more of that. But if I was still focused on finding my knight in shining armor, I'd be focused on *him*—my hero. Now, I get to focus on supporting *others*. Now I get to focus on creating a better world for *all*, rather than finding someone who can save me from the current state of the world. I'm in the process of saving myself, and supporting others to save themselves, too.

It's certainly not the fairy tale I grew up wishing, hoping, and imagining would come true for me. But it's so much richer. My life is full of purpose. I have to keep getting up, doing my best, and working through life's bullshit, because it's my duty to leave the world a little better than I found it. It's my duty to practice compassion for myself and others. It's my privilege to raise my voice and speak up in the face of bureaucracy and the status quo. It's hard work, but it fills my soul. Some days I want to give up. Some days I cry and complain. Then I need to rest and reset. I'm forced to practice and grow, grieve the constant bullshit life throws at us all, and keep getting up and trying again. My leaps are more measured and mindful, and the lessons learned aren't quite so hard.

Life and love may not have unfolded exactly as I once imagined, but it has become richer and more meaningful than I could have ever anticipated. Each lesson, no matter how hard-earned, has brought me closer to understanding my own worth and the power I hold within. As I continue my journey, I feel thankful for the lessons learned and the growth that has emerged from my experiences. With or without a romantic partner by my side, I know that I am no longer alone in this world, and I am committed to making it a better place for all.

Marie, an award-winning coach, group facilitator, and mental health advocate, interviews authors and innovators at MarieBenard.com. She promotes destigmatization, authenticity, and diversity, fostering a shared journey of learning with viewers.

CHAPTER 15

How Self-Love Healed Me
By Keri Fulmore

"Even during your darkest storms God still has a plan for you to shine bright. Don't lose faith." – Trent Shelton

"You've just got to love yourself."

Those were the words I heard as I dove deep into my inner self. At that point, my life depended on it.

I had been doing medical intuitive readings for others for fifteen years. I knew how to see, feel, and hear things. Now that I was going through what I call my "perfect storm," I had to learn to trust my inner voice to guide me through what has been my most challenging journey on this earth yet.

It all started ten months postpartum.

I had just come home from the chiropractor. I was excited to be spending the afternoon with my daughter. I picked her up to lay her on the floor and sing some songs we loved to sing together. But when I stood up, my entire body lit up like a Christmas tree with body-wide nerve pain. This pain came out of nowhere.

I remember feeling instant panic. I knew that something was very wrong. My fight-or-flight system engaged immediately. I could barely breathe. My nerve endings felt as if they were on fire. My skin burned, my muscles were twitching, and my brain felt like I was walking on a ship. Every step felt as though I were being pulled into a stormy sea.

That was the beginning of a storm I was not totally prepared for. Are we ever prepared for surprises? Are we ever welcoming of our challenges?

My journey through what became chronic body-wide nerve pain was a long one. I went from doctor to doctor, from naturopaths to psychic healers. I ended up exactly where I started; I was told there were no answers for what was happening to me. One neurologist told me I had postpartum depression, but I didn't feel depressed.

I was happy. I had a great marriage. I was married to my best friend whom I could not seem to ever get enough of. He was my soulmate, my rock, my other half. I had two amazing daughters and a career that was blossoming. Depression didn't sit well with me. It was one of those diagnoses that felt wrong in every single way. It felt like I was living in some sort of nightmare. I was told by a psychic that this was karma and that I would have this pain for the rest of my life. She told me that I was working out past life karma, and this was how it was manifesting.

I felt defeated. I felt a level of grief in my soul that I had not ever felt before. My life was flashing before my eyes when she told me this. I remember feeling helpless and hopeless. How could I go on living with body-wide, burning nerve pain that no painkillers helped? I remember praying to God to take me home if this was to be the rest of my life. All I could think was, "What will I do?

Little did I know it then, but that psychic was actually my greatest catalyst in changing the way I was thinking. I remember being so enraged when I got off the phone with her. How dare she tell me that I would have this for the rest of my life? Who did she think she was? How could you tell someone that? I immediately declared that this was *not* going to be my story. She was the gift I needed to take my power back. She was the one who lit the fire under me to put myself back in the driver's seat of my life and realize that I was not completely helpless.

I had been in chronic pain for two years at the point I spoke to this psychic. I used to cry in so much pain—soul-shattering pain—that this was happening to me. *How could this be happening to me?* I was such a good person! I felt helpless; I felt alone; I felt defeated.

I do realize now that the psychic was right in some ways. I had wondered if this might be a punishment for something I had done. She picked up on this and told me it was my karma, but I couldn't figure out what I could have possibly done to have so much pain in my body. It must have been something horrendous, was the thought circling in my head. I was like a deer in the headlights. I couldn't think my way out of this situation for the life of me.

The problem was that I was not thinking clearly at all. I was totally consumed by my emotions. I was allowing my fear and my worry (something I was very good at) to totally shape every minute of my day. Every pain that I had in my body 24/7 would just feed into my fight-or-flight system and trigger more fear and worry.

I was stuck. Truthfully, I was miserable.

I knew that I could either let this break me down or I could choose to break through. I could choose to see the challenge before me and put myself back into the driver's seat of my life. I knew that my soul had a plan for me. This may not have been the plan I wanted to experience, but somewhere inside me, I finally knew that this was happening *for* me and not *to* me.

I knew I had to change the way I was doing things. I knew that I had to turn inward and listen to what my inner guidance system was telling me. This was not easy. The thing is, stress can get in the way of clarity. It can create a fog that makes it hard to discern your intuition from your judgment. I was at a point in my life where I had been intuitively guiding people for many years; I had the framework and knew how to access my inner voice—the question was, why hadn't I been doing it? What was I waiting for? I think I had literally been waiting for the knight in shining armor of health to show up at my doorstep and give me the map.

I knew now was the time to change all of that. I had to create my own map—my own destiny—and I knew I had to start somewhere. I knew that if I was going to heal, I had to take things into my own hands. Nobody was coming to save me. As hard as I wished and prayed, this was a journey I had to take by myself, but more importantly, *for* myself. I knew that I was going to come out the other side a changed person. I could really sense that my thinking was starting to change. I was changing from victim to victor.

Each day, I would sit down and focus on my breathing. I would breathe as deeply as I could into my belly and release my pain and worries on the out-breath. Even though my body was sending me constant signals that something was wrong, I had to learn to put that aside. I had to learn to thank my body for the messages it was sending me and send love to my fear.

One day while I was working on my breathing, I could sense a new calm within my body. I felt a sort of peace wash over my thoughts—almost like witnessing the space between my thoughts. This peacefulness was the familiar place I knew to access my intuition. So, I asked my intuition, "Why do I have this chronic pain?" The answer was so swift and so light. It came in without thought or my having to try too hard. It said, "You have to love yourself". At first, the answer shocked me. My immediate response was, "*but I do love myself.*" I love who I am.

My inner voice responded with "You need to love yourself unconditionally; you don't love yourself.

That's when it hit me. I didn't love my body. All the hairs on my arm stood up. I knew that this was a truth that I had been ignoring for a very long time. In fact, I can barely remember the last time I was not trying to hide my body or make excuses for it, or feeling ashamed of the body I was in. That's when I realized that the pain in my body was the expression of pain it felt from me. My body was showing me how much it was hurting! It was showing me how I was treating it and how I had been breaking it down over time by doing so. The pain in my thoughts—how I truly felt about myself—was manifesting in my body. I was vibrating with deep truth.

I started to think about where this had begun. I am not sure it mattered where I had learned to be ashamed of my body or to judge my body so harshly, but I knew that I had to get a full understanding if I was truly going to learn to love myself.

As a child, I felt the possibility of life inside of me. I can remember feeling like anything was possible. You know the feeling you had as a child, dreaming of all that you could do and see? I felt unstoppable. I felt on top of the world! I felt like life was completely miraculous and amazing. I felt like love itself...

until I didn't. I can't put my finger on when this love for myself and my body left me, but I do remember the feeling of having it. I knew somewhere inside of me was that inner child full of self-love and adornment.

When accessing my intuition to find out where this all began, I started to unravel memories that were quite emotional. I felt tidal waves of self-loathing and grief creeping up to the surface as I gasped for air, comparison thought viruses that seemed to stretch for miles. Had I always compared myself to others as though I just didn't measure up? I knew I had always felt inadequate, as though I was being judged for my body. I always felt the need to explain why I looked the way I did. I felt embarrassed of my body—making myself small, shrinking and hiding, never feeling like those around me would truly see me for me. The thing is, I was carrying a little extra weight. I thought that it was that. I thought that the shame of the weight I was carrying was the reason I didn't love my body. But when I was looking back at photos, I realized that even in my most youthful, strongest, leanest, goddess-maiden body, I was ashamed of it. I had body dysmorphia. It didn't matter what I looked like; I could never see my beauty and that made me cry tears of bone-aching pain. Where did this start?

One of the memories that came up for me was from grade one. I remembered getting dressed in a beautiful corduroy skirt. It felt so good wearing this outfit! That day at school as I was doing some art with some of my peers, I bent over to pick up some crayons that had dropped on the floor and heard the whole class laughing at me. My underwear had been showing as I bent over. I immediately felt embarrassed and ashamed. It was like that feeling somehow shattered the energy of my body and my innocence. On top of it all, I was teased for months afterward. It was a moment that made me self-conscious of my body. It made me question how I looked and how people would perceive me. I was six years old; I was mortified—and from that moment on, I remember feeling self-conscious.

My intuitive voice also reminded me of how I never felt pretty enough. I thought that I was inadequate. I thought I was too big. This made me feel like I had to hide my body. It prevented me from showing up for myself and even robbed me of fun when out with my friends and family. For example, putting on a bathing suit. There were so many times where I didn't go swimming because I didn't want anyone to see me. I don't exactly know when I adopted this body dysmorphia. I was never big as a kid. I just know that I grew to become quite hard on myself. I would talk to myself in ways that I would never dare speak to another soul.

It was clear to me that I had been "the mean girl" to myself. I had intentionally inflicted pain on myself, not realizing at the time that the emotional and mental bodies (our thoughts and feelings) can absolutely affect our physical being. This I did know as a medical intuitive. It was something that I spoke about with people every day. I just didn't know that I was doing it to myself. I was unconscious of the way I treated myself. I never, ever thought about my relationship with myself; it had become a subconscious program.

Now that I understood what had created my body pain, the question was, what and how do I learn to love myself? The next part of my journey to wellness was a long one. You would think that loving yourself would be easy—that once you realized the issue, you could snap out of it, like waking up from a coma. You could just have that "aha!" moment and suddenly feel all kinds of warm fuzzies for yourself. That wasn't the case for me.

I tried to stand in front of mirrors and say nice things about myself. I would put on that bathing suit and work up the courage to love myself and my body unconditionally. I wrote myself love letters and affirmations that I stuck on my bathroom mirror. But I still had just as much pain. I was working on changing, but I didn't really believe it. I found myself slipping into old patterns all the time.

I believed I could re-learn how to do this. It was still there somewhere inside of me. I just needed a reminder. That is when I decided to work in a ceremony with a medicine man. There was a group healing circle that was taking place, and I just knew that this was something that would put me closer to my healing. My intuition felt strong in guiding me to this medicine man for reflection. For this ceremony, you had to come with an intention. My intention was, "Why do I have this pain and how do I love myself?" I wanted to see if there were deeper answers that could be unearthed from inside me.

The ceremonial hall was incredible. It smelled of wood and had been built on a crystal bed. The energy of the building was like a light bath from the heavens above. I could feel how infectious the group's energy was and the excitement of holding space for each other in this incredible journey we were about to go on together. Somehow this group felt like family. They felt safe.

That night, I and ten others gathered together to sit in a circle. The medicine man guided us on a journey inward. Through song and intention and the power of Devil's club that had been prayed into, the medicine man was able to guide us with his healing energy, which had been passed to him through generations of training and knowledge.

In our group meditation, which he called a journey, I quickly went into a deep inner place. I could suddenly hear my intuitive voice telling me that I just had to love myself. I heard whispers of the same thing over and over. Like a broken record of a question to which I already knew the answer, I would hear it again and again. My spirit animals showed up in this vision. They made me feel safe and secure. I know now they were there to hold me in the teaching my intuition was about to show me.

That was when I was shown my death. I know that sounds crazy, but I was shown what it meant to not be in my body anymore. It was scary to me at the time because I knew that I wasn't ready to leave my kids or my husband; I still had things I wanted to do on this planet. My vision continued, and I found myself clinging to the things that I didn't want to leave behind. I wasn't ready.

That is when my intuition or inner voice suddenly showed me that my body allowed me to be here. My body allowed me to feel the sun on my skin, the taste of chocolate and coffee, the laughter of good company, and a hug from my kids. My intuition showed me that my body allowed me to feel the warm breeze of the wind and the shoreline of water and sand on my feet. It allowed me to be here. It allowed me to feel love. At that moment, I had the most incredible love for my body. Tears were streaming down my face. These were tears of joy and a release of the pain that I had inflicted on my body for so many years. At that moment I thought I might know how God felt about each and every one of us.

I suddenly had so much love for the body that I was in. I felt changed. I felt like God had shown me what it meant to unconditionally love what I have. I felt beautiful. I felt such a great relief. I had carried around this burden of shame and judgment toward myself for so long, it was like I could breathe again for the first time. It was like my first breath all over again. I felt like I was breathing in life and it was lighting up every cell in my body. My cells felt like they were smiling with love and joy.

That ceremony changed my life. My intuition changed my life. The ceremony and the energy of the circle helped me to go a bit deeper into my intuition and helped me get out of my own way to go deeper into my self-love journey.

After that night, I noticed that the things that I was doing to help my body heal started to work. I wish I could say that it was an instant healing, but, it took some months to unravel. It was okay, though, because I knew on another level that I had healed. Little by little, the body-wide burning pain began to subside. I knew beyond a shadow of a doubt that I had found the key to my healing—my intuition and a little bit of self-love. An understanding of what self-love really is. It is gratitude for the vessel that carries your soul on this earthly plane.

I realized that our intuition is one of our greatest assets for balanced health and healing. It is something that we all have and something I wish we were taught how to access from a young age. I absolutely know that there is a power inside of each of us—a power so great that it has the ability to bring about instant healing. It connects us all. It holds all of the answers. It healed my life.

To this day, in everything that I do, I make sure that I access my intuition. I have learned that with every decision, every road traveled, and every journey I take, it is vitally important to access my inner voice. Without her, I would not have found my greatest gift.

This is the story of my perfect storm. It was in this storm of pain and heartache that I found what it meant to truly love myself. My pain transformed me, and for that, I will be forever grateful. From this day forward, I still work on daily self-love practices. After all, we are always a work in progress.

Keri Fulmore is an international Medical Intuitive and Functional Medicine Practitioner. Keri is able to relay intuitive messages from the body and blend it with holistic sciences to help aid healing. You can find Keri at www. intuitivehealthsolutions.com.

CHAPTER 16

Finding Love thru Death
By Rebecka Gregory

The opening of one's eyes at birth and seeing the world of light with a spark of wonderment infused throughout one's body is the sense with which we are born into this world. We live our lives not wanting them to end, yet so many allow their experiences in harsh environments to infuse them with fear, anger, shame, guilt, judgment, and other emotions that hinder that wonderment. Then at the time of death, we are shown the truth of what we were resisting in our lives, that is, the feeling of unconditional love and surrender to set ourselves free.

This, you see, was my journey with my father as he transitioned into his next adventure in the life cycle of his soul. For me, it was quite an epic journey that included hard lessons, surrender, release, pain, and embracing authenticity during death. It also involved learning to be selfless and setting boundaries to take care of myself.

My father was a stubborn man with a heart of gold; I guess I got that from him. He did his best to put on his happy face for others and to be jolly and full of life while underneath he lived in so much pain. This pain I speak of was trapped in the heart of his soul. That big heart was tainted by the personal prison he had created around his heart, which stemmed from his childhood and how he was raised—feeling abandoned, hurt, and alone in the world, looking for love. In turn, his holding on to all of those feelings left him with many health issues. He was engulfed in guilt and shame for his choice of how he as a father hadn't shown up for his daughters like he wanted to. I have to admit that it took me many years to see that and to forgive him for everything he did, for he abandoned me as a father in many ways, too.

Working on my own shadow allowed me to begin opening my own heart and understanding that he did the best he could with his own given resources. His emotional past was a demon he had to face, and his actions toward me were only reflections of his own inner pain. Instead of longing for his love and being disappointed due to my expectations of what I thought a father should be, I learned to accept him for who he was and celebrated the moments he could get out of his pain to show up for me. I began to slowly honor my pain, letting go of this fantasy father and loving myself for loving him. However, underneath there was a missing piece I still longed for. Taking the pressure off myself allowed me to hold this image and the intention of his actions toward me from a different point of view. In turn, he slowly began to show up for me in a different way, and I started to realize how much he had always loved me and how important I was to him. All the bundled-up anger I held against him magically began to convert into forgiveness, and our relationship deepened.

It is funny what unravels when you really start to take a look at all that has happened in your life and who you are because of it. Looking back at how I dealt with my own pain, I now see all the mirrors of things I embodied from my father and mother—and for that matter, from their past experiences. I began to dig deeply into fears that weren't mine, but that I had made mine. My head began to swirl as I started to unwind the threads of so much of my life, and I finally saw the truth of who I am and the reality of the illusion I bought into. I was continuously amazed as parts of myself unlocked, and I began to digest all that was not really "me." I began to become aware of who I am.

I was able to spend such quality time with my father during the last few years of his life. I began to understand his pain and what he lived with. He shared with me the vulnerable parts of himself and his journey. Underneath, I knew he really didn't wish to be here, and every moment was a challenge for him. There was a strength inside him that encouraged him to make the best of it, and I very much admired him for it. I thank him for not missing one of my podcasts and for his unwavering support. Even though he did not completely understand what I was talking about, he embraced it and encouraged me to excel. He was my biggest cheerleader in life, even if it took me to the end of his life to see that.

I began to release the regret I carried for not showing up for him as a daughter over the years as well. That hurt and anger continued to uncoil and opened me up more and more. This experience helped make me who I am today. At the end of it all, I have so much gratitude and appreciation for all my father took on to teach me so I could grow. I tell you all of this to encourage you to reach out and really look at your relationships with others and see what beauty lies beneath the pain that is the illusion.

My father's health was not the best and he struggled with a lot of physical pain and other issues. I knew my father's time on this plane of existence was coming to a transition. I had made peace with my father and was in a beautiful space with him. That was what I kept telling myself, to be honest. Later, I realized there were a lot of emotions I had not addressed, and they came flying out like a wrecking ball.

Something that I have had to learn is to take the time to look at all angles of any situation to see where I really am with it. Diving in with questions is my new game to play with my emotional self. Now back to the story...

My father was trucking along, not really living, just existing, waiting until it was his time... he enjoyed the moments of joy he could. He took a dive into his past and began to clear out some old pain. He opened himself to healing through energy and sound, a healing that I facilitated. He allowed himself to be in the moment, to release and cry and dig deeper into the iron wall around his heart. Taking responsibility for continuing these practices when I was not around seemed to be the challenge. He would ask all the time," Can you just heal me? I don't know how."

I gave him tool after tool to assist and finally had to stop. In turn, I began to respond, "*Dad*, this is your journey. Only you can release all your pain and heal yourself; I can only give you the tools, hold love, and support you along the way." I believe everyone's choice for a miracle lies within the soul. "If you can find a space to release all that created your physical pain then you will be set free of the burden of it." Well, on the last day of his life, that gift became reality. We will get to that part later.

Then came COVID, and the world totally changed. So did my family dynamic. I received a text from my father's fiancé that he was in the hospital with COVID. At that moment, my body was overwhelmed with this cold rush, and I knew he would not be leaving the hospital. At that moment, I accepted this outcome and asked for strength to face what was about to come. At the time I didn't realize I would be tested to the core to understand the meaning of love from a higher point of view.

Looking back, I feel my father was involved in this whole experience, making sure I saw myself and began to love myself. All I could do now was take myself out of the equation, understand this was not about me, and give my father the best send-off I could. I asked myself, "Am I making an assumption around this? Is this really happening—is my father about to transition? The struggle inside me was a fierce battle; however, when I stepped into my heart, around it, all was clear. It was my human ego preparing me for the loss and grief that I was about to embark on and what I had to experience through it.

I felt like every part of me already knew what was about to happen and all hands were on deck... I knew my father was waiting for his time to go, even though he was terrified. However, deep in his heart he was ready. I am a firm believer that this is our choice, and I wanted to celebrate my father and thank him for being my Dad. I desired that he not suffer and that he be able to *set himself free.* That was rooted and anchored so deep in me.

Now, my sister and his fiancé were in a different space around all of this and could not digest the situation and what was happening. I respected that and had to navigate what to do about it... and it did get messy. First, I had a nuclear meltdown. That is what happens when you don't allow all emotions to flow. Bam, bam goes the dam, and boy, did mine blow.

Before the dam explosion, a series of events happened to me and my sister—some explainable and some not. The universe laid out so much information, providing signs and symbols along the way, that it is hard to wrap your head around unless you experience it, which I did. Life is funny that way, the twists and turns it puts us through.

My sister and I have been at odds and have not spoken for years. Our reconciliation was something my father always wished for, and he got his wish. My sister decided to fly to me and we drove together on the six-hour excursion across Florida to visit my father. At the time, we were very fortunate to be able to see him in the ICU outside the room. My sister arrived and the great adventure began. I swallowed all the contention left unresolved with my sister and put it in a ball for another day, for I knew what was to come was going to be a challenge on so many levels and I had to do my best to be strong and keep it together. Note to self: right now, as I write this—do not stuff anything emotional down inside. Remember that nuclear meltdown I talked about? Well, here is one of the silos that exploded!

The next day I awoke to this knotted feeling in my heart space and realized I was tapping into all that was about to happen. I could not shake the feeling, so I did my best to really ground and protect myself for the six-hour drive with my sister. We get two miles down the road and the first universal sign appears: four baby ducklings on the side of the road, walking on the edge. Now, I had to stop and help these little guys. Well, three made it up onto the curb before I got out of the car and started to waddle away. However, one little duckling was smaller than the other ones and could not make it over the curb, so I started to direct it to safety. He waddled into a turn lane and had to cross another road, so I stood in the road to stop all traffic while the duckling crossed and made it to safety. I did all I could do at this time and had to move on.

As I reflected on this situation, all I could think about was that this was a sign showing me what I was moving toward; the universe was telling me that my father was the little duckling that had to go a separate way. My heart raced as I sat there contemplating and digesting all this information.

After embarrassing my sister at a rest stop by burning some sage to cleanse myself and getting strange looks while doing so, we were ready to embark on something out of a sci-fi movie. The day was gloomy and cloudy as we traveled along a highway that seemed to have no end. My heart was warmed to have this sister time and to have some laughs and enjoyment as sisters should. Part of me was comforted to know that Dad was happy his girls were together and coming to see him. Inside, a smile lit up as I thought of my father having this gift.

Little did we know, but the universe gave us another sign to move through. I felt like I was on a quest into the unknown this whole trip, which I was! All of a sudden, the phone started buzzing extremely loudly with a warning to get off the road—that we were in a flood zone. Now, at this moment, no rain was in sight and the road and sides of the road were completely dry. We kept on driving; however, the alarm went off three more times. Each time my sister's level of panic and fear increased. As the terror overcame her, her panic increased. So did the experience.

Moments later, something banged against the window, and we were flown into almost a tornadic experience. All I knew was that either I was spinning or the world around me was spinning and I could see it—it was like I was pushed out into another space and caught in a wormhole! I heard my sister yelling and all I could do was to tell her to shut up so I could gather myself and focus. I was finally able to stop the vortex around me and come back to center. And everything became calm again and the energy completely shifted. My sister looked at me and was like, "What was that, and what just happened?" I knew it was a cosmic experience we had just had; however, she would not understand. Needless to say, in those moments, time shifted, and we realized we had jumped forward in time. To this day, who knows what really took place?

Finally, we arrived at the hospital and made our way inside to see Dad. The pain in my heart was in full force and I had to take a few breaths just to get myself centered before I could make my way to the ICU. My heart was pounding, and I was completely overwhelmed at this point—and then I saw my father and all I could do was feel this incredible pain throughout my body. I was overcome and was experiencing every breath the ventilator was taking for him; this was beyond heartbreaking for me. I knew I had to keep it together the best I could. I could not breathe and felt like I was going to faint.

I had to leave the hospital to get fresh air because it was too much for me. What was I to do? I knew my Dad was not going to make it. All I could anchor into was that I did not wish to see him suffer. He had suffered enough. The doctors had indicated that due to his health, even if he beat COVID, his heart and organs were affected and would shut down. He could not undergo dialysis for his kidneys because of his state of health. This is where he was. I did not wish to accept this; however, I had to surrender to the situation.

So my sister and I had a big decision to make. I just wished him off the ventilator to allow whatever was going to happen to take place. My sister and his fiancé had different ideas. I felt daggers from both of them being shot at me—how I could even have this thought? They weren't in a space to let this happen and my back was up against a wall. I questioned myself for a moment, thinking, "What is wrong with me?" I then went back to focusing on my father's suffering and anchored into that. I knew he would not wish to live without a quality of life, bottom line.

We decided to give him the night and redirect in the morning. I felt this anger stewing up in my body, fully focused on "he should not suffer because he has suffered enough!" I remember yelling at my sister in the hospital, "I DO NOT WANT TO SEE HIM SUFFER!" Looking back, I realized that I had stuffed so much down to stay in control that it was beginning to backfire on me. My thoughts, feelings, and emotions were too wrapped up in the balance of my father, my sister, and my father's fiancé. I recalled the four ducklings on the journey. At this moment, I was the one separated from the others.

Needless to say, the ride home to my father's house was not pleasant. Doing my best to compose myself, knowing how much pain my father was in and figuring out how to navigate my sister, all at the same time …well, all that didn't last long. Remember that nuclear explosion? This is when it happened. After regrouping at the house, the conversation led to that moment. You know that moment… that moment when your cup runneth over and you snap? Well, snap I did! The only thing I remember is saying "I have had enough and am so tired of this family turning against me because I think differently!" and the rest of what I said is a blur. I know it was not pleasant, but I don't remember it; I was in complete panic attack mode. All I could do was gather my things—I could not breathe and was shaking from head to toe. I managed to get myself out to my car and just sat there and breathed to calm myself down. Once I calmed down, I remember yelling out to my father, "I did what I could do. It is up to you now! If you want out of the ICU and off this ventilator, you've gotta do it. My hands are tied!" That moment marked my surrender of the control that had overtaken me in this situation.

After driving around, I found myself at a hotel for the night. Yes, I did consider driving home; however, I knew that was not a good idea and I still had to drive my sister back to my house. Even though in my fit of rage I told her she was on her own getting home, in truth I would never have left her. Apparently, my sister didn't know me very well, because she changed her flight as soon as I left—hence why we never got along. Her vision of me is not the truth of who I am. But that's another story for another time.

At the hotel I shivered to my core due to what was happening; I knew I was required to let go of my need for control in this situation. I had to reflect deep within myself to find the courage and strength to say, "No more!" and to choose to take care of myself. There was nothing I could do; the forces at play required that I walk away. As I took a shower and reflected on the day and allowed everything to surface, tears ran down my face, turning into a substantive portion of the water that cleansed me. My heart was in so much pain and I could not breathe or stomach all that was happening.

Then something happened. In that moment, a wave of clarity came over me. I spoke out loud, stating that I would release this all. I cut all cords to the situation, and at that moment, all decisions regarding my father I give to my sister. Since she wanted to have the final word, I decided to step away and give her that wish, allowing her to decide everything from that moment forward. And in that moment, all the pain in my heart went away and I was free… I knew what was going to happen and I could not control it—nor was I supposed to. I had to surrender and detach from the situation in the moment to protect myself.

Life has an interesting way of throwing a curveball. The next morning, I awoke to a call from the doctor stating that a miracle happened; my father could be weaned off the ventilator! It seems the rant the night before, expressed in a moment of complete anger and frustration in a complex fury of desperation, was heard by my father—or so I believed. This moment did give a sly moment of relief to my heart. Now I could go home in peace and digest all that had transpired. Reflecting on this time, I realized that sometimes things can get messy; I now give myself permission to freely express myself, no matter what it looks like.

Upon my return home, my body was spent, my heart was numb, and my mind was like a twirling cyclone, digesting the events that had transpired and had left me completely drained on so many levels. My mind spun, evaluating my choices, looking at my actions, and holding support for my father's healing, all while knowing the truth of what was happening. Well, the powers that be then provided me the gift of rest, putting me in bed for five days. This time allowed me to gain the peace and inner strength to unravel all that was unbalanced within me around the situation.

I found myself with a deep-rooted anger toward my sister and my father's fiancé for allowing my father to sit and suffer, knowing that his body was slowly shutting down with each breath he took. The amazing thing was that my father did move through the virus; however, the toll it took on his already sick body left him unable to receive any other treatment besides prayers. My heart knew I could not judge, for that was their process; however, I needed to feel all the emotions popping up to gain clarity within myself. If I had not done this, I would have spiraled into another breakdown—I decided that would not be, all while asking the question within me: "Should I be in a different space around this?" I had to look at all aspects of the situation, gain clarity, and stand in the truth that all I could do was love and celebrate my father and comfort him as he began his journey home.

The call came from the doctor that his kidneys were starting to shut down and he was unable to undergo dialysis. I called my daughter to let her know it was time to drive home so we could spend time with my father for the last time. My emotions were all over the place, yet a calming peace flowed within me. All I could contemplate was how I could celebrate my father to the fullest in the time I was about to have with him. We were so fortunate the hospital allowed one person at a time to visit. I was filled with a warm gratitude of love for this gift alone, for I know many during this time did not have this option. The frantic fear began with my sister and my father's fiancé. She called me, questioning why I was going to see Dad. They were afraid I was going to "try to kill him again." Hearing that just gave me the strength not to be concerned about their feelings and just to do what was best for me. This was a huge shift for me because my earlier concerns were primarily about their feelings.

At the hospital, I had set an intent for two things. One was to get my dog Daisy in to see my father because he loved her, and the second was to open up and express, in my authentic truth, all I had to unravel with my father. Walking into the room with Daisy in tow, I saw that my father was hooked up and lying still on the bed. I could feel him and the fear he was in. I leaned over to my father and said," Dad, I snuck Daisy into the hospital for you." I received no response; however, he did open his eyes and look down to acknowledge her. I was overcome with a heart-opening love that emanated from my father in this moment of joy in her presence.

I proceeded to just allow the flood gates to open by telling him everything I felt: the pain, the hidden disappointment, the anger, and everything I had bottled up inside that I needed to let go at this time. As I was speaking, a small tear rolled down his face. I did not question the truth at that moment and allowed everything to flow. Tears were flowing from me, as I was able to release so much in this authenticity that I was unable to in the past. After that, I moved into forgiveness and released him from all of it because I knew in my heart that he did the best he could. I thanked him for being my father and gave him permission to release anything he felt about how he did me my sister wrong. I also expressed to him that he could let go and move on and be free.

I required that experience to make me who I am today. After the emotional journey, it was time to have some fun. I started to sing songs to him and of course, we had to practice having angel wings for his next adventure—now he was just watching me flapping around the room pretending to fly. My heart was so happy at that moment—a moment of truth in my soul with my father that I spent a lifetime waiting to experience. As I sat next to my father, holding his hand, he leaned his head toward me and opened his eyes and his soul looked at me. I felt this connection; my father was free and able to look at me for the first time in a space of complete unconditional love.

Tears of total joy ran down my face because I had received the biggest gift ever in that one moment of complete unconditional love that he never could give me before. I felt this release that he had moved through and healed himself and was ready with no fear. I leaned over, gave him a kiss goodbye, whispered to him that I loved him, and thanked him for being my father. At that moment he was trying to express something to me and could not talk. The nurse came in and I told her my father wanted to speak. She proceeded to remove the mask for a second; however, due to the constraints of the ventilator, he could not talk and say what he wanted. I will never know what those words were. I could only feel the love he was sending me. I asked him if he was ready to go and he shook his head *yes*. The reality of that *yes* had not yet kicked in, only that he had made his choice at that moment and the rest was his journey. All I was left with was this magical moment I had with my father and a completion of the heart.

Unbeknownst to me, the moment I walked out the door he chose to begin his journey home and transition to the other side. Those were the last moments that I had with my father on the physical plane; my body felt an elated numbness as I walked away. This feeling swirled inside me as I realized that I had just had the best last moments with my father; then came the realization those actually *were* the last moments with my father. In that moment, all I could hold onto was that love in my heart for my father and our time together; I could not face anything else.

My daughter had to get back, so we began our travels back home after the visit. My father began to shut down the moment we walked out the door and traveled home with us, providing us with signs the whole way.

First, we received a call from the hospital that he was not going to be able to be moved the next day to hospice. Second, we stopped for gas on the way home and *Another One Bites the Dust* was blasting at the gas station. I just chuckled, knowing my father's sense of humor and that he knew that would be the perfect way to get my attention. The third was that the orchestration of his passing was perfectly aligned with my glancing at a crematorium sign, as my car phone rang at the same time with the announcement that he had passed. Finally, we returned home to a nightingale outside my house singing. As tears rolled down my eyes, I sank into the experience I had with my father and the divine grace of his transition; all I could do was smile inside, for he was free. My father's fiancé exclaimed that he had passed with such peace. So, for all the suffering at the end of his life, he was able to find complete peace. Dad, I am so proud of you, and I write this to honor you.

This wave of experience has left me really evaluating myself and how I walk my path in this world. The challenges I faced opened me to the realization that in this world I had created around me, others—and doing what was best for them—had come first. *Wow!* I guess looking back, I was the fourth little duckling finding a new path for myself. One that I could walk while honoring myself and who I am. In this new path, I have compassion for others; however, it is not my responsibility to comfort their shadow selves. I am learning to set boundaries to keep my heart in balance.

How many of us in this world take care of everyone else and forget who we are? Looking back, it took me a while to stop feeling that I had let my sister and my father's fiancé down. The truth is, I did what was best for me. In the end, it was about my experience with my father and that's it. My sister and father's fiancé could not understand my position, and that is what it is. All I can say at the end of the day is that the journey to love is about your own heart's love. The rest is just part of the game we play. When you find your heart's love, then *you are love.*

Rebecka Gregory - Internationally recognized Light Expression Alchemist using her intuitive gifts, vibrational resonance and other tools is a cosmic tour director being the light for others to guide them thru the dark to the truth of who they are. www.rebeckagregory.com

CHAPTER 17

Stardust & Seawater
By Gregory Kirschenbaum

I died for a few minutes from what they call a "massive heart attack," then popped back into my body. Or… *something* happened. They told me I laid there not breathing and turned grey for a few minutes. Then just suddenly, my skin came back to pink, and I shot right up in my bed as though I were in a movie. I still remember every single moment. Perhaps that's what allows me to feel *this* level of life. I have always been an empath. But since my NDE (near-death experience), I feel like I've become almost like a character in a fantasy movie. I'm not a computer. I'm hardly exact nor can I select the winning lottery numbers. But I can sense deeply into most people's energy spheres, which allows me to, often readily, sense who is who in this world—who is a "light" person, and who is living in the "darkness."

What are we—seven, in the second grade? That's my first clear memory of standing in front of a group of boys, attempting to express why I'm so "different." There's a myriad of memories from the past; I can even remember preschool. It always strikes me when others say that they don't remember their childhood. It strikes me as sad. Or as a lie to cover their beautiful and devasted broken hearts.

That is the great tragedy. A perfectly imperfect micro-universe, literally made from stardust and seawater, poured into a human skin suit, each one walking around Earth with a broken heart. Hydrogen, carbon, gold, platinum, and everything else from the actual stars blended inside each of us, accelerated by seawater. This is what makes each of us. Each of us, who are continuously buzzing around in an atomic attempt to nullify, tranquilize, or delve deeper into that incessant vibration burning within. That "Thing." That "Feeling." That "Voice." That "Vibration." It IS certainly, "*Something*." Whatever we call it, we all have it. It is absolutely the "Thing" that we all have in common. Regardless of anything else that may appear to separate us from one another, it is that internal vibration that proves we are all ONE. *Deny, Deny, Deny,* has been the "go-to" for millennia; it may remain that way for millennia to come. But we each know the truth. We can all feel it.

People often have called me a "Dreamer." Perhaps that is what I am. It may be that all these years later, they turned out to be right. We're all living in some sort of insane fight-or-flight paradigm reminiscent of "In a Mirror, Darkly," from Star Trek. It's a world where people openly detest each other and purposely run society with the intention of hurting each other with long-term disease and chronic, multi-generational institutional violence. All the while preaching, *God, God. God*—from the handle of a gun.

It has caused me to spend the better part of my 50 years alone, a massive heart attack, and missing the blessed experience of being a husband and/or father. I have been on my own all this time. Dogs are magical, amazing expressions of God, and I have been so blessed to be a doggy Daddy for years. But dogs are not children of your own with a bride who remains by your side for the journey. Some people get to have that incarnational experience, and some do not.

There's always time.

That's the thing about being Human. When we allow ourselves to delve deeper into our shared vibration, we find ourselves more and more connected to each other and to all things with what we describe and call, "Life." Anywhere, even. This is what I call being an empath—a very hard place to live your life. And we have no choice. Once we feel the connection to the collective, it's virtually impossible to resist. Some people remain on the path of light, beaming their own positivity into that great matrix. But, of course, we all know that in fact, most people instead beam their constant negativity into that same ocean. And do whatever else they can to be general assholes to the rest of the living carbon-based entities. Selfishly. Complaining. Fighting.

Denying. Ridiculing. Is THAT how an empath is supposed to speak? Are we not supposed to be all, "Love, Peace and Yoga?"

Firstly, no. And then, secondly, no again. But that is the lesson learned the hard way. It took me almost my entire life to realize that we are all just atomic sub-particles bouncing around this galactic comedy. I was born under the misconception that every one of us was traveling on this earth for the greater good. To me, this was a great adventure—to discover as much life as there is to discover before I die. It never dawned on me that everyone else was actually out for themselves. Well, not *everyone*. Mostly everyone.

Along the way, through the years, God has blessed me with quite a lot of amazing people who have gifted me with such love and grace. Perhaps it evolved like that for me because of the destruction of my birth family. Once Mom was killed, my father ran off to find some new wife right away, and then my sister found some moron of a man for a husband, too. I was a young, immature 21 and I was left taking care of two 90-something-year-old grieving grandparents and three dogs, all while being devastatingly sad myself.

I didn't know it then, but that is when I was being taught the lesson I ultimately learned the hard way. I had no idea that even my own family members would be so selfish as to ignore their only son while they went off to find lovers to ease their pain. Hey, everyone grieves in their own way, right?

Right.

I've had a thousand lovers. Yet, no wife. No children. None that I know of.

Finding ONE lifelong partner with whom to travel could be just lovely for some people. And God only knows how I've yearned for that over the years myself. But if you do a quick Google search and type in the search bar, "What do you call a molecule with two atoms," this top result may just yield on your screen:

"What do you call a molecule with two atoms?"

Diatomic molecules form when only two atoms combine. An example of a diatomic molecule is carbon monoxide (CO), made of a single atom of carbon and one of oxygen.

Wait—isn't Carbon Monoxide a toxin and a known carcinogen? Like alcohol, tobacco, and so many other toxic substances, we simply cannot help ourselves on so many levels. It has become almost impossible to be a human on this planet and remain clean and free from poison. That includes coupling up for a romantic relationship. It is generally accepted that statistically, 50% of American marriages end in divorce within the first eight years. Speculation may allow me to claim that within that other 50%, perhaps at least half again SHOULD divorce, yet they "stay for the kids" or for any other sets of reasons. Which in most cases, creates even more damage and trauma.

Where does it end? How do we change it all, so that we can live on a planet where we all genuinely care for each other and every other living thing around us? Why do some people step aside when they see an insect walking on the ground underfoot? Why do some people intentionally stomp and kill the insect? The deer? The partner or spouse? If we hurt our own partners, with whom we share a bed and a life and children and create a genetic lineage, then most assuredly, we will cheat on our taxes, our clients, our national neighbors, and other nations' treaties and alliances. Then we'll surely, and easily, justify bombing another nation in another part of the planet. Especially, if "those people" are different.

Well, it's just a matter of time until we either truly destroy Paradise to a point of no return, or God will somehow, yet again like the stories of the Great Flood, intervene and smack us in the ass. As much as I'd love to stick around for like another 100 years and be one of the people to live to 150, it is also a very comforting thought that prior to that, I will merge back into the majesty of the cosmos. My essence will, at least, rejoin some enormity of existence. I do speculate at times, what it will be like, just as anyone else may. I had an experience to which I referred earlier when I allegedly died from a heart attack. This allowed me to truly move beyond the false pretense of humanity and look deeply into everyone's heart, mind, and soul. It allows me to see who is living in their superficiality and who is genuine.

Which sucks. Because almost everyone is faking it.

OM. Shalom. Amen.

Gregory Kirschenbaum is a nationally recognized artist and medical empath. Born and raised a native New Yorker, he made his career first as an art director in global advertising, then as they say, got out of "jail" and pursued his painting and sculpting career. After working on the Ground Zero statues, "Lunchtime Atop a Skyscraper". His work became known by millions. But his true creative passion is composing music, painting and writing stories. Greg has many sides and after his heart attack at forty-four, he returned to school in NYC and earned a degree in massage therapy. He then stayed in school and has been pursuing his Master's and Doctorate in Traditional Chinese Medicine.

CHAPTER 18

The True Meaning of Health
By Kian Xie

Note: The information contained within this chapter is reflective of the author's personal experience and is not intended as a substitute for medical care.

In 2008, when I was twenty years old, I had just finished my second year of college while living away from my parents' house. Class and work were incidental events that offered brief, half-hearted diversions from my usual partying. During this time, I didn't think much about health or sickness.

My understanding from the experiences I'd had growing up was simple: if something went wrong with my body and it didn't get better in a few days, I could go to the doctor. The doctor would tell me what was wrong, write me a prescription, and then I'd get better.

That was the year I contracted MRSA—methicillin-resistant *staphylococcus aureus*, a disease that is resistant to the usual antibiotics and is life-threatening or fatal in many cases—and my simple understanding of health was called into question. I began a new journey of deconstructing, and then reconstructing, what health really meant to me.

When "Going to the Doctor" Isn't So Simple

At first, I didn't think anything was seriously wrong. I had a rash on my hand that hadn't gone away for weeks, but I didn't think much of it because ever since I was a child, I had skin problems that came and went. I figured this rash might be unusual, but it was no big deal and would go away eventually. But it didn't go away.

I let it go on for longer than I would have if I had been sober. At this time in my life, no more than a day would typically go by that I wasn't drinking alcohol, smoking weed, or using other recreational drugs. I would drink coffee and energy drinks throughout the day to get through classes and work, then crush up a stimulant pill if I had a lot of homework to do. Then I'd smoke a bowl to balance out my jitters. On the weekends, I'd typically get blackout drunk or do harder drugs. It felt normal and easy for me to go about my life in a dissociated state, so I didn't think too hard about going to the doctor until the rash on my hand became noticeably inflamed, and one of my friends told me, in an alarmed voice, "You *have* to go to the doctor! That's infected!"

So, I finally went to the doctor.

The doctor looked at my hand and told me what was wrong: I had a staph infection.

She wrote a prescription for antibiotic pills.

I took the pills… and I didn't get better.

I returned to the doctor's office where they took a wound culture, and a couple of days later, I was informed that my staph infection was MRSA, and it was resistant to the first antibiotic I had been prescribed. The hopeful news was that the results of the culture had produced a list of antibiotics specific to the infection I had, and indicated for each one whether the infection was resistant to the drug, meaning the antibiotic wouldn't work against it, or sensitive, meaning it could work. There were three antibiotics on the list with the "sensitive" indicator, so I was prescribed one of those, assured that it would help this time. Unfortunately, the infection had by this time spread to my lips, making them sore and chapped.

I started on the new pills. I was instructed to make sure I took them twice a day and to continue taking them for two weeks until the bottle was empty, to prevent my infection from developing more antibiotic resistance. I made it all the way to the end of the bottle, and while the infection on my lips cleared up, the rash on my hand remained.

So, I went back to the doctor and received a second wound culture. Bad news: my infection had now become resistant to the second antibiotic. By then, I was starting to notice some new symptoms: fevers that would come on suddenly in the middle of the day and last for an hour or two. Pain in my finger joints, knees, and hips. And the worst feeling: an overwhelming stress on my nervous system—a sense that my whole body was on edge and fragile, like it would fall apart at any minute. I was starting to get really worried and scared.

My doctor was unavailable, so I went to the walk-in clinic, where I was prescribed yet another antibiotic, this time for four weeks. It made me feel sicker than I'd ever been. I could barely keep any food down, and I felt weak day after day. At the end of the four weeks, my skin had not healed.

I was then prescribed one final antibiotic—the last one on the list that had the potential to be effective. This one wasn't as hard on my body as the last one had been, but as I neared the end of the prescription bottle and still saw no improvement, I began to panic.

I soon learned that my original doctor had been diagnosed with cancer and had stepped away from the practice. I saw another doctor, who told me that at this point, I'd have to be admitted to the hospital for an IV. From what I had learned about MRSA, I knew what this meant: intravenous vancomycin, a "last resort" drug for antibiotic-resistant infections.

I had heard that infections like this could also become resistant to vancomycin, which would then leave me out of treatment options. At this point the infection had dug itself deeper into the joint of one of my fingers, causing a throbbing pain. At times I tried to distract myself from the pain, doing whatever I could to numb out … but underneath it all, I was a constant ball of stress and dread. Every moment of my life was underlaid with a fear of what might happen to me. What if I was admitted and the last resort treatment didn't work? Would my finger have to be amputated? Or worse, was my life in danger?

Health Invites Personal Responsibility

Later that day, my eyes fell upon a bottle of echinacea pills that was sitting on my desk. Taking herbs was not typical for me, but I had bought that bottle a while back on a whim to help me deal with an acute illness. A thought crossed my mind: "It's time I take responsibility for my own health.'

With this thought, I had an instant understanding of two things I would have to do: change my diet and give up drinking alcohol. I felt a visceral repulsion to taking the harsh antibiotics I had been prescribed over the past several months and realized I'd be willing to do anything if it meant I wouldn't have to take them anymore.

I ended up doing something a lot of people would say was dangerous and irresponsible—I did not follow my doctor's orders. Instead, I started researching natural methods to support my immune system and fight infections. I started taking a few specific herbs and supplements. I cut meat, dairy, sugar, and wheat out of my diet. I stayed away from alcohol and drugs. In just a few days, I started to notice positive improvement, even without taking any more antibiotic pills. The pain subsided, as did the swelling. My skin was still broken and unhealed, but my condition had improved significantly.

I wanted to share the news with my new doctor and see if he could continue helping me support my health. I told him I had changed my diet and the infection had improved. He responded, in a tone that felt hard and judgmental: "That's not possible. Diet has nothing to do with fighting an infection. Just drink one glass of orange juice a day, that's all you should do about that." He took another wound culture, which came back with no signs of infectious pathogens. "You don't have MRSA anymore," he said, "You have eczema. I'll write you a script for hydrocortisone."

He also wrote me an order for some lab work that wasn't covered by my insurance. I stopped by the front desk and asked about a financial assistance plan. The person behind the desk gave me a dirty look and told me I'd have to call their billing department. I felt embarrassed to hear that, but this kind of experience wasn't new to me; I was used to the complicated, frustrating process of going back and forth with providers and insurance companies, trying to get my medical bills paid. Every time someone turned me away or seemed to cast judgment due to my difficulty in paying for my care, I felt a twinge of shame. Still, I walked away from that clinic feeling somewhat hopeful—perhaps I could find a new solution and finally start feeling better.

I filled my prescription for the topical hydrocortisone cream and started using it. It seemed to work for a couple of days, and then suddenly, it stopped working. My skin broke again and wouldn't heal. Still, I had a renewed sense of motivation, and I believed that I could continue supporting my health without medication. I decided to forgo allopathic medicine and dive deeper into nutritional, herbal, and holistic approaches.

Among those approaches was a body of work on the mental, emotional, and spiritual aspects of health. Through reading various authors, I learned about the concept of people staying sick because they believed they didn't deserve to be healthy. I didn't quite understand this concept, but I was curious to see what it could mean for me, and what steps I truly had the agency to take towards better health.

There's No Simple Solution

Now the fear of amputation or dying was gone, but what tortured me day in and day out was the persistence of my symptoms with no relief. Along with the skin issues, I was still struggling with brain fog, joint pain, fatigue, and fevers that would set in suddenly at random times of the day. I had lost my trust in the allopathic medical system at this point and refused to pursue any more help in that direction. From what I had learned independently about eczema and other autoimmune diseases, the medication typically prescribed for these conditions worked by suppressing the immune system in one way or another.

This meant, according to this model of treatment, that there was no cure. I didn't want to accept the idea of my illness not being curable. I wanted to get better, and I believed I could, even if I didn't know how. I believed there was a deeper root to the problem that could be addressed if only I could find the right strategy and support. Unfortunately, as many others who deal with chronic unresolved illnesses can attest, the Western naturopathic and holistic healthcare landscape is just as complicated and frustrating to navigate, if not more so, than the Western allopathic healthcare system.

Looking back, I realize there are deep reasons for this that have to do with our society's oppressive history. But I didn't have perspective on that at the time: all I knew was that trying to get the care I needed was expensive, and it was overwhelmingly confusing to figure out which way to turn. Different books and practitioners would give me drastically different explanations as to what was really going on with my body. Some people claimed they could heal me in just a few sessions of their particular modality. Others said I'd have to undergo a litany of tests to check for hidden allergies and food sensitivities. Others still said that those tests would tell me nothing, and the only solution was to go on an extended restricted diet or fast. Then there were those people who believed that healing was all in the mind, and all I'd have to do was think more positively.

I tried dozens of approaches, spent thousands of dollars—all of my attempts frustrated me. Nothing felt quite right. A proposed solution might work for a short time, then suddenly become ineffective, and my practitioners couldn't explain why. I relied heavily on restricting my diet to keep my symptoms under control, but over time it seemed like I had to restrict myself more and more; the list of foods I had negative reactions to grew and grew, changing week after week. Allergy tests and food sensitivity panels yielded a series of conflicting and complicated results—at one point it seemed like I was "allergic to everything." I experienced persistent feelings of wrongness, not being "good enough" at healing, and a sense of misalignment—of never being quite right.

Some people said I'd just have to stay the course. I thought: "Which course?"

The confusing, frustrating process of trial and error went on for several years.

Do I Deserve Health?

At the same time I was on this health journey, I was also exploring my spirituality and questioning whether I could have a relationship with a higher power. Both of my parents were atheists, and I had been raised with no religion. While I don't think any spiritual belief system or lack thereof is objectively right or wrong, I found that my own "lack thereof" was leaving me feeling lost and alone as I continued to search for answers on how I could get healthy.

Of course, my interest in holistic health ultimately provided some exposure to the spiritual aspects of healing. The "New-Age" schools of thought intrigued me, especially the idea that I could change my reality by changing my mind. I tried saying affirmations like "I am healthy," "My body is functioning with ease," and "I deserve thriving health." But saying these words always frustrated me because they conflicted with what I saw and felt in the moment. I thought maybe the affirmations and mindset techniques weren't working because there was something wrong with me. Maybe I wasn't saying the words earnestly enough, maybe I wasn't feeling the right feelings or thinking the right thoughts. What started out as an effort to be more positive turned into a spiral of self-blame.

In 2011, after three years of dealing with health issues, I became a Christian and joined a fundamentalist church. Here lay another promise of spiritual healing. Reading in the Bible that God had the power to heal, and that Jesus was an especially notable healer, I wondered what healing there could be for me. I delved into inquiry, through worship services and Bible study groups, around my feelings of guilt and shame, and God's promises for deliverance and salvation. It seemed that hope and love were available to me, at least in the eternal sense. But I struggled because I wanted health in my body now. Once again, I turned back to the thought that it was somehow my fault I wasn't getting better, just as I had thought while exploring New-Age practices.

What made things really tough about being a Christian is that I'm also transgender. Even after I completed my medical transition in 2012, of which most of the physical changes involved are irreversible, I was pressured by many of my peers and mentors in the church to "de-transition" ... or at least to break off my engagement to the woman who is now my wife and commit to a life of celibacy. I had no desire to do either of those things, yet every day I carried a feeling of shame and regret, wondering if I was doing the wrong thing in the eyes of God.

One day, I was reading the Bible and came across a story in the Old Testament of a person who was being punished for "sexual immorality." Not only was that person being punished, but their whole family line was punished as well, with a persistent illness that could not be cured. I stared at those words in the scripture, wondering if it really was the truth that God was punishing me for wanting an intimate relationship with the woman I loved while being the way I was.

Feelings of doubt and shame followed me everywhere. I repeatedly found myself in a cycle of being unable to stay sober; I would stay completely on track for a few months at a time, and then return to drug use as a way to suppress those persistent feelings of shame. I had a deep discord within my spiritual beliefs: on one side was the belief propagated by New-Age practitioners that I somehow "deserved" health. On the other side was the repeated message from the Christian church that I was a sinner by nature, and while I could be redeemed in Christ, I would be blocked from true salvation if I did not conform to the "correct" prescribed behavior.

Health Is Ongoing Growth, Not Perfection

There were many parallels in the types of treatment I received from different people as I pursued health:

- Judgmental remarks from doctors who didn't believe that I could influence my own health by changing my diet.

- Disdain from clinic staff when I asked for help to pay for my lab work.

- Critique from holistic practitioners who thought I just "needed a better mindset" to get better.

- Admonishment from fellow Christians for not living a lifestyle that they believed was in line with God's plan.

In all these cases, the people who offered me judgment, critique, disdain, or admonishment had placed themselves in positions of authority over others' lives, including over my own. But more importantly than that, I had placed those people in positions of authority over how I would choose to see myself. In my journey to take personal responsibility for my own health, my biggest challenge was taking personal responsibility for how I determined my own goodness and worthiness of good health.

It took many challenges like this to help me finally see that I was the only one with the true power to judge myself as good or bad. Furthermore, I could accept my own goodness without needing to be perfect in every way. As I overcame many of these challenges, I noticed my health improving in phases, turning one corner after another.

There's a reason and intention behind how I describe each phase of healing as "turning a corner" rather than "finding the cure" or "getting healed." While I had hoped for years that there would be "one thing" that could save me—that could help me get better once and for all—in reality, that was not the case. It tried my patience, but it also taught me that health is about ongoing growth, not perfection, and there is a broad and rich spectrum of experiences of health, not just the simple binary of "sick" versus "healthy." The positive pattern of healing inspired me to grow more courageously with each corner I turned.

I chose to leave my fundamentalist church and discovered I could introduce meat back into my diet—this time from local, sustainable farms—and it was nourishing to me.

I reconnected with members of my family with whom I'd become out of touch. I cried when I realized what it truly felt like to be loved. I understood now that healing was not just about doing the right things for my individual physical body, but also about creating connection and community, experiencing real love, and being who I really am.

I gained more energy and strength and was able to enter a new career—in corporate healthcare, of all places. I faced and dealt with my moral conflicts around my work, and discovered how I could show up and help people honestly, even in an environment that supported a type of healthcare I disagreed with.

I reinvigorated my passion for social justice and continued to learn about and face the reality of the world around me. I realized I could find goodness in any situation, as well as many people who genuinely cared for others, while also acknowledging the realities of injustice and pursuing meaningful change.

As I grew to understand this truth, I also met a new allopathic doctor—one who didn't criticize how I chose to support my own health, but who enabled me to take the agency I needed to take while supporting me in those areas of allopathic care that I needed for diagnostic purposes. This new practitioner also supported my use of hormones as I stabilized in my transition. Most importantly, it was helpful to have someone I could check in with about how my health was progressing—someone who genuinely respected me without judgment.

Today, my health isn't "perfect," but I am thriving. I no longer have joint pain or intermittent fevers. My skin is mostly clear, with very minor irritations on occasion that serve as guides for when I need to care for myself better. I no longer need to severely restrict my diet; although I eat nourishing and nutritious foods on a regular basis, I can also feel free to indulge in some "unhealthy" foods from time to time.

Where before I struggled to perform everyday physical tasks, I'm now able to enjoy vigorous exercise several times a week. I no longer drink alcohol or use recreational drugs; I am able to stay consistently sober. My mood fluctuates from day to day, but I'm able to stay happy in the big picture, and

I no longer feel weighed down by feelings of shame. I surround myself with friends and loved ones who genuinely care for me, and my relationships are defined by mutual respect and goodwill. I no longer place it in anyone else's hands to judge my life as right or wrong. I embrace my imperfections and always seek to grow into a more authentic version of who I am.

Putting Health into Perspective

My specific case wasn't as dangerous as that of many others who have contracted MRSA. I was never hospitalized because I went against my doctor's instructions. And because the alternative solutions I tried worked, the infection itself remained confined to small areas of my body and eventually was resolved.

However, what wore me down over time was the persistence of symptoms that arose after my extended antibiotic treatments and the prolonged time I lacked answers, going from doctor to doctor, and not getting the clarity I needed. That persistence of illness turned what many might call a series of "minor" symptoms into an ongoing drain on my energy, leaving me incapable of living my life to its fullest potential for over ten years.

As I grew in my understanding of how to support my own health, I received training as a health coach, herbalist, and health advocate. I am not currently a professional healing practitioner, but I've gained skills to support members of my community as they grow in their own agency to direct their own healthcare and personal healing journeys. These are the skills that I believe anyone can gain and grow with on a daily basis—skills that we can all use to support each other as we direct our own paths, individually and together.

I believe everyone's path to health and healing is unique, so I won't place myself in a position to determine what "should" work for others. However, here are a few things that helped me immensely on my journey, and still help me as I grow in my own health and healing:

- Delving deeper into my cultural and ethnic roots: learning where I came from.

- Reconnecting with my extended family of origin and remembering how it feels to be loved.

- Learning to love myself and accept my own desires and needs.

- Taking a look at my feelings of guilt and shame and finding my own personal perspective on worthiness and deservingness.

- Understanding the impacts of colonial and imperial trauma on my family lineage.

- Learning about the effects of trauma, both generational and in this lifetime, and getting support to grow and heal around those traumatic experiences.

- Facing the truth that the Western concept of health—including holistic and naturopathic health—is heavily influenced by systemic oppression and violence.

- Recognizing the moments in my personal life where I had the power to effect change and taking constructive action in those moments.

- Standing up courageously for myself when I was being treated unfairly.

- Taking that courageous self-care and translating it to advocate for justice for my beloved family and community members.

- Doing the work to support social healing to reintegrate a more supportive understanding of health, not just as individuals, but as an interdependent community.

Healing was not a linear path for me, and while there were many difficulties that arose, I am glad to have experienced this rich journey. The reward I have received comes with a sense of freedom and agency in knowing who I am, the ability to embrace my own needs with acceptance and support, and the experience of relationships with others and my community at large that also reflect that inner love and acceptance.

It's an overall sense of personal responsibility, yet also a calling to care for others and understand that we all need each other. We all deserve love, care, and happiness. We all deserve the journey of health—not absolute perfection or reliance on that promised "one thing" to solve all our problems instantly—but a journey that calls us to growth, courage, and acceptance of who we are now and who we want to become.

Kian Xie is a corporate healthcare strategist, business consultant, and career educator. He is passionate about reimagining new ways to work and care for each other in rapidly changing times. www.kianxie.net

CHAPTER 19

How Tics Turned our Life Upside Down
By Dr. Johanneke Kodde

Sometimes life can appear to be ticking (and in our case ticking) along and you don't even realize you are way off track. And even though the shit has hit the proverbial fan, it needs to fly in your face before you start to take notice.

This particular Monday was one of those moments where it hit me square in the face. It was a rainy Monday afternoon in late November, and I had gone for a walk to the river to take a small offering for the little soul that had left my body at age seventeen, as suggested by my new massage therapist. There was some unfinished energy going on in my womb, you see. I was getting desperate for anything that would make sense and improve the dire reality that was going on in our world. But the flower offering had swirled around in the same spot, being held up by some branches and debris, so it was hardly the ceremonial goodbye I had envisioned. I was feeling as rudderless as the flowers in the river, not sure whether we were on the right path for our daughter. There was a missed call from my mother-in-law, but I wasn't in the mood to speak to her, so I ignored it. Then my husband rang.

"My dad is dead. Dropped dead in the hospital whilst going for an eye appointment. They say his heart has stopped. I am coming home now and then I'm going to Holland to see my mum." Oh God. Shit. That's bad. A sinking feeling came over me. I hadn't been particularly close to my father-in-law; he struggled to show love and affection and was resentful that his health had gone downhill since he retired, but he was always there when we visited and we all loved his cooking. I knew this was going to hit my mother-in-law very hard. "Okay, see you in a moment," I said.

It was also the day we had decided to finally keep our twelve-year-old daughter out of school until the Christmas holidays. As soon as she restarted school in September, after months at home during the pandemic, she developed florid tics, leading to worsening anxiety and eventually, seizures. No doctor or psychologist seemed to know what was going on. The tics were relentless, starting from the moment she woke until she fell back into a deep sleep at night. Nonstop. Clapping, gestures, high-pitched noises, profanities, shakes, dropping to the floor, hitting herself.

The school had embraced her new "disability;" the class was educated on Tourette's and the teachers tried to make allowances. But she still spent more and more time on her own, in a side room, petrified of anything and everything. We had to drive her to school because the school bus was too much, and she had started hitting herself in the face. She could have tic attacks, where she would tic and shake incessantly and then get scared of her inability to stop. The situation was escalating, and we didn't know what to do.

So this Monday, she had finally dropped out of school. And then my father-in-law dropped dead, and my husband dropped everything and left the country to be with his mum. The only way for me to look after our daughter was to drop my work commitments and be at home. What started as a slightly confused Monday ended in a nightmarish one.

That week we found ourselves at home: no work, no school, no dad, no grandad anymore. It was in the dark weeks before Christmas. I decided to let go—let go of what we should be doing, feeling, or saying. It was as if the shock of that fateful Monday had finally broken through many years of living in a carefully constructed reality. The ground that I thought was firm had become quicksand. The walls were crumbling. I decided to throw out the parenting rule book. I had to start again, once and for all. To go back to peace. So that our daughter's body, mind, and soul would have the space to find peace as well.

How did we get to this point? How had I become so fixed in my way of doing life that I hadn't even realized my daughter was silently twisting herself in a million different knots to appease the world around her? Sure, we knew she was a sensitive child. She had not left my breast as a baby, nor my lap as a toddler. She had eczema and allergies. She was quiet and shy but appeared happy with her friends and adored dressing up, dolls, gymnastics, the usual. Primary school had been a little challenging but overall, she appeared to be a happy girl. If anything, I thought she could do with a bit of toughening up. A bit more assertiveness. Like that time she didn't use her twisted ankle for a week and it started to go limp and purple, only to do cartwheels again the moment the X-ray showed there was nothing going on.

Maybe I had become too comfortable in my profession as a doctor and in my role as a mother. I had not been an overly confident child, either. I remember clearly how hard it was in primary school to find my identity: a favorite color, a favorite song, a favorite writer. Such slippery, tricky questions! I needed to have a style I liked, a look—an identity of *some* sort. I liked Mel and Kim and Madonna, but I mainly liked them secretly in my own bedroom, recording songs from the radio on my little tape recorder, then playing them back and trying to erase the DJ's voice during the intro. I remember practicing dance moves in front of the mirror, wearing multiple bracelets and putting my hair up. But I only shared my favorites when it was safe—if someone else suggested they liked it first.

Secondary school was even more of a minefield. You see, my boyfriend played the guitar and grew his hair long and curly, which was pretty cool. And he had a group of friends who dabbled in the really cool grunge zone. But I also loved Friday nights spent playing clarinet (not very well, but hey…) in the local town band with a group of other friends. Less cool, but loads of fun, nevertheless. And I absolutely adored ballroom dancing with one of my close friends (now husband, but that's a whole other story), and this involved yet another, vastly different crowd. One of my girlfriends was in that group; she knew about fashion. I was usually wearing something second-hand with holes in it, to my mother's despair. And then there were the friends I had made in Taize, a multifaith community in France—the alternative, slightly churchy, but still cool ones.

So I had to stay somewhere in the middle. Not too obviously this or that. Not too specific about any one style or type of music, or it may not be right. It may mark me down in their eyes somehow. Or so I thought. Secondary school progressed, and I had to start planning my future career steps. I had no idea. (You see, I have recently discovered that in a system related to astrology, called "Human Design," I have an "open Identity Center." This indicates that I am not designed to have a strong sense of identity or direction. Basically, it really doesn't matter. Life will guide me. But no one told me this.) I was convinced I had to find an identity. Put on a certain outfit and wear it for the rest of my life.

Out of desperation for the lack of direction forthcoming from my teenage brain, my parents paid for a really expensive profiling test. It tested all my abilities and matched them to a set of people who had done the same test and were successful in certain professions. Sounds reasonable, doesn't it? Somewhere deep inside I had an inkling of what I might want to do, but I hadn't expressed it. Become a doctor, maybe? So off we went to a dingy, musty-smelling office room with a computer where I had to tap with two fingers whilst verbally answering all sorts of tests. In my memory, the room was yellowy brown, like a seventies scene. And after I had done this for an hour or so, a report was generated, and the moment supreme arrived. My top match was… to be a librarian! I cried all the way home.

And I became… a doctor. Something inside gently pushed me in that direction. I was interested in people and their behavior and wanted to do good in the world. And I had the brains and tenacity that could probably pull it off. At age seventeen I was drawn to all things alternative, so I decided to—swiftly—become a doctor and then go down the alternative route. This was not quite how it worked out. But at the age of thirty, I had managed to get married, become a qualified family doctor, and have my first child. My open Identity Centre was happy. I had colored within the lines of my profile and filled it with *three* identities: wife, mother, and doctor. It was as if a weight of insecurity was lifted from my shoulders. I didn't have to try so hard or morph all the time. I could lean in a bit more. And to be fair, once I had a screaming baby and met other sleep-deprived mothers, a lot of preconceived ideas fell away anyway. So for about fifteen years I was quietly and confidently building and solidifying my career, family, marriage, friendships, and fitness—until it was time for my carefully designed solar system to tremble when our daughter's body and mind started to slip away from us all.

Back to that fateful, shitty Monday when everything dropped away. From the moment I decided to throw out the parenting rulebook, our daughter's demeanor changed visibly. We went on little adventures: we bought her painting materials and constructed an outdoor studio, so the tics could be as messy as they wanted to be. We bought new wallpaper, and I had our bedroom refurbished. She picked up her brother's guitar and taught herself to play some chords. We decided to get a dog and went looking at puppies at a nearby farm. She baked chocolate balls and then made an advent calendar to put them in. The seizures stopped. It felt as if her creative, late grandad had somehow gifted us a couple of weeks to tap back into our senses of self and connection. It was a strangely sad and magical time.

Over the next months, with the help of Hazel the puppy, numerous professionals, a lot of patience, muddy dog walks, super noodles, and copious amounts of love and faith, our daughter slowly improved. Her predicament created many idle hours where we had to be in the house while she was in her room, or we had to wait in the car when she went to an appointment or tried a few hours of a special school. In the void, this period where time seemed to slow down, I was inadvertently drawn into my own process of soul-searching. My once revered job as a family doctor lost its shine and I started to wonder who I really was, what was the purpose of all this, what could I learn from this turmoil? I was excavating, diving in, and learning new ways of looking at myself and others, for example through astrology and Human Design. Winter turned to spring and then summer. Our daughter's progress remained slow, and I had embarked on my own personal journey of transformation, with no idea where it might lead.

Late that summer, I gathered with a wonderful circle of women and mothers for a full moon ceremony. The evening was chilly as the summer weather waned, and the sky was overcast and drizzling, which caused our fire to smoke excessively and hide the moon behind the clouds. As the wind kept turning, we couldn't help giggling at our attempts to be serious about our ceremony which, by most standards, wasn't turning out to be much of a ceremony after all. Here I was, after months of soul-searching, talking to friends about what I wanted to release under this full moon. Well, I didn't know what I wanted to release. I had no idea about anything anymore: if my job was right for me, if I was any good at this parenting thing, if I was going in any kind of direction with all my navel-gazing. I felt like I was wading through treacle. I felt totally and completely in the thick of a pile of sticky, slimy, gooey fudge—which didn't even taste nice!

So all I could do was cry. I sobbed and sobbed until one of my friends suggested that this might be what it feels like for a caterpillar to be in the mush of the chrysalis while turning into a butterfly—completely stuck, unable to move, slowly transforming into something that is still unknown. Wow, that's a nice way of seeing it, I thought. Because this is pretty unbearable. That evening I came away feeling like a little bit of my new shape had started to form. Only a tiny little bit, very slowly, still invisible to the outside world. Still a long way to go, but the imaginal cells were beginning to initiate the new shapes, sizes, and colors that were destined to come out if I dared to follow my heart and soul. What a relief!

And so we muddled on. After the summer holidays, fraught with attempts at family time, thwarted by our daughter's tics and anxiety whenever we had any expectations, she started a new school. A special, temporary school, with only a handful of children per class, all with their own problems. She couldn't eat with anyone, so we would return to the school at lunchtime with a toastie from a specific coffee outlet and a particular smoothie, which she would consume in the car. Then we had a couple more hours' time to pass before returning home. I filled my time with reading, studying spirituality, and finding the best coffee shops to hang out in nearby. We were now into our second year of highly charged, tricky-to-maneuver territory. Any whiff of expectation of our daughter's progress was squashed with some kind of drama. If I had the audacity to plan something for myself, it would need to be canceled or rearranged due to an unexpected turn of events at home or at her school. But despite that, she did, very slowly, improve along the way. But it was hard work to remain positive and upbeat without any expectations while still trusting in a good long-term outcome.

By February, cracks were appearing in my carefully maintained positive demeanor and calm composure. I was actually on the verge of burnout, which particularly affected my work as a doctor. I was disillusioned, tired, disinterested. After two years of navigating turbulent waters—first with the adrenaline rush of being at the frontlines of a pandemic and then the emotional turmoil of having a very unwell teenage daughter in and out of school—I was done with it all. During a work business meeting I had rolled my eyes and shrugged my shoulders at every point that was raised. The shrugging of shoulders wasn't entirely unusual when trying to run a business in a healthcare system with an ever-changing landscape, moving targets, changing protocols, money pressures, staff needs, and ever-increasing patient demands. But that wasn't my style. I was more of a "Let's sort it out and don't dwell on it" type. Ever the optimist. It will be fine one way or another. My practice manager counted on me for that—keeping the spirits high.

But I couldn't do it anymore. So, I shrugged and rolled my eyes and didn't even try to hide that I really didn't care. Whatever. After that meeting, the practice manager came into my room and asked, "Are you okay?" A fatal question if you are NOT okay. The floodgates opened. "I'll be okay; I'm just tired," I said. "Do you need some time off?" she asked. I looked at her incredulously. "What do you mean? I can't take time off. That's not a thing I do. I have reduced my days; I manage my own stress levels. I won't let myself get to that point...." I cried some more. "That would be amazing," I said.

"Does your husband know you feel like this?" "Not really. Not that it is this bad. We've had so much going on, we're both just trying to keep going," I responded. "Go and talk to him and let me know what you want to do," she offered. "Thanks, Tracey," I said.

So I spoke to him and made a plan to tag a few weeks of extra leave onto the Easter holidays (in a month's time). And when I presented my plan, my colleagues looked at me incredulously and sent me home the next day. That week I went to a conference (to lift my spirits) and caught COVID-19. And then I crashed. I finally gave in, although terrified that if I did that, I would never get up from the sofa again—that I would turn into a blob. My friend, a burnout coach, laughed and asked me what I would say if someone else had that worry. I said, 'Don't be ridiculous; of course you will get back up when you are ready." Over the following weeks and months, I rested, read, meditated, and relaxed. I had readings, recharged, and had several sessions with a coach.

Eventually, it was time to go to Costa Rica for a retreat. This trip sealed my recovery and allowed me to break out of my expanded, but still limited, belief system. The butterfly was finally ready to emerge. I was out of the box. My worldview had expanded; possibilities seemed endless. I was re-energized, optimistic, enthusiastic. It was mid-summer. I felt as radiant as the sun, as abundant as nature at this time of year, and my acupuncturist said that my energy was a bit like a Formula One car or a racehorse. "Bionic," she called it. It felt good. I was charged up for bigger and better things. In my absence, the practice had decided to increase appointment lengths from ten to fifteen minutes. When I came back after three months off, they made allowances, so I was able to preserve my enthusiasm and it all felt light and pleasant. I also nurtured the seeds of new ideas and a new way of working, independently. Anything was still possible, the road still unpaved. I was beaming.

This could have been the end of this story. But life is rarely linear, and another curve ball was waiting for me. Our daughter had done so well that she was now ready to go to a "normal" school. We had found a small, supportive, private school that she felt comfortable with. She wasn't ready to go on the school minibus, so we drove her there every day, 45 min each way. I was slowly developing my idea of working independently and during a sleepless night the name and logo 'Body Mind Soul Doctor' came to me. I talked to another coach, and I was planning a possible new future career, all very much in the early stage of ideas, with little commitment or practical understanding of how it would all unfold.

Summer turned to autumn. Our practice was under more pressure and appointment length reduced back again. A colleague announced her retirement for the following spring and attempts were started to find a replacement for her. With the busy season, my work environment was darkening again. And it continued to get gloomier, colder, and more restricted.

Around that time, I embarked on a course to learn how to read the Akashic Records, which fit beautifully into my plan of becoming this body, mind, and soul doctor. I finally found a way to tap into the abilities that I apparently had, according to the psychics and intuitives that I had consulted along the way. This was exciting, and I shared some of my enthusiasm with my closest colleague at work, who merely giggled at my next level of witchiness. With the winter encroaching and my future self-continuing to grow came the realization that sooner or later, I would have to announce to the practice partnership that I couldn't see myself staying there forever. I had created a new Instagram account with my new name and was considering how I might make some money from this new incarnation. A website idea was forming. There seemed to be two vastly different seasons playing out in my world: a spring meadow feeling of new opportunities and ideas and a distinctly frosty winter land, bereft of green shoots, but desperately longing to find a path forward in the snow.

At the practice, we interviewed, went to career fairs, and had doctors come to see the practice. We talked to every trainee and otherwise vaguely interested person about how wonderful it would be if they would join us. I waited and waited and *waited* for that one person who would rescue my morally responsible self from the agony of having to announce that I was leaving as well. But of course, that person never came. Exactly a year after I was rescued from full-blown burnout by the practice manager, I had to make the decision to rescue myself. Because the feeling that was coming over me, again, was one of disinterest and disillusion, although this time it wasn't so much physical fatigue. I felt imprisoned by my own sense of duty. In the car, on the way back from dropping my daughter at school, the feeling of constriction made me gag and I cried out of frustration. (Oh, and I was about to go to Spain for a weekend with my parents and siblings to celebrate my birthday. The trip was canceled at the last minute, so there were some tears for that as well.) I decided that it could wait no longer, and I wrote an email to announce that, with a heavy heart, I had made the decision to step out of the practice partnership that I had lived and breathed for 15 years, in order to preserve my health and to create a different future for myself and my family.

Six months later my notice period was over, and I was a free bird. I had committed to help the practice for a bit longer if needed and to keep the bank account healthy, but life as an independent practitioner was beckoning. I had birthed a new version of my professional self! I was really becoming the body, mind and soul doctor—complete with logo, website, social media presence—and most of all, a real desire to work in the way I had always tried but had never fully succeeded at within the constraints of the UK National Health Service. My appointment times had become fifty-plus minutes, instead of ten. I developed the Body Mind Soul Method, with which I help my patients (or do I call them clients now?) understand their symptoms as messages from their bodies that they are living out of balance. I dive into their life stories, uncover hidden patterns, and help them re-ignite their passions and purpose. Along the way I give lifestyle advice, but only in the context of self-awareness and understanding. And if they are interested, I use Human Design or read their Akashic Records. I love working in this way.

More importantly, I have discovered a very different version of my personal self in the past three, often harrowing, years. A kinder, gentler, more intuitive, and more embodied version. One who recognizes when she is in her mind too much and knows how to bring herself back into her body. One who checks in with her heart and soul regularly and is not afraid to talk about it. One who sees her outer world as a reflection of her inner cosmos and (most of the time) no longer takes things personally or finds fault in others. One who realizes that she has infinite potential and creativity but can get a bit stuck in orchestrating the details, until she remembers to ground and center herself to find the wisdom within. In other words: a more balanced, body-mind-soul aware version, but of course, still a work in progress…

Dr. Johanneke Kodde is an experienced family doctor who believes that the awareness and integration of body, mind, and soul will help many people to better understand their symptoms, face mental health challenges and uncover and follow their hidden desires and passions. www.bodymindsouldoctor.com •Instagram: @bodymindsouldoctor • Facebook: Body Mind Soul Doctor (business) • LinkedIn: Dr Johanneke Kodde

CHAPTER 20

People We Hate to Love
By Jara Lindgren

As a six-foot-tall demi-god of a Swedish woman, I never thought it would be a five foot four, twenty-nothing-year-old, Mexican man, that would be the vessel to bring me to the depths of my soul. But he was, and those stats about him may be all wrong because I hate his guts and pay no attention to him at all. I definitely have not noticed any stupid details about him that I am annoyed to be aware of; like how he has a suntan line on his face from his sunglasses, or how he's in love with Harvard and his hometown. I also haven't noticed that he seems to love donuts, he's self-conscious about his belly fat, super loves his mom and his throwback Jordans. I've noticed nothing. And if I could, I would never see him again. I feel towards him like Alfalfa's misread letter to Darla in Little Rascals, I hate his stinkin' guts. He triggers in me every inadequacy I had worked my entire adult life on healing.

Before I met him, I thought I was in a solid place, feeling comfortable in owning who I was and excited that this next phase in life was looking like I could find space that would allow me, better yet require me, to be 100% authentically me. Big, Bold, Badass Bitch who leads with love and compassion, and who is always ready for a challenge. But he blew all that up. What makes it worse, he wasn't even trying. He doesn't even have an ounce of malice in him, nor does he even know the reverberating impact of him just showing up in my life has had on who I am.

The first day of class I walked in, saw the man presumed to be the professor, and in a half condescending tone, thought, "Oh how cute, he's so young. He's even still got adorable chubby cheeks. Hehehe, he even looks like several men on my dating roster, except short!" I chuckled at myself because of this observation. And instantly felt my ego grow bigger because if it's one thing I knew from dating so much, and lived life experiences, I make impressive first impressions. And something inside of me wanted his.

On the second day of class, each student took a turn explaining what they wanted to do for their yearlong project and received feedback on how to refine it. Normal procedure for this type of class, and exactly what I was in this class to do.

I shared what I wanted to do, which was a culmination of hours of research and analysis melted together by my passion for its importance and contribution to society. I had eagerly been awaiting this very class my first two years of law school, waiting to be guided and instructed on how to accomplish big ideas. Finally, an opportunity for me to be big and bold and free, in a space that could hold it. I was filled with so much excitement and passion to begin this journey. Eager for feedback and help on how to make it possible, and ready for the work ahead. His feedback came, and all I heard was "that's great but too big, others in higher positions, and more qualified than you, have already tried and failed."

"I know that already and I've been looking at it and found where they went wrong." I asserted hoping to win his favor.

"Start with smaller steps to build upon," and then he gave a few ideas of where to start and to do more research. I smiled politely and said thank you, putting on the mask of social graces that came second nature to me in these situations. Never let them know it hit hard, be grateful they're even patronizing you with they're help. That's how you deal with men. Right?!

I left pissed. Who is this mother fucker to tell me that my idea is too big and to take fuckin baby steps? Essentially the Mofo, as I now called him, told me I was too much, too big, and not enough all at once. I felt sideswiped. This wasn't what I was here for. I was here to expand, not contract. What a waste of my time. I should have done an internship, at least then I'd be gaining employable skills. But I wanted to do this! THIS was the class I came here for. Why did this feedback even trigger me so hard? I'm an athlete, a fitness competitor, I literally pay people to tell me how to improve my skills. I enjoy getting torn apart to rebuild better. That's what it takes to be elite. But this hit really hard. He, specifically he, hit me really hard.

He doesn't know who I am. He doesn't know what I can do. He doesn't know that my first year of law school I coached 6 sports teams, fundraised thousands of dollars for those teams, am a single mom of 4 kids and dealing with aging parents, at the gym at 4:30 am every morning, have a six pack, and still managed to be middle of the pack in law school rankings spending only a few hours studying, which sure may not be top but that's because I have a mortgage and responsibilities while all the other 20 nothing babies are only focused on school. I can hang cabinets on a wall perfectly, BY MYSELF for godsake! I can do anything if just shown how!!!! I wasn't asking his opinion, nor his permission, I was letting him know what I was doing so he could guide me in doing it.

Breathe in. Breathe out. Meditate.

'Let's not change course just yet. Let's get more insight on some of his ideas and why he thinks them. Show effort on my part, a little bit of my fighting spirit- even though I hate to waste it on a losing cause. Besides, short ass mother fucker may just know what he's talking about, it is why the school hired him. Let's see if I can make something work and ask how I can articulate it differently to garner support, since we have to work in groups.'

I swallowed my jagged pride and emailed to set up a meeting. He sent three times that would work for him, and I chose the appointment right before next class. He never confirmed, so I showed up as scheduled anyway just in case, so at least I couldn't be the one to blame for things going south. He wasn't there. There were people in the room, they were just ending a class, but no one I recognized, so I left.

Now more than ever I felt like this was a waste of time. Taking a W at this point seemed like the better option. How was I supposed to get advice from someone who couldn't show up. This was my marriage all over again. I did so much work, read so many books, went to so many conferences, sought so much help, but it was never going to work because he did not show up. That ended in a painful divorce. Just three months ago I gave my heart to another man who wanted me to be his "Everything," and then somehow was too busy for me once I became exclusively his. Not to mention the hundreds of men I have dated over the past four years that have said they saw something long term in me, but their admiration waned unexplained. Now this. He's just like every other man.... a lying disappointment.

He's supposed to be here to help me, guide me, teach me. I can't receive advice from someone I don't trust. And to top it off, now I was feeling agonizingly disrespected, and dumb as rocks, for believing he could be different because he was my professor, but not only did he look like the men I date, now he was showing up like them. My ego can't take this. I won't pay exorbitant money to feel belittled and betrayed. I can only take so much.

I left and was on my way to the registrar's office when I happened to run into a friend and gave her the super digest version of events as we walked to her destination, the bookstore. She listened, and I listened as I spoke. Almost as if I was an observer of my own life and thoughts. Everything inside of me said it was time to cut losses, change course, and run. But then there was the part of me that was listening as my friend, and it was also asking, 'is that an old story pattern that was running or was that my truth? A topic that had interested me for a while. Our instincts are always right, but our engrained energetic patterns are not – they just think they are keeping us alive. For the first time in…like ever…I was questioning my reasoning for quitting something. Reasonings for everything I had previously quit were socially acceptable; But were they really acceptable to my soul?

I stood outside the building to my classroom, and I thought hard, deep and quick. So many other events came to mind. Opportunities where I was faced with something (a feeling I can't name) or to run. I could see a pattern I had too often chosen to run and play the victim to circumstance. What was I going to do now? Was I previously always right in these situations? What would happen if I stayed instead of run?

So, I walked in and went to class 3 feeling so awkward, so uncomfortable, so painfully unsure of myself because I was doing something I hadn't done before in a situation like this, it went against every fiber of my being… I let go of control - and my ego started breaking.

I walked into class with whatever smile I could muster, "well you broke me professor!" was my greeting. Half-truth and half comedic jest just trying to relieve my own body's tension with humor.

"I didn't mean to." The look on his face led me to believe he meant it with total sincerity. Like from the depths of his being. Which also kinda annoyed me that he believed he had the power to break me.

"I was here before class but didn't see you," I responded.

"Oh, Professor Chase was here." He said.

"Oh, I had no idea who she was, there were other people here in the room, and since I'd never met her before, I didn't realize she was who I should have been looking for." The class was always structured with two professors, but Professor Chase had been gone the first two classes.

Everyone went around the room giving updates to inform the new professor on our projects. I asked to be skipped - because that's what you do when you feel uncomfortable; you make the situation even more awkward by not following protocol. I'm not sure if it was already pin-drop quiet in the class, but I swear I could hear someone's very loud thoughts say "uummmm, is she allowed to skip?" Professor Chase asked me to repeat myself because even she was caught off guard by the request. "Can I be skipped please; we can come back to me at the end if there's time." We ran out of time for me to speak which I was sooo grateful for.

"Jara, I'm sorry we didn't have time to get to yours today." Said Professor Chase. To which I just politely smiled, not a single word. Well, I just made a great first impression, I'm sure. Way to go Jara. To top it off I had run with haste immediately after the class for a family event which I'm sure looked like I was just avoiding them. At some level I probably was.

A few days passed and I was still being triggered. The pain was so real and agonizing. I figured now was the time to withdraw from the class.

Breathe in, breathe out. Meditate.

'Why was he triggering so much? Why is this hitting the very depths of my soul??'

It had everything to do with him and at the same time absolutely nothing to do with him. It at least had nothing to do with what he said. It had everything to do with everything he was, and that the universe was using him as an archetype to symbolize all the masculine energies in my life combined into one. It was a very cruel joke. He was my single mom, whose validation I would never receive, my father's apathy I could never break through, my ex-husbands insecurities that I had to shrink my truth for, he was the patronizing patriarchal religion of my childhood whose fucked up indoctrination cost me years in therapy, and he was my misogynist uncle who told me, at 14, I had to apologize to my 16 year old male cousin whom I had beat in arm wrestling. I was too much, too big, too strong, too visible, too powerfully female for them all. And now, here, all those old wounds – wounds I thought I had healed- culminated up again like a multi-headed beast and took shape in one unsuspecting man.

Breathe in. Breathe out. Meditate.

'What if he was actually a friend? What if him showing up was to expand you, not contract you? What if this is a beautiful gift for you to break your ego's false narratives and create space for you to emerge as your big self? What happens if he's a friend?'

Then, like a wave crashing into the shore I was hit with intense sense of wonder, excitement, curiosity. I smiled. Now the tension of pain was met with an unexplained sensation of expansion. It felt delicious.

Such a beautiful gift to be given the opportunity to heal such deep wounds in such a safe and loving way from the universe. Right? Because I didn't really have to interact with him like I did other men in my life this could be safe. He couldn't actually hurt me. Right? Purely by being conscious of these feelings I could move through this. Right? Just give gratitude that it's being triggered through a simple means and not a catastrophic life event. Right?

I wanted to relish in this new feeling, it felt good, amazingly so, like exhilaratingly so! Exquisitely so! I had no words. But it was so new, it felt so delicate. And as much as I wanted to live in this new space it also felt awkward and uncomfortable because I didn't know how to BE in this new space. I could still very much feel my old patterns pushing for space in my being and the very real pain that still electrified my body at the thought of having to be in his presence.

Breathe in. Breathe out. Meditate.

'Why are you really taking this class? To learn how the game works and to learn the skills needed to play it. Yes. And must it be your project that you learn it with? No, I guess not. I'll stay in and I will try one more time to get their insight on my project. I have such a strong feeling of urgency to do this work. I just have to swallow my pride and be in this new space of being'.

I had to let go of my ego's attachment to how my journey was supposed to look. I felt so vulnerable and raw and yet so expansive and delicious. There was something pulling at me to keep going on this new path. I knew that to meet my soul I'd have to pursue this project. And I knew that to pursue my project I needed whatever it was that I was to learn in this class. I'd have to do whatever was required, and what was required was to let go of the control and keep moving. Plus, I wanted more of this new feeling. I was so curious about it.

I needed to meet with the professors again and ask for advice. This was huge. I don't generally allow myself to be vulnerable a second time with people that I feel disrespected my being. I don't generally give second chances on allowing people to show up when they've already shown me they can't. I wasn't following my normal script; my ego was going crazy and causing a pain tight in my chest.... but that new amazing feeling, the one wherein we are friends, and that feeling of being expansive, was enticing me to step into this uncomfortable space and ask. So, I opened my computer to email the professors for help. What are the odds? There was an email from him, checking in. Maybe he really was friend not foe. It at least made it easier to ask. So, I set up an appointment to see them and seek advice, again.

I was very prepared for this meeting. I had all the numbers and stats, and the pathway I wanted to take. I had everything outlined that I wanted to bring up to discuss. I was ready to tell them all the reasons why my project was important and why I should be able to do it. I brought it all.
Them: "It's a great idea. But you have to do it in a group because it's a lot of work."

I already knew no one in the class was ready for this with me. I wanted to do it myself.

Me: "So, what you're saying is I can do it myself, but it will be a lot of work."

Professor Chase: "You won't get a good grade in the class if you do it alone because team participation is part of the grade."

Me: "So, what you're saying is that I can do it myself, but I will get a bad grade."

Main Professor: "No. It's a great idea, but it would be negligence on our part if we let you do it alone because it really is a lot of work. A senator once told me 'If you can't convince the people around you to team up with you, why should I?'"

WOW! This Mofo just can't stop! If there were any wounds left in my soul to trigger this did it.

"If I can't convince one of these puppies from class to join in a big dog fight then I wasn't enough?" I WASN'T ENOUGH?????!!!! I wasn't enough for my too big idea. That hit like an arsenic cocktail to my body. Every defense mechanism went up to hide my authentic emotions and self. Protocol kicked in: Just smile. Say 'thank you for your time, I really appreciate it.' And leave. Which I did in the absolutely most lumbersome way possible. My social graces were hit by a Mac truck and didn't even know my left from right and I ran into a door…that I had just opened!

Breathe in. Breathe out. Meditate.

'Why am I doing this? To learn the game. Breath in. Why does this hurt so fucking bad? Breath out. I CAN'T BREATHE!!!! Think of him as your friend and this as a gift to heal from.'

Instantly that amazing feeling was back that I wanted to live in, an expansive place where I could show up as a big, bold, badass and it was rewarded and honored. The place where I didn't have to hide any part of who I am to be validated and seen.

'Work on your project on your own. They can't stop you. Remember why you are here. Learn to play the game by teaming up with another project. Play the game.'

God this was confusing. The same entity that was causing a morbid pain-screaming out for me to hide, was the same entity that sent waves of orgasmic emotions down my body - a deliciously exquisite expansiveness pulling me to keep showing up.

*   *   *   *   *

"Mom!! I can't find my black shorts for basketball!!" Said with as much sass, attitude, and entitlement as only a fourteen-year-old girl can.

In my head I am repeating my mantra for dealing with her as a conscious parent as she's growing, 'It's just a phase. This attitude and frustration over life's little things is developmentally appropriate. Deep breath. Negotiate and solve the situation.'

Once centered, I respond like all moms do, in a tone of pure love laced with annoyance of having to repeat the obvious for the thousandth time, "Did you check your draws or the laundry pile?"

"YES!! Of course I did!!"

"Did you check your siblings' drawers? Sometimes laundry gets put back in the wrong place."

Time was running out, we needed to be leaving. I join in the search ransacking my own drawers trying to find some black shorts that could make do. But to no avail, the few I found were too big, too small, or the wrong style for the fashionista.

"We can stop at Walmart on the way to the game. No guarantee what they will have but they will have something. But we need to be leaving now to make it to your game on time!" Seriously, let's go already is what I was thinking.

I kept searching as she kept looking and whining about not finding the shorts that she wanted. I found a pair of black soccer shorts that were her brother's and handed them to her.

"Try these." I said as I was stretching the waistband to show they could fit her.

"They're too long!!"

"Well then just 'roll them like seven times'"". Mocking a reference she had made the other day about overhearing ridiculous girls at her private school in the bathroom consulting each other on how to shorten their uniform skirts.

"Ugh. I don't want toooooo," she complained as she took them out of my hand.

I turned to go finish making sure everyone else was ready to leave, had shoes, snacks, water, you know the basics of getting kids ready to go anywhere they don't want to go which is what going to older siblings' sports tournaments is for the younger kids. And I was still looking for the lost, apparently magical, black shorts.

As I am maneuvering through the house getting stuff ready, picking up clothes and shit to quickly put away (because seriously who lives in this pig stye! And when I'm in a hurry it's apparently the time to clean??!!!) I see her in front of the full-length mirror in the living room with her brother's black shorts on.

Finally, we can go. She may not be ecstatic about it but at least we can now go. I was feeling slightly relieved that we might hold to today's schedule.

"How do they fit?" I half asked knowing I would get some comment about the fact that they are not the 'right ones' which would be accompanied by eye rolling and sighs. She turned around and faced me.

"They don't fit right!!!!" her eyes were welled up with tears and she was beginning to cry, and this is when I. Lost. My. Shit!

Like an ocean wave coming to capsize a pirates ship I let my mouth speak what my heart and soul yelled. "Are you fucking kidding me?!!!"

Everyone in the house became intensely quiet anxiously witnessing the unfolding of this show they knew was going to be hot because the beast in mom had just been let loose and would not be backing down.

"Are you seriously going to stand there and cry about the fact that your fucking SHORTS don't fit right!!! Your SHORTS!!!!!???? Fuckin SHORTS!!!!!!! You want to quit now because your shorts don't fit? You want to give up on your dreams, over shorts!" I was hot and on a roll.
"Well, here's your origin story. This is it!!" She rolled her eyes as I had began again.

"Don't roll your eyes at me. I know you think this is a joke. It's not. The brothers from Rise. They had to SHARE SHOES!!! Fucking SHOES!! And you're complaining about your shorts not fitting right! Your origin story is being given every single opportunity in the world [hands slapping together for emphasis]and deciding what you're going to do with it."

My voice and entire being filled with rage, and anger at her entitlement in this situation. She had no idea the sacrifices and struggle her father and I made to give our four kids every opportunity to succeed. We were divorced and living together for God sake.

"Your dad and I make HUGE sacrifices for you to have all these opportunities. And no, this is not a guilt trip. We don't care what you chose to do in life. Be an author. Be a chef. Be whatever the hell you want to be. But I can guarantee you this: at some point of chasing any dream you won't have the right pen, you won't have the right pan, there will be something that won't be just right and, in that moment, you're going to have to choose whether you're going to keep going or give up. You have to choose. Are you going to let that be what breaks you?"

In that moment I saw past her into the mirror she was in front of, and I saw me, at 15, faced with a dream crushing dilemma that I did allow to break me.

Tears filled my eyes and I continued to lay into her "I wish. I WISH, I had someone fighting for me when I was your age. I wish I had someone to tell me to keep going. Keep chasing my dreams! I wish I had someone fighting for me. I was depressed for two years after getting mono thinking that my basketball D1 dreams were dead. For TWO years. And NO ONE fought for me or my dreams. NO ONE!"

For a split second I caught my own reflection, I saw deep into my own eyes in the mirror behind her once again. Realizing that it was now me, at 42 years old and triggered by some rando Professor man who kept showing up to (what felt like) bash me down in my adult dreams, that I was giving this speech too. I may have been looking at my daughter, but I was speaking to me.

The tears kept coming as my voice changed, becoming more tender and earnest, and laid into it with every part of my heart, "Baby girl. You were born to be an elite athlete. You were born to be fucking amazing. You were born to do great things, but it's not going to be easy, and it *HAS* to be *YOUR* choice. There's always going to be something that's not just right. And you have to decide if you give up or if you keep fighting. But know this, whether you like it or not, *I Will NEVER QUIT FIGHTING* for you and your greatness. *I will never quit*!!!!"

The tears were streaming down my face at this point, and I knew what I told her was the speech that I had wished my mom gave me, even now, that I wished she would give me as an adult. But really the only one who needed to give it to me was also the one that needed to hear it. I knew what I had to do. I had to keep showing up and fighting, even though it wasn't "just right'. But it was my dream, and **I** had to choose to fight.

*   *   *   *   *

I continued to go to class and joined a fantastic group with two others. I was learning and playing the game. And I avoided my professors as much as I could while still showing up as a solid group member. I felt so awkward, so uncomfortable. I was sooo awkward in this class. I didn't know how to *be* in this situation. I felt so vulnerable and raw all the time. And there was still this weird tension in my body. On the one hand there was the visceral agonizing pain of my ego collapsing which forced me to deconstruct my belief systems in every faucet of my life having been triggered to the depths of my soul. And on the other hand, there was a new sensation that would wash over my body, taking my breath away, that was truly safe, expansive, exciting, and fun. What made it most interesting is that it was the same person who brought about both.

I started my passion project on the side, and it had taken off on its own, but differently than I had anticipated. The universe kept giving me gifts of insight and shifts to help it take shape especially as I let go of the need to control it. It was exciting and big. It was requiring all of me. The real me. The big me. It felt awkward, and uncomfortably new. I was beginning to see why the universe didn't allow me to pursue it in the class; its form was meant to take shape differently than the class structure would have allowed. I was meant to take shape differently. The more I let go of my ego and stepped into the expansion the more my project took shape. The more of my true essence took shape.

Breathe in. Breathe out. Meditate.

'What am I supposed to do with this project? It's becoming more than I currently have the skill set for. It's taking a shape I'm not sure where to go with. I need someone to tell me what I should do. Ask him for help. *HELL NO!*'

What little was left of my ego screamed throughout my body that I would never ask the enemy for help again. The Mofo has now *TWICE* almost emotionally killed me. Besides, I can do this alone- finding my own help, I don't need him, I will prove to him this was not 'negligence' to do it myself. The dialogue in my head was going crazy for two weeks. I knew I needed his insights. I knew I needed his help. But how do you ask an enemy for help? But wasn't he now a friend? I don't know. Both feelings resided within me, and I had just become fine with how awkward, uncomfortable, and unconfronted they were.

Finally, at the urging of a former professor, I set up a meeting to ask The Mofo for insight and help.

I felt so conflicted. In my personal life I had been on my soul's journeying through such huge excavations of my beliefs – all triggered by this man. In my professional school life, I had just put him behind a glass door, purposely avoiding interactions with him if I could, even if that meant being agonizingly awkward at times. Always being late and always leaving fast. My ego hated him. My expansion loved him. I was sure to die in this meeting and I was sure to be seeing my best friend. I sound like I'm batshit crazy!! Seriously, who does this?! But I wanted my dreams more than I wanted my ego or even for him to like me, so I met him for help.

Any part of my ego that thought it was going to need to fight had now been dispelled. He showed up at the meeting and sincerely wanted to help. He saw me, vulnerable and raw. I had no plans. I had no control. I had nothing but a vision and hope and lots of amazing pieces I didn't know exactly what to do with. But he saw what could be done and gave me advice on how to do it, and what those next steps could be, for my dreams to come to fruition.

No, we're still not real friends in life. I walked away still feeling excruciatingly uncomfortable and feeling all sorts of awkward. Classes still cause me moments of panic and insecurities. But I did it and am doing it. I chose my goals over my ego, gave space to my soul, and I lived. Turns out my ego had been wrong; I didn't need to hide. I needed to keep showing up for myself and dispelling my own myths.

The project is still taking shape and building into a wondrous manifestation of my heart's desires; almost surreal. But it is happening. And to be honest, there is still an inner fight between my old patterns and my new being on who's going to win in each moment. There's still a tension in my body between avoiding my professor as much as possible and wanting to be besties. The human relationships part of things is still causing anxiety. But I'm grateful. I'm grateful that a short Mexican man inadvertently showed up, and the Universe used him as a gateway; opening a path I then journeyed down, exploring a depth of my soul I'd never ventured before. I really love who I am finding there. She is everything, and she is wild and free. Big, Bold, Badass Bitch who leads with love and compassion. Her essence feels magnetizing.

And now, for the most part, I'm freed from my ego. Where once I would have ran instead of feeling awkward and uncomfortable, I now consciously look at the situation first.

So, what am I now without my ego leading? Who am I without my past stories dictating my every move? Simply put, I AM. And it's exciting and scary. It's wonderful and big. It's exhilarating and orgasmic. It's jumping off a cliff to soft waters below all the while holding your best friend's hand. It feels incredibly safe, and still totally awkward as fuck. I'm learning to receive help and trust the Universe, who has since brought into my life several amazing men who are the total opposite of what I had previously believed men were. They are supportive, see all of me, and expect me to succeed in very badass big ways. I am having to learn how to choose my success over my victimhood. Relearning how to pursue my truth. But what I've learned the most is that the Universe will cross our paths with the most perfect (often unexpected) people to trigger our ego, ask us to delve deep, and expand our soul; and we will hate that we love them so much, only hoping to someday be able to thank them for simply existing.

Jara enjoys the peace of living out in the country in Sacramento CA, where she is happily navigating a new stage in life as a single mom to four amazing kids and pursuing her dream career.

CHAPTER 21

Know When to Walk Away, Know When to Run, Know When to Stay — a Job Hopper's Cautionary Tale
By Alison Hill

Denver, Colorado, Spring 2000 — "I *want* to go to the library!" He spits the words out, grabbing my throat and pressing down hard. I can't breathe, let alone scream for help. Cold, rage-filled eyes glare down at me. Panicked, I try prying his bony fingers off my soon-to-be crushed windpipe, but he snatches my thumb and bends it back. Miraculously, it doesn't snap. Who knew digits were so flexible? Eventually, he lets go, sneering at me. No remorse. But I still need to take him home; I'm in charge of his welfare. It's my job. Wheezing and shaking from shock, I glance around the bus depot, desperately wondering what to do next. I realize nobody even noticed the struggle—and this is in broad daylight, well before iPhones. "Not worth the health insurance," I tell myself, wondering how to describe the event in an incident report—a slight misunderstanding? Altercation? Attempted murder?

Denver, Colorado, August 2000 — He pulls up beside me, tilts his head, and peers through the illegally tinted windows of my tan Honda Accord. I glance at the photo laid out on the passenger seat. Yep, that's him alright. The guy I'm supposed to surveil. He nods, laughs, and speeds off while I'm still fumbling with the video camera. What a burn. Humiliating. I guess it's funny in hindsight. I'd left the house super early for my first assignment, while it was still dark. Maybe next time I should check that my headlights are switched off before trying to be incognito. I was hoping he wouldn't start following *me*. Who knows if he was armed...

Undisclosed location in North Carolina, late 2000's — I feel physically ill around him. Every word out of this person's mouth is condescending and accusatory. I can't write a thing. His looming presence sucks out all my creativity. Nothing comes out right, and I've been a journalist for what, almost 15 years? I should have walked out sooner, before it became a shouting match. PR isn't really in my wheelhouse anyway. The "last stand" was probably a shock to other staff members, who either scuttled away like fleeing cockroaches or stared down at their computer screens, pretending to look busy. Someone told me later that it was entertaining to watch—probably the first time anyone had called him out. Yeah, thanks for the heads-up and moral support. Feel free to back me up next time. The half-pint tyrant still owes me money for time served.

As they say, it's all in a day's work.

There's a term for this now, of course — a toxic work environment. But back then it was yet to be defined. You just got on with it. I was also unfamiliar with the words *narcissist*, *sociopath*, and *gaslighting*. I'm not one to quit straight out of the gate and will give each job the good old college try, at least for a few months. Even when the universe screams at the top of her lungs, "Get the hell out of there! Right now! It's not worth it."

We spend a third of our lives working and after a while, our jobs begin to define us. Work issues inevitably bleed into our home lives, and since the two are interconnected it's imperative that we seek balance. At the very least, a job should be bearable. It shouldn't put you in jeopardy, become a burden, or affect your mental well-being and physical health. The pursuit of a career, disappointments, fear of failure, office politics, and the stress of job searching can pile up and take a huge toll.

A little forward planning could have saved me from most of the job-searching stress I've experienced and the frustration of doing work I hate. For example, it's best to have something lined up if you decide to move countries, or states, or quit a hard-to-attain career job. This way you can avoid desperation or settling for something far out of your comfort zone, including finding yourself in dangerous situations.

Just like most people, I did odd jobs during college and straight after graduating, but I took on many 'between career' positions because I moved around so much. If I'd stayed in one place, my working life could have been much smoother, and this piece would never have been written.

I left a great career in television, a position many people spend a lifetime pursuing. It's probably one of my biggest regrets. Not only did I leave my job, but I also left my family, lifelong friends, my country, and my culture for the second time since graduating college. And for what? A dream. An adventure. Skiing on the weekends. Don't get me wrong, I love living in America, but it hasn't been easy.

My dad died a month and a half before I boarded the plane. We even had to postpone the funeral because of my London-based green card interview. Looking back, I should have stayed longer. But everything was already arranged. It was September 1999 and my husband had been in Denver for months. The only thing I *hadn't* planned was a new job. This wasn't my first rodeo. I'd emigrated to the US before, newly married, straight out of college. I should have known better. I had trouble finding meaningful work back then and did everything from working in a library and several daycare centers to waiting tables and selling lingerie in Dillard's. I even tried selling Cutco knives. But I figured this time, with my media experience as a newspaper reporter and an investigative journalist for a primetime current affairs TV show, it should be easy to snag a great position in the US. Boy, was I wrong! I was a small fish in a very big sea. I didn't grasp the truth of this statement at the time.

But back to those particularly toxic jobs, which are the focus of this piece and the lesson I'd like to share. To sum it up—if your work sucks, leave as soon as possible. Find a way. It's not worth jeopardizing your physical and mental health. We're never taught at home, in school, or in college, when or how to walk away—from a relationship, a bad situation, or a job that's destroying your self-worth. The more you linger, the worse it gets.

I'm a serial job hopper turned freelancer. It's been challenging monetarily as well as mentally. I tried adding up how many jobs I've had since I first entered the working world at the tender age of sixteen. The count is twenty-six, if you include my four waitressing jobs, washing dishes at a New Hampshire children's summer camp, and scraping plates in my college refectory (canteen to Americans). Then there are all the temporary jobs I've held. This isn't even counting my numerous freelance gigs or contract work.

Being a job hopper wasn't easy in the past when resume gaps screamed instability, inconsistency, and no loyalty. Today's youngsters don't understand. Now it's normal to job hop, but back then, working somewhere for a year or less was almost as bad as doing time. So why did you leave your last position?

I don't know… toxic short-man syndrome? Dangerous workplace? Psychotic client'?

I've had crappy jobs that were okay. Just a means to make money. But the ones I mentioned at the beginning of this piece were the most challenging and character-building.

When I became a private investigator, I thought it might be the start of a fun new career. I trained in Denver and spent four days at the corporate office in Phoenix, in the August heat (around 110 Fahrenheit), less than ideal for sitting in a car all day.

During my training, I was tasked with going out into a parking lot and choosing a random person to follow for the rest of the day. When they got home, I was to approach them and start up a conversation without raising suspicion. I'd already trained as an investigative journalist in Wales, including undercover work, so I nailed it. But I soon realized that I wasn't cut out for this type of life—even before getting burned on my first assignment. It was all surveillance work involving insurance fraud, mostly worker's compensation cases. You spied on people who had suspicious claims and collected visual evidence. For example, we pursued a guy one night to a bar, where he spent several hours drinking and playing pool, yet claimed his back was injured and he couldn't work. We secretly filmed him the whole night. I almost felt sorry for the guy.

There was one glaring issue with surveillance work that affected females—how to urinate while on surveillance. You could pull up to someone's neighborhood, settle in, and wait hours until they emerged. One day my boss said to me, "Can you turn around for a moment so I can piss in this bottle?" I didn't learn about that stuff in college. And I didn't realize until I was training in Phoenix that this was a male-dominated profession. I was the only woman there.

"Do you think she's ready?" a colleague asked my boss before he sent me on a difficult first assignment. "Sure she is," he said, smiling at me. Unfortunately, it was a complicated case. The guy lived in a four-story apartment complex with two entrances and owned three different cars. I drove around several times just trying to locate his vehicles. I couldn't find them, so I parked in a spot where I could monitor both entrances/exits. Ten minutes later the target pulled alongside me laughing. Someone could have seen me driving around and tipped him off, but I still had my headlights on, and it was a bright Colorado morning. I also had my windows tinted limousine black. I may have been slightly noticeable, especially if he was a seasoned, habitual scammer.

It's funny in hindsight, but at the time I was scared and vulnerable—a lone female pursuing a man suspected of insurance fraud. Some private investigators carry a firearm, and I can see why. It looks glamorous and exciting in the movies, but being a PI wasn't the life for me. I'd had misgivings earlier and felt bad when I called my boss to tell him I wanted to quit. He was a nice guy, enthusiastic about the job, and very thorough with the training. It was the circumstances that were problematic.

The next thing I knew, the owner of the company called me. A few months earlier he had hired me on the spot. "You're perfect," he said. "You can blend in. It's not like you're some blond bombshell who gains attention." Yeah, dude, thanks for the compliment. He must have noticed the crestfallen look on my face. No woman wants to be told they don't stand out in a crowd. "Oh, you're very attractive," he quickly—and inappropriately—jumps in. "I just mean that you don't draw attention to yourself." And you're smart, he added. "Look at you scribbling away in shorthand!"

He tried to convince me to stay, probably because they paid for my flight, hotel, and training. Maybe he thought I had potential. But I was done. This time I couldn't be swayed. Not only did I feel like I'd done a bad job, but I also didn't like the prospect of sitting alone in a car all day spying on people. I was hoping there would be some missing person casework, but they stuck strictly to insurance fraud. "Just do it for the money," my boss said. "Everyone wants to say they're a private investigator." That's true. But we're not all cut out for the work long term. And I can't pee in a bottle.

Thank goodness my temp job took me right back. I had a new appreciation for not having to hold, and I had access to a bathroom that I could use anytime. And to be honest, I relished getting dressed up for work. And no offense to men, God love 'em, but it was nice being around other females again.

Then a friend said she could help get me a job at her workplace, which takes us to my next debacle.

You may be interested in my opening paragraph. Who was trying to kill me? I'm not exaggerating. This really happened, but I must tread carefully here as I don't want to reveal too much about this position. Let's say I worked with vulnerable adults. I wasn't trained or qualified. It was a job to get out of another job. My efforts to find something in journalism had been futile. It would be another year before I became a producer at PBS. I was interviewed at various news stations but never managed to clinch the deal. My experience in television was specific—investigative, long-form programming, and didn't really translate well into daily news positions, which were the only ones available.

So I found myself in a very stressful and demanding role. People depended on me. Vulnerable people I wasn't equipped to serve, although I tried very hard and truly cared for them. The worst part was being on 24-hour call for a week each month. One night I found myself rescuing an adult individual with Down syndrome while his caregivers were in the middle of a vicious argument. Many of my "clients" were on specific medications, and I was frantically trying to find all his pills while the poor man stood bewildered in the middle of the living room as a shouting match ensued. I quickly removed him from the house, but because it was after hours I had nowhere to take him. We went to my small apartment, and I gave him something to drink, while I tried reaching a manager. I didn't know what to do and it was hours before someone helped me. Again, I'm not trained in social work or in working with vulnerable populations; it was a very stressful time.

Another person on my list had been moved around a lot and there were previous incidents that should have been addressed. This young man was smart, but his behavior was very concerning. One afternoon I was told to train him on the bus system, showing him how to catch a bus to and from his workplace, the library, and other locations he frequented. On this occasion, he just wanted to go straight to the library, and I insisted we stick to the plan. It didn't sit well, and he tried to strangle me. I'm not sure if he intended to cause my demise, but his eyes said it all, *I want to go to the library, and you can't stop me.* I honestly don't recall how I got him home. But I think we took the bus back to his house. I refused to be alone with him after that. There was no sympathy or debriefing back in the office. I learned later that the managers blamed me for trying to force him on the bus, yet they had specifically asked me to train him on how to use the bus system. Apparently, this was not the first time he had displayed violent tendencies. Nothing was done. We'll leave it at that. The point is, I should have left right then, but I stayed. I wouldn't just be leaving a job, there were vulnerable people under my watch. I stayed for their benefit, not that of the company, whose staff treated me with utter disdain. There were other troubling things about this situation that I can't divulge. I still shudder when I look back on my time there. It was awful.

I was left traumatized by that job. Shortly after, I had a car accident. It was my fault; I didn't see the red light at an intersection. The other driver's arm was broken as a result, and I was so distraught at having caused someone harm, that it led to a major anxiety episode. I was diagnosed with PTSD.

Then there's the third event on my list. There's not much to say except that my intuition and my body (I got the runs most days minutes after stepping into the building, sorry for the TMI), were yelling at me, "Get out! Like now!" To be honest, I wasn't quite sure what I was supposed to do, except for promoting a particular client. It was very confusing, and if I asked a question, there would be some kind of smug response such as, "You're the experienced journalist; you should know the job." Even at the "interview," when I said I couldn't start for a couple of days since I had a ski trip planned (and paid for), he became petty and indignant. "That's fine," he smirked, "I guess we'll all work around your schedule." This was temporary and freelance, and I had other gigs. I should have left. Forget about alarm bells—air raid sirens were going off full blast. But I shut them down. The money was too good. My husband even urged me to try to stick it out. Days after starting this position, I became very ill, but I still showed up. I was in a constant state of anxiety, that feeling when you're on a fairground ride and your tummy flips.

This pompous fool would stand like a wannabe Roman emperor in the middle of the floor and publicly criticize my work. Just like Steve Carell's character in *The Office*, he was completely oblivious to the feelings and needs of his staff. There's little wonder the company has such a high turnover rate.

One morning I slept later than usual after doing a 2 a.m. live interview with the BBC. I missed the initial call asking about the whereabouts of documents I shared with a colleague the previous day. Because I hadn't responded, there were several follow-up messages, progressively nastier, ultimately threatening not to pay me. They already *had* these documents, which I spent many hours preparing, so I was livid. I marched into the building and headed for the corner office. He was in the doorway, and I tried to explain the circumstances with the early morning BBC interview—that I had sent the work in—but he didn't want to hear it. "You only respond when I mention money," he accused me, and that's when I exploded. I told him exactly what I thought of him. A preternatural silence descended on the room. People scuttled away as softly as possible, lest they too come under fire.

The Universe tried to warn me off the bat. When I approached the reception desk during my initial interview, the first thing I noticed was a zebra rug. It was real. Repulsed, I should have turned around right then. Lesson learned.

Sometimes it's not worth staying in a job if it doesn't make you happy or fulfilled. It's not worth it for the prestige or power. If you have misgivings, niggling doubts, and it feels wrong, don't ignore those instincts. They're usually true. Just find a way to leave. And if a job makes you physically ill, quit immediately. There can be no *buts*, *maybes*, or *what-ifs*. Don't stick it out for the money, the benefits, or because your partner, parent, or best friend says you should stay. Resign if it starts affecting your mental health. And it's especially important to walk away if someone tries to strangle you at a bus stop.

I feel battered, weathered, and exhausted from all these experiences when I could have been enjoying a comfortable, well-paid, prominent journalism position in Wales this whole time. It's a smaller pond over there and I was already in the club; all I had to do was keep showing up. Then again, it's been quite an education, an adventure that I never would have experienced if I had stayed at home. I'm resilient and more adaptable than ever. It may even have ushered me along the road to enlightenment; adversity can, after, all teach you a lot about yourself, other people, and the world. But one thing's for sure, it's all great fodder for personal essays.

Alison Hill is a writer, journalist, Emmy-nominated producer, and the author of The Writer's Digest Guide to Journalism. A twenty-five-year media veteran, she's done everything from hosting TV shows and speaking on live radio, to filming undercover. As a freelancer, she writes for various print and online publications, including a monthly column for WritersDigest.com, and is also a New York Times stringer. Since 2001 Alison has been a guest commentator on BBC Cymru radio news shows. Before going solo, she produced and directed studio discussion shows for PBS and was an investigative journalist for an ITV Wales current affairs series. An avid hiker and kayaker, Alison grew up in the mountains of north Wales and speaks fluent Welsh. She now lives in South Carolina with her husband, ten-year-old daughter, two rescue cats, and a dog.

CHAPTER 22

Embracing Authenticity: A Quest for Personal Truth Within the Mystery of the Ultimate Truth
By Kerry Jehanne-Guadalupe

My beloved husband, Krishna, had a dream about me in which three questions were posed: *What are you afraid of? What are you most attached to? What are you willing to live for?* I was intrigued by the questions and decided to ponder them. After a few weeks of reflection and sorting through superficial responses, one answer to the three questions arose from within me: *truth*.

I am afraid of speaking my truth.
I am most attached to knowing the truth.
I am willing to live for the truth.

Speaking my truth

When I was a child, classmates made fun of the speech impediment I had while growing up. I wasn't bullied because I had a speech impediment. To say I was bullied *because* of my speech impediment puts the cause of the bullying on me. I was never the *cause* of other people's cruelty; I was not the reason they became bullies. Yet, I did not understand this as a child. I believed I was the cause, I was the problem, and that something in me provoked darkness in others. Consequently, the fears I had to sort through concerning speaking my truth related to being verbally attacked, followed by being outright rejected and shunned.

I emerged from childhood as a passive participant in my life. Often, I would not share my truth, even to state my needs, opinions, or preferences, out of my fear of being slaughtered by the words of others. In many of the moments where I did not speak up, I experienced mixed emotions: both the relief of keeping myself safe from perceived or potentially real threats, as well as a sense of self-betrayal. I avoided external conflicts by creating severe internal struggles. Becoming inauthentic to be accepted came at a significant cost, including a crisis of self. This pattern worked for me for some time because the self-betrayal felt easier to manage than the possible threats. Then, there came a time when the cost of the internal struggles was unbearable; I could no longer act out of fear of rejection for who I was by keeping myself hidden within a perceived sense of safety.

When I was finding my voice, I was emerging as a 'truth-teller,' though I did not know about such roles at the time. The truth-teller within a family or community is the one who says, "Hey, there is some weird, toxic, funky stuff going on here that we should look at." It turns out that not everyone wants to be aware of unhealthy patterns. Speaking my truth has come with a huge learning curve, as I went from being passive to pissing people off. Though it wasn't often that I aggravated people, when I did, they were often terrifyingly explosive. Violent responses were frightening for me and could shake me to my core. I became aware that I had to resolve the terror left in me from the years I endured being bullied as a child, as harsh responses triggered deep inner wounds.

Family members were not the only people reacting to my truth and perspectives. Many years ago, I downright agitated most of the staff I supervised when I was a director of an education program. Upon being hired, I remember walking the premises and telling the executive director, "This place feels like home." Little did I know that was a foreshadowing of that place feeling like the home I grew up in. In my role as director, all I was trying to do was bring awareness to some dynamics that were detrimental to the program. The staff did not want me to question the workplace dynamics; they wanted me to find a place within the dynamics—to be the director of the dysfunction, not the dismantler. It was only in looking back that I realized I was in the truth-teller role in that job, just as I was within my family.

I now recognize that I play the truth-teller role from time to time and better understand behavior patterns. More recently, I met a man disguising himself as a shaman, but in truth, he was a sexual predator. When I figured out his game, I knew the moment I started to speak the truth about him and warn people would be the moment he would attempt to make me look like I was crazy, dark, or both. Sure enough, he did. When a predator, much like a narcissist, gets called out on their behavior, they turn on the truth-teller and attempt to make that person look insane or evil to others in the community. They flip the story to make themselves the victim while sharing their perfected "poor me" response. There is something so utterly liberating about knowing this pattern.

I am not the cause of someone's cruelty, though I am sure to expect it if I choose to speak my truth within any highly dysfunctional home, workplace, or even a retreat center. It took me many rounds in the truth-telling ring, many rounds of being flattened, to even realize that I was occasionally embodying the truth-teller archetype. If I enter the truth-telling ring with someone who does not want a truth to be exposed, they will likely throw some verbal punches and make grand attempts to defame my character. Fortifying myself with my truth, I have learned to decide what words from others enter my heart. Before learning to do this, I would let myself be destroyed by the words and behaviors of others, along with their perceptions of me.

Self-determining who I am has been essential so that a void is not left within me where others' perceptions can take root. This not only pertains to moments when I have found myself in the truth-teller role but also pertains to my everyday life. Part of allowing my truth to emerge has been the subsequent slide down the bell curve of "socially normal" into an outlier position. In this outlier position, I have had to self-determine what this means. For example, in my work, I function as a channel of light language. Being a channel of light language comes with many perceptions of me, some of which are benevolent, while other perceptions are far from kind. Standing in my truth, I can dismiss the comments of others who unreservedly believe that people who function as channels are doing the work of the devil. It feels like a miracle that I can stand in my knowing of who I am and not even be fazed by such perceptions.

In a moment of aligning with my truth, I found the courage to write a letter to family members sharing what I do for a living, along with my worry about being disowned. I bared my soul, and most of them didn't even respond, which only confirmed their rejection. My human needs for acceptance and approval and the corresponding sense of safety and security from belonging have not always aligned with my soul's aspirations. I chose to journey through the immense pain of losing people in my life instead of losing myself because I can no longer sell my soul to blend in and be accepted.

Diverging from conformity and establishing a sense of safety on the outskirts of normality has come hand-in-hand with learning to feel safe in conflict, as well as feeling safe in being unloved, unwelcome, or even abandoned. It is one thing for me to have different values, perspectives, and ways of living, but feeling secure in those differences is essential for me. If I am different without self-assurance, without being content and comfortable within myself, I am not free; I am tethered to fear, insecurities, and my desire to be accepted. My need for acceptance and approval diminished as my sense of self increased. I stopped fearing that people would leave me because I broke the habit of abandoning myself so others would not abandon me.

I realized that being safe is not about playing small but in aligning with my truth. I feel super safe being nestled into my truth. This includes basic things like choosing which words work for me. For example, for many years, I would get a sense of what words people used for the Divine and adjust myself accordingly. I altered my vocabulary to be in alignment with other people's truths, mainly to prevent rejection, as the word *God* lands with people in vastly different ways and for a plethora of reasons. Now, I no longer worry if people will tune me out or judge me because I use the word God. The fact that I no longer adjust my vocabulary, my truth, to be heard or to prevent judgment is profoundly significant for me. As my truth is expressed, it will land in the context of people's lives as it will, and I have grown comfortable with this.

As I have grown older, I have been learning to use my voice to remain true to my nature and live according to my rhythms. At my core, I love joy, gentleness, and connection, and I am rather allergic to conflict and drama. Staying true to myself has been learning to speak and assert myself in my life in a way that keeps me aligned with my inner truth, such as using my voice to kindly extract myself from interactions that are not good for my heart.

Speaking my truth has been quite the journey. In grade school, with my speech impediment, I never wanted to speak; in fact, I could get through the entire day without speaking to anyone. I was there physically, but I had no voice. I lived in isolation right in the middle of people. Today, I belt out light language, and I have grown to use my voice to speak my truth. I even wrote a book, *The Devil's Yoga: A Woman's Journey from Entrapment to Freedom*, that details the horrific experience I had with the false shaman who was, in truth, a sexual predator. The fact that I published this book after growing up without much of a voice is a miracle.

I am most attached to knowing the truth.

When answering the questions from Krishna's dream, I was amazed that the three questions had the same answer, as I was expecting three unique responses. I was even more surprised that the thing I was most attached to was something positive: *truth*. I assumed the answer to the second question would be linked to something I was afraid to let go of or something my ego was attached to. Being attached to truth made me realize that being attached to something is not always limiting but can foster determination, bravery, and even liberation. I acknowledged the cultural conditioning of thought I fell into—having a negative connotation related to being attached to anything.

Though I would absolutely love to know the ultimate truth of the universe and the nature of reality, that might not be accessible to me while my spirit is incarnated in human form. I do believe that there is an ultimate truth of who I am that resides within me, and I strive to increase access to that inner truth. What is honest to my essence, my ultimate intrinsic nature, is the foundation of my truth. My truth is rooted in my essence, not in my mind or culture. Ultimately, I want to explore this life while being uniquely Kerry—allowing my essence, the holder of my truth, to be expressed through my personality.

Being attached to knowing my truth has meant venturing into the confines of my mind. Examining my own psyche—the good, the wonky, and the prison—has not only been about witnessing how I have been programmed by external influences like media, education, religion, mainstream culture, or countercultures, but where I have internally tethered myself with beliefs.

I have been an expert knot-tyer.

My gallivants into cul-de-sacs of my psyche and internal prisons have shown me that I had twice-over tethered myself: I had not only reined myself in with negative beliefs about myself that have kept me small and confined at the personality level, but I had also created a psychological prison that kept my essence locked up. My knot-tying skills gave new meaning to "losing oneself in thought." I lost myself at the personality level (who I can fully be as Kerry) within the bombardment of negative thoughts, and I also lost contact with my essence; I literally lost myself in thought.

I have been mind-locked with negative thoughts and heart-locked with destructive emotions that, in turn, have kept me soul-locked. Living (well, more like surviving, as I really can't call it living) without feeling a connection to my essence was pure madness because all I had access to were my thoughts, which were mostly negative and rampaging through my mind, and my emotions, which were a hot mixture of fear, resentment, and rage. I grew up with a traumatized mind that was aligned with my wounding, not my essence—a mind that convinced me, at two different times in my life, to attempt suicide.

After many decades of depression, which started in early childhood, my brain developed a neurobiology of depression, which greatly influenced my thinking, including the conclusions I formed about myself. Many conclusions became beliefs; my beliefs created notions of truth, and my notions of truth created horrible perceptions of myself. Though my perceptions about myself have often been far from accurate, I trusted all the negative beliefs to be true. I trusted the "truth" of the loud, self-deprecating thoughts related to self-loathing as well as the more subtle, insidious thoughts that ran in the background. This only tied the knots tighter.

In many ways and for many decades, my mind steered me away from my essence. I felt my essence was distant and inaccessible. I had zero concept of it. To get to my essence, I had to get through my mind and into my heart, and well, the passage through the mind was a doozie! Learning to use my mind as a navigation tool into my heart has been essential. My mind needed a proper job rather than running wild. It wasn't about closing shop but about giving my mind a way to access wisdom from my heart that leads me to expand and bring out the best in me, instead of listening to the noise that makes me shrink and suffer. This is an ongoing dance of watching my mind conjure up nonsense and then using my mind to allow my essence to provide guidance. Using my mind as a navigation tool into my heart has been a life-changer and a lifesaver, literally!

From time to time, I continue to get captured by my thoughts and feelings. Yet, when my essence knocks at the door of my personality, it hands me a key. The key is not in the hands of my personality, as my psyche cannot release my psyche, only my essence can. I am continuing to learn to get myself, at the personality level, out of the way and allow my essence to provide the guidance and required energy to break me out of any hypnotic rhythms of thought and emotional patterns I have used to entrance myself. Anchoring to my truth has included a continuous dance of breaking free and finding more tethers I didn't know were there, identifying where I am holding myself captive, and learning to untie the knots.

It has been the work of my essence to ensure that I am honest with my own truth and in alignment with my inner wisdom. This has included not only untying the internal tethers but also the external tethers like socialization. At certain times in my life, I have felt conditioned beyond measure, like a walking puppet of culture, void of myself, removed from my truth, and full of indoctrination. This started early on in my life. Like many kids, I was a sponge. I learned how to think, feel, and behave from people around me, including family members, educators, and coaches, along with television personalities, the advertisement industry, the diet industry, the church, the news media, and so on. From what I learned, I thought, felt, and behaved accordingly. For example, I was taught to fear God, and I was fearful. I was in alignment with the teachings that had very little to do with my truth, but the notions of truth handed down to me.

After decades of regurgitating information from grade school to grad school and following all sorts of cultural norms, breaking the shackles of socialization and releasing internalized customs and ideologies has been part of my path to accessing my truth. As I strive to be honest with my own truth versus what I have been conditioned to believe, it has been imperative to examine what my truth, values, and perspectives are based upon, including countercultural influences. There have been times when I did not follow a traditional course, such as when I dropped out of college and taught environmental education on a sailboat that functioned as a floating classroom. I assumed that since I was not following mainstream society, I was somehow living my truth. Yet, I was simply following another set of norms while believing I was free. Socialization can be incredibly insidious.

External tethers have not only appeared through socialization but also through well-disguised fabrications of truth. The retreat center where I met the false shaman/sexual predator had many well-disguised horrors, yet it came with rave reviews. The center was supported by prominent authors, thought leaders, and proclaimed healers, many of whom were world-renowned. I assumed that if these individuals supported the center, it must be reliable, trustworthy, and honorable. Thus, I handed over my discernment well before I stepped foot on the land. If I had tuned into my knowing, I might have been able to discern something was off and access more of the truth of the center.

Instead, I trusted the perceptions of others, many of whom were unaware of the dark undercurrents of the retreat center.

While at the center, I endured being taken advantage of while in a vulnerable state. Getting through my horrendous experience with the false shaman required me to name the experience truthfully rather than engaging in spiritual bypassing: utilizing spiritual principles to evade integration and healing of trauma. I do believe, on a higher plane, that there are no victims; yet, in the third dimension, we as humans can experience being victimized. My essence and my personality can live these two truths simultaneously and be at peace within the multidimensionality of truth.

If I applied a higher-dimensional truth to my third-dimensional reality, I would have inadvertently led myself down a path of spiritual bypassing rather than true healing. While I have no interest in living in victim consciousness, I also don't want to spiritually bypass any experiences and suppress trauma. Processing the experience of being victimized through feeling what was true for me: anger, confusion, grief, and fear, until these emotions were integrated, led me to feel empowered, liberated, and *truly* free from the trauma.

The evolution of my truth corresponds to increasing my connection to my essence. It is a loving intelligence that I am learning to be more present with. Connecting more and more with my essence has allowed me to distinguish between my truth and cultural notions of truth. It has helped me access the wisdom of my body instead of referring to a metaphysical book. My essence has helped me to trust the information coming through me as I work as an intuitive while knowing not to trust everything my mind says.

My essence holds my truth, which can then be reflected through my personality. The more I connect to my essence, the easier it is to bring forth the principles that are core to my being, such as integrity, honesty, and respect. This connection helps me to stand by such principles, yet not stand in a way that is too rigid because my principles can be, at times, contradictory. I honor commitments I make, and yet there have been times when I needed to break a commitment. Though my core principles remain steady, much of my truth has been fluid, ever-changing, and contextual. What was true for me in one year was not true for me in another, such as the kind of work my soul felt called to do. My views on certain topics have changed, along with my biorhythms, ways of interacting, my needs, my response to life experiences, and more.

My truth is an ongoing dance between the "I" and the "I am," between my personality and my presence.

I am willing to live for the truth.

Growing up, my relationship with God was bizarre and distorted at best. Like many, I grew up believing in a wrathful God. I saw "him" as very masculine, mean, and out-to-get-me. "He" felt more like a demon with a destruction story than a God with a creation story. When people would say, "Don't worry, God is in control," or "Let go and let God," I would cringe, as I did not find relief in such statements. Let go and let God do what exactly?

It was difficult to trust life when I didn't trust the maker of life.

Hell was tangible to me. When I was in 6th grade, I was digging under a tree in my backyard. Within six inches or so, I came across the tree's roots, which were red. I instantly thought that was the entrance to the devil's home as if hell was that close and that easy to enter. I quickly covered up the roots. I had been well indoctrinated into the constructs that God was vengeful, which made hell a real possibility. I can see now that this wasn't my truth; it was an insidious indoctrination that covertly impacted my life.

When I started to no longer resonate with the church's teachings, I began to be open to the idea that a good, benevolent, and loving God exists. Though my mind was starting to come around, my heart still had zero faith or trust in God. Intellectually, knowing that God is loving did nothing to open my heart. Opening myself to experience a loving presence has been a journey in itself.

I carried my lack of trust in God into adulthood. When I was learning to meditate, I realized that I did not feel safe leaving the confines of my mind, regardless of how crazy my mind was. If I started to melt into and merge with spaciousness, I would come to full alertness with a hyper-vigilance, not of my mind, but of the nothingness, as I feared what I was melting into and wondered if it was safe to experience. Better the devil I know—my crazy mind—than to reach out to what was unknown. I did not feel safe reaching out to something greater than me to help me free myself from my mind.

As the construct of a wrathful God was dissipating, I was starting to experience God as loving. Yet, when I perceived God as loving, I realized how unworthy I felt of Divine love. I didn't need to think about receiving God's love when I understood God as unloving. Yet, when I began to experience God as a Mysterious Loving Presence, I discovered that I believed I was unlovable; an untruth that felt like an absolute truth. What I have come to believe is this whole notion of being or not being worthy of love is a human construct that has nothing to do with God.

Though I left the church in my early teens, the church lived on inside of me. Inadvertently, I found spiritual communities that had a distinct overlap with the religion I was raised in. It was as if some notions of spirituality were born out of religion, and therefore, I unconsciously resonated with the similarities because they felt familiar. I journeyed from handing over my power and seeking answers from church authorities to seeking answers from psychics. I still used an intermediary between myself and the Divine: in the church, the priest, and outside, the healer. I was still controlled, just through different doctrines and tactics. I still felt guilt and shame, just for other reasons. Ritual practices went from sacraments to ceremonies, some of which were extremely mismanaged by "elders." All in all, I felt very accustomed to hierarchical structures, corruption, misuse of power, and abusive behavior of leaders in the world of spirituality because of my years in religion.

Though I am very aware of the tremendous harm from some religions that are devastating to the human soul, to say the least, I have learned through personal experience that some spiritual communities have become cults, and some "shamans" or "gurus" have been identified as sexual predators. I have also witnessed how spiritual communities can be places where people co-create their reality with their own set of facts and truths, reject information that contradicts their perceived and constructed worldviews, and feel like their truth is what is true in general, just like church!

This is why I have learned to question what my truth is based upon. This is not self-doubt. This is knowing that we, as humans, can feel we have escaped or are beyond a certain level of consciousness yet unintentionally carry over what we think we have escaped from to another version of the same consciousness. I know that I can be insidiously indoctrinated in ways I cannot see, and therefore, I have learned to make sure that what is in resonance is from my heart and not from what is familiar. I have learned to trust myself to challenge notions of truth, especially culturally constructed notions of truth, spiritual or otherwise.

I don't know the mysteries of the universe and the ultimate nature of God, though I would love to know. It is easy to trust when there is a degree of certainty and knowing. But since I don't know the ultimate nature of God, I need my faith to cultivate trust. Trusting or not trusting an all-loving presence is not a reflection of God but of me. God is solid, and therefore, questioning the reliability of God feels unnecessary to me. The real question is: how much can I surrender to trusting God? This is on me.

I have had some extraordinary experiences where I felt that I had surrendered fully to the love of God—experiences where I have felt very little concept of myself as Kerry but as an essence that is part of all that is. I have been cracked open to love with the brilliant white lights and all, only to clamp down and disconnect within days or weeks after my experience. I would start to doubt that what I experienced was God; how do I know if what I experienced was true? Am I deceiving myself? I could not find my truth, even through my own experience.

At some point, I had to get really honest with myself. This was not a healthy self-doubt. This doubt acted as a sword that cut through the connection. This was no longer about the church or spiritual communities. This was about me. I was the one holding the sword and standing between God and me. When I took an honest look, I realized that not trusting myself and my knowing was a mask to my resistance to letting go—knowing God gets in the way of me keeping my story.

Though I am most attached to knowing the truth, and I am willing to live for the truth, I have come up against resistance to the truth because brushing up against any level of Divine truth comes with a crumbling, a deconstructing of notions of myself and my reality. I cannot walk toward truth and remain intact. My essence might be attached to the truth and willing to live for the truth, but that comes with my human self being willing to deconstruct / "die" to the truth—not dying physically, but a death of certain aspects of my personality that keep me in notions of separation. Since I don't want to be more attached to my story than to knowing God, connecting more and more with God has come with increasing my willingness to untie the knots, being willing to recognize myself beyond my personality, beyond the straps I have tethered myself with.

The ultimate truth may only be accessible after my physical death, where my essence might have access to infinite wisdom. Yet, while alive in my physical form, being willing to live for the truth—like *really* live—means letting go of the past and feeling joy. Allowing my essence to be more present and expressed through my personality is to feel the feelings of my essence, like joy, love, connectedness, and gratitude.

Though my relationship with God is constantly evolving, I had to get this God thing sorted out to some degree in order to function in this world. I now trust God, and I now trust life, even when the nature of reality feels utterly bizarre at times. Within all the wonkiness that comes with being human resides my connection to God; at whatever beginning level that connection is, it is there, and for that, I am grateful. For that, I can live more freely as I journey with an ever-evolving personal truth, within the ultimate truth, which remains an ongoing mystery.

Kerry Jehanne-Guadalupe is an author and a holistic practitioner of wellness modalities, including *light language*. Her background includes organic farming and beekeeping, as well as adult education within academia and organizations. https://www.kerryjehanne.com

Other Works from Betsy Chasse and Rampant Feline Media

Tipping Sacred Cows
Killing Buddha
Dancing in the Unknown
The Documentary Filmmaking Master Class
Stories of Becoming Myself

Learn more at www.betsychasse.net

Contributing Authors:
    Vanda Mikoloski, Robert Plagmann, Dr. Theresa L. Smith, D.C., Claudia Micco, Kerry Jehanne-Guadalupe, Kelly Sophia Grace, J.D., Allisun Sturges, Marie Benard, Rebecka Gregory, Kian Xie, Tobias Forrest, Jennifer McLean, Vienne Cordet, Roberto Páez, Rissy Lynn Smith, Mary Adams, Alison Hill, Jara Lindgren, Wayne D. Carter, Keri Fulmore, Dr. Johanneke Kodde, Kristen Marie, Gregory Kirschenbaum

Milton Keynes UK
Ingram Content Group UK Ltd.
UKHW020649040324
438885UK00017B/981